Better Lessons in
A-level hist

GW01606882

Diana L

Acknowledgements

With thanks to the fantastic history team at The Sixth Form College, Farnborough.

Thanks, also, to Vince Bramley, who gave generously of his own time to talk about his experiences of the Falklands War.

The Publishers would like to thank the following for permission to reproduce copyright material:

Text credits

Chapter 1: p.14 extract from a letter by Nigel Kingscote to Henry Mapleton (Crimean War Society Mapleton archive) from *www.crimeanwar.org/cwrsentry.html,* reproduced by permission of G. P. Walker; **p.33** extract from *A Message from the Falklands* by Lieut David Tinker RN, compiled by Professor Hugh Tinker, © Hugh Tinker 1982, reproduced by permission of Sheil Land Associates Ltd; **Chapter 4: p.82** David Nicol, extract from 'Principles of good assessment and feedback: Theory and practice' from *REAP International Online Conference on Assessment Design for Learner Responsibility* (29–31 May, 2007), reprinted by permission of the author; **p.94** Patrick Finney, extract from 'The romance of decline: The historiography of appeasement and British national identity', from *Electronic Journal of International History* on *www.history.ac.uk/resources/e-journal-international-history/finney-paper* (Institute of Historical Research, 2000), reprinted by permission of the author; **Chapter 5: pp.100 & 104** Patrick O'Brien, extracts from 'An Engagement with Postmodern Foes, Literary Theorists and Friends on the Borders with History' from *www.history.ac.uk/discourse/pob.html* (Institute of Historical Research, February 1999), © Professor Patrick O'Brien, reprinted by permission of the Institute of Historical Research; **p.101** Alun Munslow, extract from 'The Postmodern in History: A Response to Professor O'Brien' from *www.history.ac.uk/siscourse/alun.html* (Institute of Hisorical Research, Feburary 1999), reprinted by permission of the author; **pp.103 & 104** Sigurdur Gylfi Magnusson, extract from 'What is Microhistory?' from *http://hnn.us/article/f23720.html* (George Mason University's History News Network, August 2006), reprinted by permission of the author, and Sigurdur Gylfi Magnusson, extract from 'Social History – Cultural History – Alltagsgeschichte – Microhistory: In Between Methodologies and Conceptual Frameworks' from *Journal of Microhistory* (2006), reprinted by permission of the author; **pp.113 & 114** Wanda Newby, extract from *Peace and War: Growing up in Fascist Italy* (HarperCollins Publishers, 1991), reprinted by permission of the publisher; **p.120** Victoria de Grazia, extract from *How Fascism Ruled Women: Italy, 1922–1945* (University of California Press, 1992), © 1992 by the Regents of the University of California, reprinted by permission of the publisher.

Photo credits

Cover Mary Evans Picture Library; **p.16** © Punch Limited/TopFoto; **p.69** Wikipedia screen grab reproduced under Creative Commons Attribution-ShareAlike License, Photo Courtesy of U.S. Army/photo by Staff Sgt. Brandon Aird; **p.85** © Pictorial Press Ltd/Alamy; **p.109** © Keystone/Hulton Archive/Getty Images.

Every effort has been made to trace all copyright holders, but if any have been inadvertently overlooked the Publishers will be pleased to make the necessary arrangements at the first opportunity.

Although every effort has been made to ensure that website addresses are correct at time of going to press, Hodder Education cannot be held responsible for the content of any website mentioned in this book. It is sometimes possible to find a relocated web page by typing in the address of the home page for a website in the URL window of your browser.

Hachette UK's policy is to use papers that are natural, renewable and recyclable products and made from wood grown in sustainable forests. The logging and manufacturing processes are expected to conform to the environmental regulations of the country of origin.

Orders: please contact Bookpoint Ltd, 130 Milton Park, Abingdon, Oxon OX14 4SB. Telephone: +44 (0)1235 827720. Fax: +44 (0)1235 400454. Lines are open 9.00a.m.–5.00p.m., Monday to Saturday, with a 24-hour message answering service. Visit our website at www.hoddereducation.co.uk

© Diana Laffin 2009

First published in 2009
by Hodder Education,
an Hachette UK company
338 Euston Road
London NW1 3BH

Impression number 6

Year 2013

All rights reserved. Apart from any use permitted under UK copyright law, the material in this publication is copyright and cannot be photocopied or otherwise produced in its entirety or copied onto acetate without permission. Electronic copying is not permitted. Permission is given to teachers to make limited copies of resource sheets marked © Hodder Education, for classroom distribution only, to students within their own school or educational institution. The material may not be copied in full, in unlimited quantities, kept on behalf of others, distributed outside the purchasing institution, copied onwards, sold to third parties, or stored for future use in a retrieval system. This permission is subject to the payment of the purchase price of the book. If you wish to use the material in any way other than as specified you must apply in writing to the Publisher at the above address.

Typeset in Garamond Light Condensed and Helvetica 35 Thin
by Phoenix Photosetting, Chatham, Kent
Artwork by Barking Dog Art

Printed in Great Britain by Hobbs the Printers

A catalogue record for this title is available from the British Library

ISBN 978 0340 97546 6

Contents

Introduction

Results, results, results

History teachers are under intense pressure to deliver results. Performance management, league tables and departmental assessment reports all require us to ensure that our students achieve the top grades. At open evenings parents are increasingly pressing in their enquiries, asking about the proportion of A grades or value-added data. When students are asked why they take the subject, their responses all too frequently stress their need for particular grades for a law degree or a place at a good university. It would be foolish to pretend that results do not matter. Of course they do.

This has always made me feel a little awkward about promoting the broader goals of history teaching in the examination years. Hard-pressed teachers, struggling with an increasing burden of administration and government-imposed changes, do not need a privileged idealist to tell them that their courses should be based on higher aims than good results in the next set module. But a personal experience in the summer I finished writing this book has renewed my confidence that history education cannot, and should not, be driven by a narrow concentration on the approaching assessment.

Going off-piste: what will students remember of their history lessons?

In August 2005 my son received his A level results. Bristol University required him to gain three A grades to win a place on their economics course. But the computer screen told him that he had two As and a B. The B was in history and he had missed the A by one solitary mark. It was a bitter blow and one he took some time to get over.

Three years later, the same son squashed into an overloaded student car and did a tour around England. The holiday revolved mainly around testing the relative merits of bars and pubs of university towns such as Birmingham, Newcastle and Leicester. When driving home on the motorway, however, this gang decided to turn off and explore the site of Bosworth battlefield. They spent two hours there. My son is not an enthusiastic reader, will never be a subscriber to *History Today* and did not study the Tudor period at A level. His mates are similar. Yet their experience of learning history was enough to set them on this detour and question the museum curators about the factors which swayed the outcome of Bosworth.

Students who return to college some years later confirm that, in the long term, it is not marks in exams which live on but the times the teacher had the courage to go off-piste. They remember trips, funny moments, heated discussions, experiments that went well and, even more, the experiments that went wrong. More broadly, their experience of learning history has left two important legacies. One: the belief that history is fun. The other: the belief that history matters.

This conviction is the principle that underpins this book. The chapters are not based on particular specifications or assessment criteria but rather broader goals such as independent learning, meaningful source analysis and thoughtful engagement with interpretations. As far as possible I have tried to focus on how to develop young people as good historians. The suggested activities, however, are ones that are used in my college courses in preparation for coursework and examinations. In the end, examinations are not the enemy. The higher levels of examination mark schemes summarise the skills that deeper learners acquire naturally. A broad and long-term view of examination criteria does not conflict with a creative and ambitious scheme of work.

Using student learning time to the full

Finally, there is the issue of time. When I am running training workshops, the most frequent point raised is the problem of finding time to incorporate active learning and deeper enquiries into overcrowded syllabi. While there is no easy solution to this, a good starting point is to ensure, right from the beginning, that the acquisition of knowledge is mainly the responsibility of the student. If the teacher supplies factual revision booklets, sets frequent knowledge tests and overloads students with handouts, the class will soon become dependent. Insisting on reading preparation before lessons and a list of references on all essays, and assuming a baseline knowledge in discussions, may frighten some of your less motivated characters but will be worth doing for the learning time released.

This book is written in the context of major changes to the AS/A2 examinations in England and Wales and the introduction of new qualifications such as diplomas and the Pre-U. My experience of twenty years of teaching tells me that there will more changes in the future. At a time when many teachers will be writing new schemes of work or adapting old ones, this book suggests some fun and challenging ideas to include which should stand the test of time. There is a combination of longer term lesson sequences to support planning with standalone activities which could be lifted for use in any course or context. Whether you are dipping in or making longer term plans, I hope you find something useful.

CHAPTER 1 Planning the big picture

Chapter summary

- This chapter considers ways of teaching a 100-year study with particular focus on historical significance and change over time.
- The problems of teaching military history are discussed and addressed.
- The chapter suggests ways to provide students with a clear overview so that they can get to grips with the 'big picture'.
- Examples are also given of thematic depth studies which allow students to develop deeper knowledge and understanding.
- A final team investigation weaves together the main themes of the study.
- The scheme of work finishes with a plenary debate which focuses on the nature and extent of change.
- The chapter suggests how the following 100-year enquiry might be planned:
  What were the most significant changes in the nature of warfare in the years 1845–1991?

Context

Patterns and trends: the problem of change over time

On 22 June 1941, German troops attacked the Soviet Union. On exactly the same date, 129 years earlier, Napoleon had attacked the same territory. It has sometimes been suggested that if Hitler had studied his history better he would not have made what many believe to be his biggest blunder in the war. This is a mistaken view. Hitler was a keen historian who had ordered his generals to study Napoleon's campaign prior to Operation Barbarossa. He was deeply aware of Napoleon's failure, even superstitiously avoiding the same route as his predecessor. His repeated insistence in orders that there should be no going back was based on the view that early retreat had been Napoleon's mistake. Yet, despite some differences in the campaigns, the general pattern was repeated: early success followed by terrible hardships in the Russian winter, and final defeat.

'Those who cannot learn from history are doomed to repeat it,' stated the Spanish philosopher, George Santayana. Yet it is usually very difficult to learn from history. Certainly, in history, what goes around comes around – but it comes around in a different form, in a different way and in a different context. Tackling the challenge of the process of change over an extended period of time is at the heart of any attempt to explore a long period of time, such as the 100-year study, currently a compulsory module in post-16 history courses in England and Wales.

Whether it is possible to detect patterns and trends in history has been a perennial source of contention (see Figure 1.1). In this postmodern age, we have the coincidence of massive change with the unfashionability of the whole idea of 'general trends'. The scale and impact of change has developed at a staggering rate; just consider, for instance, how the Internet has influenced mass communication in little over a decade. At the same time historians seem to have become deeply suspicious of grand narratives or large overviews, unless it is the story of an offbeat aspect such as cod or personal hygiene. Instead, micro history, the personal experience or small community seem to be the style of the moment.

The 100-year study presents the opportunity to explore big issues and themes, with an open mind as to whether a trend or pattern can be found.

Figure 1.1 *Extract from Thomson, D. (1957)* Europe since Napoleon

The English liberal historian and politician, HAL Fisher, prefaced the famous *History of Europe* which he completed in 1936 with the words: 'men wiser and more learned than I have discerned in history a plot, a rhythm, a predetermined pattern. These harmonies are concealed from me. I can only see one emergency following upon another as wave follows upon wave, only one great fact with respect to which, since it is unique, there can be only generalisations.' I, too, detect no plot or predetermined pattern; but I can see certain rhythms of movement and certain patterns of change. They might better be called 'general trends', provided they are not regarded as flowing from eternal causes or proceeding to infinity. It is no part of the historian's duty to be a prophet; but it is his duty to take advantage of his great privilege of hindsight to elucidate what came to pass, even if participants in the events were not always aware of the consequences that would follow from the decisions they took or the course of action they pursued.

Thomson (1972: 16–17)

Harris and Kitson (2002) have argued convincingly, from their own practice as history teachers, that the best approach to this type of study is not through a detailed chronology but through a clever weaving of overview and depth in the manner of basket weaving. Most of the examination boards have provided ideas of thematic approaches and warned against getting stuck in a morass of factual content at the expense of a view of the 'big picture'. There is also plenty of good practice to build on from Key Stage 3. In his article on the importance of meaningful enquiry questions, Riley (2000) included examples of planning which created resonance through repeated conceptual themes. Also working at Key Stage 3, Banham (2000) used Shemilt's work on the second-order concept of historical change to show how rigorous consideration of the nature of change can transform the focus of students' learning when analysing change and continuity over time (Shemilt, 1980). I would argue that these ideas should also underpin planning of an effective development study at post-16 level.

A dominant requirement in any examination specification focusing on long-term development is the concept of historical significance. The longer term study is the ideal module with which to tackle this key concept as it encourages students to place their historical knowledge in a broader context, making connections with past and future. Thinking about significance has moved on in the last few years, with many writers encouraging teachers to think beyond the equation of significance with consequence. Many history teachers will be familiar with Counsell's 'Five Rs' (Counsell, 2004) and her use of this model to investigate the significance of Josephine Butler's campaigns. Counsell suggested that pupils needed to develop their own criteria for weighing historical significance and that this could be fostered by suggesting some starting criteria that they might apply and critique. (See Figure 1.2 for Counsell's suggested schema.) Another successful example of an investigation into significance is Hammond's (2001) structured plan for teaching the Holocaust which promotes a blend of longitudinal study of anti-Semitism with a depth study of the Second World War in order to place the Holocaust in a meaningful context. This helped her pupils to move their thinking beyond immediate moral reactions and a focus on numbers, to a deeper and more thoughtful appreciation of the meaning of the Holocaust today. Certainly at post-16 level, students need to be challenged about the nature of significance, a concept which will require them to consider why they are studying history at all.

Figure 1.2 *Five Rs for thinking about historical significance*

- **Remarkable** (the event/development was remarked upon by people at the time and/or since)
- **Remembered** (the event/development was important at some stage in history within the collective memory of a group or groups)
- **Resonant** (people like to make analogies with it; it is possible to connect with experiences, beliefs or situations across time and space)
- **Resulting** in change (it had consequences for the future)
- **Revealing** (of some other aspect of the past)

Counsell (2004: 32)

Remembrance and commemoration: the problem of history, memory and war

> A critical historiography has to stand at a distance from memory in all its senses, and by the same token it must be both connected to and estranged from the present.
>
> *Megill (2007: 40)*

One work that I have found illuminating while considering the role of memory is Megill's *Historical Knowledge, Historical Error*. Megill (2007) suggests that history used as tradition, or for memory or commemoration, can be a way of 'evading history' rather than creating it. Memory is strongly affected by the person remembering, by their current context and by their purpose in bringing back past experience. The historian uses memory in order to 'get beyond it', put it in its context and seek corroborative evidence. Megill emphasises the fact that commemoration is an intentional, communal desire to remember the past in a particular way, often employing religious ritual and symbolism to do so. Most historians and history teachers would agree that both need to be treated with caution in history education. Northern Ireland is a familiar case, where a version of history is both remembered and commemorated to perpetuate a historical divide.

The teaching community is not always consistent, however, in seeking to differentiate between memory, commemoration and history education. In my experience, in topics such as the Holocaust and the First World War, the immensity of the suffering often seems to push aside the normal model of critical appraisal. The desire to commemorate may be a powerful and legitimate one but it can lead to teaching which is based on the assumption that students should learn why the war is significant in the current moral and cultural context, with the use of both memory and commemoration to support that premise. This can inhibit any attempt to 'go beyond memory' and question the nature and extent of the war's significance for participants, their families and their descendants. For me, one of the most revealing aspects of the Imperial War Museum's *Last Post: The Final Word from our First World War Soldiers* is that, for several of those Great War veterans interviewed, the war was not necessarily the most significant event of their lives. These interviews describe their experiences before and after the war and, for many of these remarkable men, their work, their family life and their hobbies were the most important things they wanted to record. Arguably, the memoirs of these survivors are just as representative a legacy of the 1914–18 conflict as the Menin Gate. Horror at the loss of life, followed by a 'Never again' reaction, is always a natural response to war, especially, perhaps, to the merciless killing of the First World War. But it can be a barrier to good historical thinking. Look at the letters and diaries, look at the inscriptions on the stones, and you will find few soldiers or families who talk of the futility of war.

In a brave article, another history teacher, Lyon (2007), challenged the uncritical integration of remembrance into teaching about the First World War and suggested ways to help students to reflect in a more disciplined way while studying the topic. His use of different kinds of 'thinking hats' helps students to differentiate between their emotional response, information gathering and critical thinking while learning about the war. This is a sensitive way of acknowledging their emotional reactions while encouraging other forms of response alongside them. When looking back on wars, it is usually the premature deaths of young men which influence our thinking. However, when studying war in a historical context, the history teacher needs to negotiate the coexistence of emotional engagement with a broader analysis of the significance of the event.

Military history has also suffered from a particular kind of selectivity. It is the First World War, and almost exclusively the Western Front, which invariably predominates. In both the local parish churches in my neighbourhood there are touching memorials to men who lost their lives in colonial conflicts, especially the Boer War. At a rough calculation, almost as many died in these wars as did in the Second World War, and the scar in my local community must have run as deep. The First World War, with 'brave little Belgium', Wilfred Owen and body lice, has the educational fizz of champagne. For many teachers, the Boer War is an uncomfortable and distant squabble over stolen property. In this war the British invented concentration camps, hundreds died of undramatic diseases and were ambushed on dusty plains. It has little educational appeal and is more or less absent from the school curriculum. Even within the teaching of the popular world wars, there is a tendency to focus on appealing aspects rather than the broader context. Coman (1999) has shown how concentration on the home front gave primary school pupils a very uneven view of the Second World War, portraying Germans as persistent aggressors and the British as primarily defensive during the conflict. It is quite possible for secondary students to study the First World War in some depth but emerge with little understanding of what went on at Salonika or Mesopotamia, both hugely important for the subsequent history of Eastern Europe and the Middle East.

On the whole, the teaching community is not comfortable with military history. Their attitude is akin to the Victorian view of sex. It is acceptable to talk of courtship, marriage and the birth of children but it is vulgar to mention what happens in between. Thus we spend ages weighing up long- and short-term causes of war, touch upon its impact on civilians and evaluate its effects. But, apart from the odd foray in the First World War, weaponry, tactics and events on the battlefield are not quite nice. This reflects a national ambivalence. We wear our poppies with pride but hold aloof from military parades, are suspicious of service personnel visiting our schools and neglect our military museums. Dead soldiers can be tolerated, even revered, but living ones must be kept at a distance. A recent debate (March 2008) about the military in schools revealed the attitudes of some members of the National Union of Teachers, one of whom said: 'Teachers and schools should not be conduits for either the dissemination of MoD propaganda or the recruitment of military personnel.'

Teaching materials on the war in Iraq, produced for the Ministry of Defence as a web-based resource, were also attacked by the teaching union and in a statement a spokesman felt impelled to point out that the resources warned that 'war could be dangerous' (BBC News Online (Education), 13 March 2008).

There are several barriers to the teaching of military history at secondary level. One is a genuine concern that learning about war could glorify violence in an age when there is widespread concern about physical aggression amongst young people. Another is the prejudicial view that the world of tanks and guns is one for nerds in anoraks. Many school teachers are women, similar to myself, who find the intricacies of the Sherman and Panther tanks a big turn-off and think their pupils will too. Yet what happens in a battle can be pivotal and many students (yes, mostly boys) find warfare fascinating. In my college at Farnborough, we cannot shy away from military matters because we are at the heart of them. Aldershot and Sandhurst are a stone's throw away and there are barracks and shooting ranges dotted around the neighbouring countryside. A good proportion of our students have military connections and there are numerous military museums on our doorstep. At the time of writing, the television news regularly reports the deaths of British soldiers in Iraq or Afghanistan. Young men are dying in their twenties, many of them trained only a few miles from my college. I have always believed that history courses should have local resonance. Studying war and its impact is a natural choice for us. But it is not an easy one.

Here are the three key objectives in the 100-year study module listed by the examination board I currently use:

- to analyse significance
- to evaluate source material
- to explore the process of change over an extended period of time.

Adapted from Edexcel (2007: 9)

In this chapter, suggestions are made about how to integrate these objectives into an effective teaching module.

Activities

This section comprises three sets of practical activities:

- a series of overview activities
- two in-depth investigations
- a concluding study.

All these activities are drawn together with one big enquiry question:

What were the most significant changes in the nature of warfare in the years 1845–1991?

The focus of this 100-year study is continuity and change in warfare, with a particular emphasis on technology. The danger is that this will result in eager investigations into tank or aircraft development which follow an unquestioning model of linear progression. The word 'significant' in the question is deliberately placed to put these developments into a broader context which picks up on three out of the five features of significance that Counsell (2004) suggests: 'resonant', 'remembered' and 'resulting in change'. The military significance of war, in terms of technology, tactics and leadership, will be the main area of study, with evaluation of how far each conflict resulted in change. This is then contrasted with how war is remembered in a broader sense, encouraging students to place their studies in a wider and more meaningful framework.

To introduce the whole unit you will need to give your students an overview of the concrete, factual aspects of British military history. Alongside this, you will need to develop critical thinking about the historical significance of warfare, especially in terms of resonance and memory.

Planning and teaching the scheme of work

The plan given in Figure 1.3 describes how this study can be taught chronologically, with concentration on one particular theme for each major conflict studied. As there is not the space here to go through each war in turn, there is an example of one depth study on the Crimean War (Investigation A) focusing on leadership, and an explanation of how the unit might be pulled together in a study of the Falklands War (Investigation B). The Crimean War example shows how the teaching can focus on one aspect while also providing a broad overview and a grasp of the key significance of that war. This could then be used as a template for the subsequent studies of the First and Second World Wars with different themes.

Anyone teaching an exam course involving a 100-year study will have to make some hard decisions over content. The conflicts and themes selected here seemed to make the best sense for my students in our context, with the focus on mainly British conflicts fought overseas for a significant period. A commitment to plough through all British wars for the 140-year period would lead to serious content overload and real difficulty in identifying key issues and themes throughout. However, the selection of the most relevant examples must be left up to the school or college involved. It is arguable, for instance, if the Falklands War was the most important of the post-war conflicts, and other centres might choose Korea or the Gulf conflict in preference.

Comparison studies

In order to encourage wider reading and exploration of conflicts outside the main teaching, the scheme of work includes recommended comparison studies. Students should pursue the main theme in the classroom study in more depth, with a detailed evaluation of an example of the same theme in a different conflict. Insist that each student completes one comparison study per topic, with at least one before 1914 and one after 1945, making a total of three completed before they reach the final Falklands topic. Give them some flexibility over the form their studies could take: essay, PowerPoint, movie, podcast or detailed mind map could be suggested. Create a drop box on your intranet for students to deposit their work and then choose the best contributions to share with other students. Use lesson time if you have it or set peer review as a homework exercise and remind students that these assignments will play an important role at the end of the module.

Overview activities

Rationale

The purpose here is to give students a clear introduction to the main wars of the last 100 years in terms of time, extent of involvement and the technology used. The outcome is a rather crude and simplified three-dimensional timeline, but it will help your students to achieve a sound factual foundation for what follows.

Activity 1

Chronological overview of military technology

Timelines are a very helpful tool for overview work and most teachers utilise them in all sorts of forms: pictorial, computer based or even kinaesthetic. For military history, a 3D model timeline is ideal. Your students will have fun constructing it and will be able to summarise key elements of continuity and change using the finished product. Duplo is the ideal means for construction. It is expensive to buy new but can be bought second-hand or borrowed from someone with young children. The finished timeline can remain as a source of reference (if you can find the space) and be recorded on paper for students' files as well. See Figure 1.4 for instructions on how to organise this.

Figure 1.4 *How to make and use a Duplo timeline*

1. Ask your CDT department to cut the large square bases into strips so that you can make a long line. I cut three bases into three equal strips, making nine bases in total.
2. Organise your Duplo blocks into colours and put them in separate boxes. You can label them if you like or simply create a key on your whiteboard, e.g. Red = Casualties.
3. Lay your base in a line, pushing together desks or tables to make an even surface. Label the years with cards from 1850 to 1990. With my bases, this makes 15 years for each base with 24 nodules on each. You cannot be too particular about the exact years within each base as it does not work out evenly, and some wars, like the Falklands, were very short but will need at least one block (two nodules) on which to build.
4. Divide your students into groups, with one group for each major overseas British conflict against a foreign opponent. What you include and what you omit will always be difficult and you should make this decision

● **Figure 1.3** *The changing nature of warfare, 1845–1991*

Big enquiry question: What were the most significant changes in the nature of warfare in the years 1845–1991?					
Broader study	**Depth study conflict**	**Theme**	**Mini questions**	**Activities**	**Recommended comparison studies: How important was … in the … war?**
War on land and sea in the 19th century	The Crimean War	Focus on leadership	How significant was leadership compared to other factors in the conduct and outcome of the war? How far did the war result in changes in the nature of warfare? Do we remember what is most significant about this war?	Preparatory map work; interpretations study; Charge of the Light Brigade case study and reassessment; evaluation of the role of leadership compared to other factors; review of the military effects of the war; review of parental questionnaires; discussion of the wider significance of the war.	*Either* Kitchener at Omdurman *or* Haig on the Western Front in the First World War *or* Montgomery at El Alamein in the Second World War *or* De la Billière in the Gulf War
The First World War	The Western Front, 1914–18	Focus on technology	How significant was technology compared to other factors in the conduct and outcome of the war? How far did the war result in changes in the nature of warfare? Do we remember what is most significant about this war?	Preparatory map work; evaluation of the use of tanks, machine guns, gas and aircraft on the Western Front; review of parental questionnaires; discussion of the wider significance of the war.	*Either* Rifles and artillery in the Boer War *or* The role of aircraft in the Battle of Britain *or* Computer-based technology in the Gulf War
The Second World War	The Allied Invasions, 1944–45	Focus on tactics	How significant were tactics compared to other factors in the conduct and outcome of the war? How far did the war result in changes in the nature of warfare? Do we remember what is most significant about this war?	Preparatory map work; evaluation of the role played by planning, intelligence and strategy in the D-Day landings and the Italian campaign; review of parental questionnaires; discussion of the wider significance of the war.	*Either* Planning and strategy in the sieges of Mafeking and Ladysmith in the Boer War *or* The Gallipoli campaign *or* Operation Musketeer (capture of the Suez Canal in 1956) *or* The Battle of Imjin River in Korea
Warfare in the nuclear age	The Falklands conflict, 1982	Evaluation of all major factors	How significant were leadership, tactics, technology and other factors in the conduct and outcome of the war? How far did the war result in changes in the nature of warfare? Do we remember what is most significant about this war?	Preparatory map work and teacher explanation; *Apprentice*-style investigations and boardroom finale; dartboard card sort; study of views of the war; structured seminar on the significance of the Falklands War today; review of parental questionnaires.	
Plenary session					

for yourself. For the purposes of simplicity I have omitted imperial conflicts such as Kitchener's Egyptian campaign, internal strife such as Northern Ireland and shorter disputes such as Suez. The Russian Civil War has also been omitted because of the difficulties in finding accurate statistics or a clear definition of the British role within it. Statistics for deaths in war are always approximate and sometimes controversial. In the interests of clarity I have focused just on British deaths, not wounded or other nationalities. As far as possible the British figures refer to UK forces not Empire.

I recommend simplifying to the following:

War	Dates	Duration	British casualties (Estimated numbers of those killed in action, rounded off)
Crimean War	1853–56	3 years	3,000
Boer Wars	1880–81	4 months	20,000
	1899–1902	3 years	
First World War	1914–18	4 years	700,000
Second World War	1939–45	6 years	400,000
Korean War	1950–53	3 years	1,000
Falklands War	1982	6 weeks	250
First Gulf War	1990–91	6 months	25

5. Within each group give your students a number. Number 1s should go to the red box and construct a tower in the correct place on the line of British war dead for each conflict. Use this as the basis for discussion about which wars had the highest casualties and why.
6. Allocate the remaining students in each group two forms of military technology to record.
   To simplify this, give them this code:

   A new weapon, not yet well established and prone to problems → One block high

   An established weapon which played a useful role alongside others → Two blocks high

   A widespread and important weapon which played a dominant role in the war → Three blocks high

   A war-winning weapon (crucial to the outcome of the war) → Four blocks high

   Then allocate the weapons:
   rifles (blue), machine guns (green), tanks (orange), aircraft (yellow), other (black).
   Require each team to research their war and make a group decision about the bricks for each weapon.
   The 'other' category can be used for important weapons that were rarely deployed or just associated with one war such as gas or the nuclear bomb. Again for the purposes of simplicity, naval technology has been omitted but you could add submarines and dreadnoughts if you wish.
   Ask students to build towers for the technology adjacent to the existing casualty tower.
7. Give them a simple outline chart to record the bar graphs and use this as the basis for an initial discussion about the relationship between casualties and wartime technology. Encourage students to make hypotheses about this and record their ideas to return to at the end.

Activity 2

Location and extent of wars

Provide a world map for each student on A3 paper so that each country is clearly defined. Provide a colour code for each of the major conflicts (Resource 1A).

When studying each war in sequence, ask your students to complete some preparatory map work. They should shade the main areas of conflict in light but solid colour and then draw light stripes of the same colour in the participating countries. When war recurs in the same area, instruct students to shade on top or add extra stripes. As we are looking at British conflicts, the United Kingdom will end up looking like a multi-coloured zebra.

This activity will give students a geographical framework and a sense of which areas of the world were repeated areas of tension.

Activity 3

How are the wars remembered today?

Picking up the other strand of the module, ask students to record their parents' answers to a simple and short questionnaire (Resource 1B). Emphasise that this is not a general knowledge quiz and leaving questions blank is perfectly acceptable. Asking them to interview their parents orally and jot down their responses makes this less formal and wordy. Ask them to do it off the cuff and not allow any looking up, as this would defeat the purpose of the exercise.

Make the responses anonymous, gather them in and summarise them to use at the end of each wartime study.

RESOURCE 1A *Overview map details*

Shade the main areas of conflict in light but solid colour and then draw light stripes of the same colour in the participating countries. When war recurs in the same area, shade on top or add extra stripes.

War (and colour code)	Dates	Main locations	Main participating states
Crimean War BLUE	1853–56	Crimean Peninsula, the Balkans, the Black Sea, the Baltic Sea	France, Britain, Ottoman Empire, Kingdom of Piedmont and Sardinia, Russian Empire
Boer Wars ORANGE	1880–81 1899–1902	The Transvaal in South Africa	Britain, British Empire (Australia and New Zealand), Orange Free State, South African Republic
First World War RED	1914–18	France and Belgium, Austrian–Italian frontier, Mesopotamia, Armenia, Gallipoli, Galicia, Poland, Balkans, German colonies in Africa	Britain, British Empire, France, Belgium, Russia, Italy, USA, Balkan States, Ottoman Empire
Second World War GREEN	1939–45	Most of Europe, North Africa, South East Asia (Burma), the Middle East, the Mediterranean, the Pacific	Britain, France, Low Countries, Scandinavia excluding Sweden, USSR, USA, Japan, China, Poland, Germany
Korean War PURPLE	1950–53	Korea	North and South Korea, China, USA, Britain, British Commonwealth
Falklands War BROWN	1982	South Atlantic	Britain, Argentina
First Gulf War PINK	1990–91	Kuwait and Iraq	Iraq, Kuwait, Saudi Arabia, coalition of mainly USA and Britain

RESOURCE 1B *Questionnaire on the memory of British wars, 1850–1990*

What do you remember about each of these wars today?

1. THE CRIMEAN WAR 1853–56

2. THE BOER WARS 1880–81, 1899–1902

3. THE FIRST WORLD WAR 1914–18

4. THE SECOND WORLD WAR 1939–45

5. THE KOREAN WAR 1950–53

6. THE FALKLANDS WAR 1982

7. THE FIRST GULF WAR 1990–91

 © HODDER EDUCATION

In-depth investigations

Investigation A

The Crimean War

For each wartime investigation, one theme from the module (see Figure 1.3) is selected and then considered alongside other key aspects of the war. For this study it is leadership.

The Crimean War lasted two years (for the British), and the casualties amounted to the same as the combined US casualties in the two world wars. It involved naval battles in the Baltic, a British attack on Siberia, two long sieges and the preparation of defences in Hong Kong and Australia. Despite all this, it is chiefly remembered for one unsuccessful charge during one battle on the Crimean peninsula and an English nurse called Florence Nightingale. Few wars have such a distorted legacy.

Dixon is forthright in his verdict on the Crimean War:

> As an example of protracted incompetence at high levels of command the Crimean War, is not, unfortunately, unique. It was, however, the prototype for subsequent ineptitude. Though small in number in comparison with those of later wars, the 18,000 who died owed their untimely demise to an admixture of poor planning, unclear orders, lack of intelligence (in both senses of the word) and fatal acquiescence to social pressures on the part of their commander. They died because they were mismanaged by men whose positions in the military hierarchy owed less to their ability than to their wealth, their place in society, or their reputation for 'fitting in'. They died because soldiers were too readily regarded as expendable objects.
>
> *Dixon (1994: 50)*

There is lots of evidence to support this view. In his famous poem on the Charge of the Light Brigade, Tennyson wrote 'the soldier knew/ Someone had blunder'd'. In this infamous and misguided action, out of 673 involved, 113 were killed and 134 were wounded. Lord Raglan, the senior commander, was, according to one historian, 'unfitted for command of an army' (Pemberton, quoted in Troubetzkoy, 2006: 167). Battlefield experience was a distant memory for this one-armed 'perfect gentleman' (Troubetzkoy, 2006: 167), who, in absent-minded moments, often referred to the enemy as the 'French', forgetting they were his allies this time round. Lord Cardigan, after a series of incompetent incidents, had been removed from his command of the 15th Hussars only to be allowed to purchase the post of Lieutenant Colonel at the cost of £40,000 two years later. One writer commented that the youthful Lord Cardigan had a glorious golden head with 'nothing in it' (Woodham-Smith, 1953: 15). He certainly showed more interest in his soldiers' tightly fitting cherry-coloured 'pants' than he did in military strategy. Unattracted by the hardships of war, Cardigan spent a large part of the Crimean campaign aboard his yacht, suitably equipped with a feather bed and French cook. Lord Lucan, only slightly more able than his hated brother-in-law, Cardigan, was nicknamed 'Lord Look-On' for his failure to direct his cavalry from the front. War correspondent William Russell rightly pointed out the inadequacies of logistics: shortages of basic supplies in the harsh Russian winter, which resulted in terrible suffering. All the evidence seems to confirm that the Encyclopedia Britannica is right, it was the most 'ill managed campaign in English History' (Dixon, 1994: 36).

This is how the Crimean War is remembered, if it is remembered at all in the twenty-first century. But it is not how it was remembered in the past. A few miles south of my college, in the garrison church in Aldershot, is a rather grand memorial. It is to Sir James Scarlett, the man who led the charge of the heavy brigade at the Battle of Balaclava. In this engagement, Scarlett led 800 horseman against a Russian force of 1600, causing them to flee. Scarlett's leadership in this action was faultless: courageous, intelligent and decisive. English losses were insignificant compared to the enemy's. It was, in the words of one historian, a 'genuine victory' (Troubetzkoy 2006: 260) and a French commentator even described it as glorious. Scarlett, commander of the heavy brigade, was of the same rank as Cardigan, commander of the light brigade. Both led charges in the Battle of Balaclava. But we only remember the one who failed.

This makes a good starting point for an investigation into military leadership.

Activity 1

Mini question:

How significant was leadership compared to other factors in the conduct and outcome of the Crimean War?

You will need to spend a couple of lessons setting the scene for your students as they will come to this with very little knowledge. After their map work, cover briefly the causes of the war and Britain's military, diplomatic and political situation at the time. Make them aware of the broader campaign in the Baltic and the Russian invasion of Moldavia and Wallachia but focus mainly on the Crimea. Provide them with a basic chronology and a summary of the key participants as a foundation.

Stage 1: The traditional view

The common memory of the Crimean War focuses on three failures: the failure to give the men adequate supplies, the failure to care for the sick and the failure to lead them in battle. The Charge of the Light Brigade is used as a prime example of the weak leadership of stupid aristocratic generals.

RESOURCE 1C *Role play on the Charge of the Light Brigade*

Extract from *The Charge of the Light Brigade*

'Forward, the Light Brigade!'
Was there a man dismay'd?
Not tho' the soldier knew
Someone had blunder'd:
Theirs not to make reply,
Theirs not to reason why,
Theirs but to do and die:
Into the valley of Death
Rode the six hundred.

Alfred, Lord Tennyson

1.

LORD RAGLAN
COMMANDER-IN-CHIEF

You are on high ground above the battle, where you can clearly see the enemy forces and your own men. It takes up to 30 minutes for a horseman to deliver messages from your post to the front line. Russian forces greatly outnumber your own and they have powerful artillery entrenched in the North valley. However, Scarlett has just led a successful charge, turning the battle in your favour.

You are frustrated to see Russian soldiers creeping forward in the central causeway to retrieve their guns. Lucan's cavalry could prevent this with a speedy attack. You are in a hurry so you tell General Airey to write down your instructions.

Tell Airey to write this down:

'*Lord Raglan wishes the cavalry to advance rapidly to the front and try to prevent the enemy carrying away the guns.*'

2.

GENERAL AIREY
QUARTERMASTER

You are under pressure to record the commander's instructions quickly. You pull out an odd bit of paper and scribble down his words, using your sword scabbard to lean on.

You hastily sign the note *R. Airey*.

You select Captain Nolan to take the note as he is renowned for his horsemanship and will deliver it quickly.

© HODDER EDUCATION

3.

CAPTAIN SIR LOUIS NOLAN
AIDE-DE-CAMP

You are a very skilful horseman and take the note at speed, deftly guiding your horse down the steep paths.

You had not listened in to the commanders' previous conversation and only picked up on the note of urgency that Lucan should attack with all speed.

You have total contempt for both Lucan and Cardigan, calling them 'Lord Look-on' and 'The Noble Yachtsman'.

You arrive out of breath, not bothering to hide the contempt you feel for Lord Lucan. You are frustrated by his slow response and shout at him:

'*Lord Raglan's orders are that the cavalry should attack immediately.*'

When he asks you, '*What guns?*', you do not really know the answer. None is visible from Lucan's position in the valley. However, you are too proud to admit to uncertainty, and make a vague gesture towards the North Valley where the enemy are based, with the words:

'*There, my lord, is your enemy. There are your guns.*'

4.

EARL OF LUCAN
IN CHARGE OF THE CAVALRY DIVISION

You receive the note and study it carefully. For such an important order it seems puzzling that it is signed by Airey not Raglan and that it is written on a scrap of paper. Furthermore you are insulted by Nolan's lack of respect and you reciprocate his dislike.

The order makes little sense as to attack the main enemy guns with your small cavalry forces and no infantry support would be a foolhardy mission. You express your uncertainty but Nolan shouts back at you. You respond:

'*Attack, sir! Attack what? What guns?*'

As he appears to confirm that the order is to make a full-on attack on the North Valley, you accept this. You do not want to appear to be indecisive to a man who clearly holds you in contempt. It is beneath your dignity to question him further.

When Cardigan questions the order, you answer:

'*I know it but Lord Raglan will have it. We have no choice but to obey.*'

5.

EARL OF CARDIGAN
IN CHARGE OF THE LIGHT BRIGADE

When you see your commanding officer, Lord Lucan, approaching, you observe proper military etiquette and salute. He gives you the order to advance down the North Valley with the Light Brigade. Although you have hardly spoken to Lucan in the past 30 years and dislike any appearance of evading orders, you feel you have to remonstrate:

'*Certainly, sir; but allow me to point out to you that the Russians have a battery in the valley on our front, and batteries and riflemen on both sides.*'

Lucan agrees with your assessment but replies that you have no choice.

Your loathing of Lord Lucan and your proud character prevent you from arguing any further. You prepare your men for their suicidal mission without any further query.

Provide some background to the Battle of Balaclava and establish that Scarlett's charge had repulsed the Russian cavalry under Ryzhov. The British commander, Raglan, could see the Russians regrouping, with the possibility of recapturing their abandoned guns, and wanted to prevent them.

Start off with Tennyson's magnificent poem – it is worth reading the whole thing or, if you don't want to, there is an original recording of Tennyson reading it on YouTube. Reinforce this with a clip from the 1968 film, which confirms the image of incompetent and callous generalship. Involve students in the story by selecting your outgoing characters to take on roles for enacting the way Raglan's message was distorted as it passed through the hands of a series of proud men who loathed each other. Evaluate what this incident suggests about British military leadership as an introduction to your investigation.

To prepare for the role-play activity, set out the classroom as the battlefield, with Raglan high up in a distant corner and Airey and Nolan close by. Set up the Russians with some massive guns (improvise with cardboard tubes from wrapping paper if you like) in the 'North Valley' and Lucan and Cardigan at one side. Place the abandoned guns in a position that can be seen by Raglan but not by the generals on the ground. Five role-play cards and a rough plan of the battle are provided on Resources 1C and 1D.

After the role play, carry out an analysis. Review the chain of events and list all the failures of military leadership that it reveals. Give the students Dixon's assessment of the Crimean War provided at the beginning of this investigation.

Stage 2: Reappraisal

Now is the time to evaluate that traditional view. A good starting point is an extract from a letter from Nigel Kingscote, third aide-de-camp to Raglan, writing to Henry Mapleton in November 1854. This is provided on Resource 1E.

Ask your students to highlight the reference to the Light Brigade Charge in one colour and any other military engagements in another to make the point that contemporary observers did not place enormous weight on this one incident.

Follow this up with a lively account of Scarlett's Charge of the Heavy Brigade and then a summary of the Battle of Balaclava in general. Now ask your students if the event in the Crimean War which is most remembered is actually the one that is most significant.

Stage 3: Interpretations

Provide the information sheet (Resource 1F) and the cartoon (Resource 1G) so that students can be made aware of the context of these interpretations. This is not the main focus of this study but essential background if students are to reach their own well informed conclusions.

Stage 4: Judgement

Now set your students the challenge of making their own assessment of the leadership of the Crimean War. Divide them into six groups with one military leader each: Lord Raglan, Lord Cardigan, Lord Lucan, Major General Colin Campbell, Charles Napier (commander at sea) and Brigadier General James Scarlett. Widen the scope of the study from the Battle of Balaclava to the whole campaign, including tactics and logistics.

Give them extra reading and research time (see the Bibliography for useful titles) and ask them to complete the competence barometer (Resource 1H) for each general, putting a comment with quotes and examples under each category and summing up at the bottom. Collect in their completed forms and issue as a class booklet.

As a written plenary, ask the class to assess whether Dixon's view of the military leadership of the Crimean War as the 'prototype of military ineptitude' is a fair judgement.

Stage 5: Evaluation of other factors

At this point you will need to bring in the range of other factors influencing the war: technology, tactics and other aspects such as the opposing forces, logistics, weather and terrain. The easiest way to do this is through a pack of reading matter but you could mix in a DVD, and a trip to the National Army Museum at Chelsea would provide a range of other, rich material as well.

Mix your students into new groups. Give them Resource 1I and ask them to fill in points under each category. Follow this up with further research in the students' own time to add more depth and detail. Provide them all with a clear summary of the war (Browning, P. 2002: 53–57 is recommended), which includes an explanation of the importance of technological developments such as the Minie bullet and the rifled barrel, and ensure they consider the naval war including the Baltic blockade.

When it is complete, ask students to highlight any points on their chart that are linked to leadership of the campaign. Share these in small groups and ensure they all write down several examples. Use these ideas for a final class discussion about how much leadership influenced other factors and how far it influenced the war as an independent factor.

RESOURCE 1D *Rough plan of the Battle of Balaclava*

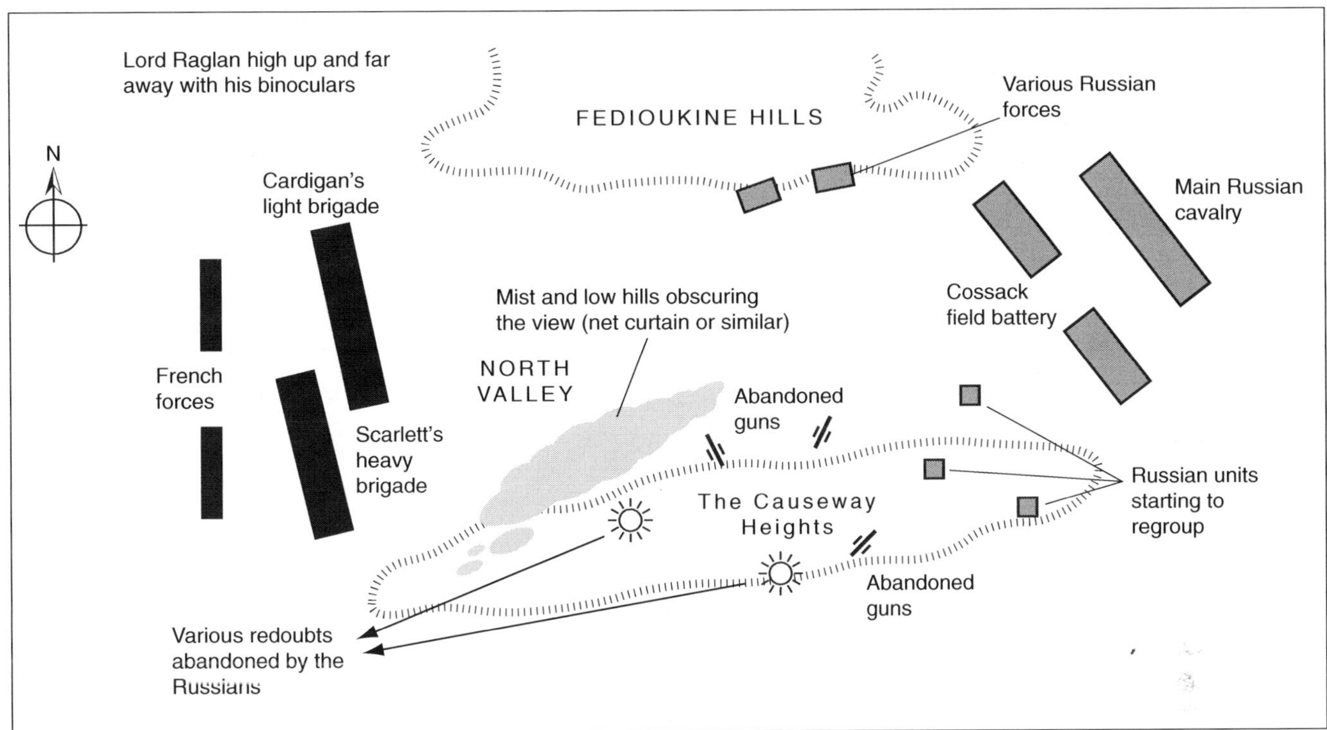

Battle plan adapted from Sweetman, J. (1990) Balaclava 1854: The Charge of the Light Brigade, *p. 71*

RESOURCE  *Extract from aide-de-camp's letter to Henry Mapleton*

The action of the 5th was as hard-fought a battle as ever took place and how our *single* line of troops stood before the masses of Russians that came up against them I know not, and one (*sic*) or twice it was touch and go, indeed some of our artillery men were bayonet (*sic*) at their guns but we lost none of the guns. The French came up at the nick of time and fought well but would be better with a turn more dash. The Russians brought up a *mass* of cannon and threw shells like hail, indeed they do nothing without lots of Artillery and some day or another I prophesy they will get into a great mess when we have licked them and we are able to follow them up. What we want is more men and everything has fallen upon us as yet.

I am thankful to say we all came safe out of the fight on the 5th though under a heavier fire and for a much longer time than at the Alma. Poulett had his horse shot under him and poor Genl. Stranways (*sic*) was killed close by my Lord's side.

Those brutes of Turks, as you well know, bolted from the redoubts round Balaklava at almost the first shot and consequently the Russians got our guns. We would have taken the redoubt again but I suppose his Lordship did not like to loose (*sic*) men for a trifle.

The charge of Heavy Cavalry was splendid and so exciting, the old 'Plungers' covering themselves with glory. Nothing could have been more spirited than the charge of Light Cavalry on the same day, the 25th, but alas with great loss and very little result, the fact was poor Nolan, who took the order, exaggerated it very much, though written, but I cannot exonerate Lord Lucan for listening to him.

The siege just crawls on, but we want to be as slow as possible now and wait till we get further reinforcements of men and guns, the French the same, but I do not for a minute doubt we shall be in this town sooner or later. The sooner the better if we had a chance of getting away as soon as it is all over, but I am afraid that is out of the question and we must make the best of being cooped up here all the winter.

Crimean War Society Mapleton archive.
www.crimeanwar.org/cwrsentry.html

 © HODDER EDUCATION

RESOURCE 1F *Interpretations of the Crimean War*

Immediate: Alfred, Lord Tennyson and W. H. Russell

Tennyson's poem was an immediate response to reading an account of the Battle of Balaclava in *The Times*. It was the prose of William Howard Russell, writing to inspire his middle-class readership, that led to the famous poem. Russell, an Irishman who enjoyed drinking and singing with the troops, certainly adopted the viewpoint of the soldiers. This led Raglan to forbid his generals to talk to him. It should be remembered that both Russell and Tennyson had mixed motives: ambitious careers as writers to protect and service to the demands of a patriotic public.

Short term: The political climate and the Administrative Reform Association

The Crimean War came at a time of debate and flux in British politics. The franchise had been extended in 1832 and there were demands for further reform. Campaigners set up the Administrative Reform Association in 1855 to introduce more meritocratic government, such as entry to the civil service through examinations. It was in the interests of this pressure group, who were highly influential in the media of the time, to portray the privileged army leaders as incompetent bunglers. They wanted to end the buying of commissions (army positions) and make the army more open to promotion through the ranks. After the war they pressed for an enquiry into the management of the campaign. The Roebuck Committee's report, published in April 1855, was a strongly worded attack on the army leadership and was widely reported in the papers. The *Punch* cartoon of November 1855 captures the accusatory attitudes of the time.

Longer term: Cecil Woodham-Smith, *The Reason Why* (1953) and the 1969 film *The Charge of the Light Brigade*

Cecil Woodham-Smith was an Irish writer whose interpretation of the war focused firmly on the characters and life stories of the main generals. With a background in writing advertisements, she had already published a book on the Irish famine and may have felt hostile towards Lord Lucan for his harsh treatment of tenants on his Irish estates. Although her book, published in 1953, was a bestseller, it has been criticised by historians for its focus on personalities and the tendency to blur fiction and biography into a historical account. Her book was used extensively by the scriptwriters for the 1969 film, which portrays all the army officers, apart from Nolan, as buffoons. Produced at a time of great social change, this film was directed and written by 'angry young men' of the 1960s, who were also keen to attack a privileged establishment.

RESOURCE 1G *'Grand military spectacle'*

GRAND MILITARY SPECTACLE.

The Heroes of the Crimea Inspecting the Field-Marshals.

John Leech, cartoon, Punch, *3 November 1855*

On return from battle, the generals traditionally inspect the troops. This cartoon shows the reverse with weary and wounded soldiers reviewing their superiors, looking immaculate in their uniforms.

http://lts.brandeis.edu/research/archives-speccoll/events/crimeanwar/Aftermath.html

RESOURCE 1H *Barometer of military competence*

NAME OF LEADER:

ROLE IN THE CAMPAIGN:

For each category put a dot on the line with a comment underneath. Leave blank any that do not apply or you do not have information about.

FEATURES OF AN EXCELLENT LEADER		**FEATURES OF A VERY POOR LEADER**
Effective deployment of human and other resources, e.g. does not risk life unnecessarily.	↔	Wasteful of human and other resources, e.g. shows disregard for human life.
Good use of intelligence, e.g. finds out about the strength of the enemy.	↔	Poor use of intelligence, e.g. relies on prejudice or hearsay.
Strong relationship with his men, e.g. maintains a distance but stays in touch, communicates well.	↔	Poor relationship with men, e.g. appears authoritarian and distant.
Decisive but flexible, e.g. gives clear orders but reviews them in the light of new information or events.	↔	Indecisive or intransigent, e.g. fails to give clear orders, sticks to old techniques even when they are not working.
Leads by example, e.g. models the behaviour he wants, shares danger and hardships.	↔	Sets a poor example, e.g. avoids the risks and hardships of battle, treats subordinates poorly.
Receptive to new ideas, e.g. use of new technology or new tactics.	↔	Unwilling to experiment with new technology or tactics.

Summing up his competence:

List compiled from ideas in Keegan, J. (2004) The Mask of Command: A Study of Generalship *and Dixon, N. (1994)* On the Psychology of Military Incompetence

RESOURCE 1I *Factors which influenced the conduct and outcome of the Crimean War*

Technology	Tactics	The enemy	Other, e.g. logistics, luck, terrain, weather

 © HODDER EDUCATION

Activity 2

Mini question:

How far did the war result in changes in the nature of warfare?

Stage 1
With students working in small groups, ask them to come up with some ways in which the war might be significant for future wars.

Stage 2
Provide them with a set of extracts (Resource 1J) and a plain sheet of A3 paper. On the A3 paper, they will need to map out a grid along the lines shown in Figure 1.5 below. Direct them to highlight any relevant points in the extracts, cut them out and colour code them according to author. They should then write an evaluative sentence for each category, assessing the nature and extent of the change. You can then shrink the resulting grids on the photocopier and return them to the students for future reference.

Activity 3

Mini question:

Do we remember what is most significant about the Crimean War?

Finally, return to the responses in the questionnaires and pull together the main ways the war is remembered. Provide students with the summary sheet on costs and consequences of the war (Resource 1K). Draw out the contrasts between the two.

As a quick plenary, ask each student to sketch a design for a memorial to the war, which captures what they consider to be its most significant aspect.

Figure 1.5 *Possible grid*

How far did the Crimean conflict result in changes in the nature of warfare?

Factor	Main points from the extracts	Evaluative sentence
Technology		
Tactics		
Leadership/army organisation		
The role of the public and the press		
Overall conclusion		

RESOURCE 1J *Assessments of the significance of the Crimean War*

The sufferings, the courage, the endurance displayed in the Crimean War were not wasted. It had been a small war, an unsuccessful war, a horribly mismanaged war; but it proved to be of enormous importance. After the Crimean War a change came in military affairs – even the incompetence of the Crimea bore fruit. A new age of Army reform began not only in England but in Europe and the United States of America: staff colleges were set up, the conditions under which commissions and promotion were obtained were reformed, medical and hospital services, supply, clothing, cooking were all investigated and improved. Above all the treatment of the private soldier was changed. The bravery, the stubborn endurance of private soldiers, reported in newspapers for the first time during the Crimea, had been a revelation. At the beginning of the campaign the private soldier was regarded as a dangerous brute; at the end he was a hero. Army welfare and Army education, Army recreation, sports and physical training, the health services, all came into being as a result of the Crimea. The agony had been frightful, but it had not all been useless.

Woodham-Smith (1953) The Reason Why, *pp. 273–74*

The logistical difficulties of the war prompted army reform in Great Britain. The first, and most important, was the rationalisation of the chain of command for organisation in the field (from seven to one). One civilian minister (the Secretary of State for War) and one military officer (the Commander-in-chief) now controlled all aspects of personnel, supply and ordnance. A Staff College was set up in 1862 at Camberley to improve staff work within the army. The support services in the field were rationalised. A Mounted Staff Corps became the army's police service, whilst the Land Transport Corps became the Military Train and later, in 1870, the Army Service Corps.

Johnson (2002) The Changing Nature of Warfare 1792–1918, *p. 78*

The introduction of first the Minie rifle and then the Enfield, revolutionised the battlefield. The ordinary infantry soldier now possessed a weapon long-ranged and accurate enough to enable him to operate it independently. He need no longer manoeuvre in line and fire in volleys to compensate for the inaccuracy of his musket. To that extent the thick skirmishing line into which the Light Division dissolved at the Battle of Alma during its attack on the Great Redoubt, far from being an aberration, foreshadowed the tactic which, out of necessity, came to be adopted on the even more lethal battlefields of the Franco-Prussian War sixteen years later.

Massie (2004) The National Army Museum Book of the Crimean War: The Untold Stories, *p. 254*

 © HODDER EDUCATION

Comparing the Crimean and Boer Wars

Dixon has just pointed out two differences between the two wars: new technology and a different enemy.

The chief benefit of the British nation was the reform of the British army. This war, fought at the mid-point of the nineteenth century, had many elements that would have been familiar to those who fought under Wellington. There were as many new elements introduced which would have been equally familiar to the soldiers of the Great War. Rifled firearms and artillery, conical bullets and shells, the electric telegraph, iron-clad, steam driven warships, railways, war photography, war reportage: all of these developments, new at the start of the war, were accepted as normal by its end. Tactics changed dramatically; both cavalry and infantry learned to adopt more open formations, and relied far more on firepower, which itself was far more predictable. The Minie rifle had been replaced in the latter stages of the campaign by the Enfield, which were so effective that they were soon being sent out to India, to be issued to the sepoys.

...

Above all, the Crimean War was the training ground for a generation of young officers. Some of those serving in the Crimea as young men became generals of the future: Hamley, Gordon, Adye, Wolseley. Midshipman Evelyn Wood became a Field Marshall, and Sergeant Luke O'Connor, who had refused to relinquish the colours in the Great Redoubt, died a Major-General and a KCB. These were the men who went on to extend, defend and police the Empire, and in general, they did it well.

Spilsbury (2005) The Thin Red Line: An Eyewitness History of the Crimean War, *pp. 322–23*

These two differences between the wars would not have mattered had those who ran the British army managed to keep up with the times in their thinking, and shaken off the habits acquired over the preceding five hundred years. This they seemed unable to do. For a start, officers were still so busy being gentlemen, in and out of gorgeous uniforms, that they had little time for their men and a total absence of concern for the latter's welfare. ...

Progress in adopting new military techniques was also conspicuous by its absence. Right up to the outbreak of war, training manoeuvres were characterised by a disregard of new weapons. 'The accent was on solid line formations, mechanical precision, rigid dependence on order, firing strictly in volleys at a word of command.'

The position as regards artillery was little better. According to one writer: 'The artillery doctrine of the time was older than the guns, older almost than the Crimea. The artillery galloped smartly into action, unlimbered in the open (for it had no notion of indirect fire), and opened fire over primitive sights with no vestige of a gun shield to protect its crews.'

Considering its inadequate handling of the Crimean War, one might have expected that the high command would try to rehabilitate itself with a rigorous training programme during the ensuing years of peace. Evidently it did not. According to Kruger: 'Only two months a year were spent training. For the rest a man was parading.'

Dixon (1994) On the Psychology of Military Incompetence, *p. 53*

RESOURCE 1K *The costs and consequences of the Crimean War*

The human cost	
British servicemen killed in action	2,755
British servicemen wounded/died of disease (estimated)	2,019 died of wounds 16,323 died of disease
Leaders killed	3 generals died at the Battle of Inkerman. The commander-in-chief, Lord Raglan, died of natural causes.
Allied deaths (French, Sardinian and Turkish troops as well as British from all causes)	Over 500,000
Russians dead (from all causes)	About 522,000
The financial cost	
Cost of the operation (for Britain)	About £50,000,000
The political/diplomatic consequences	
British politics	As a result of the public concern about the war, the government of Lord Aberdeen fell from power and was replaced in February 1855 by one led by Lord Palmerston. The Roebuck Committee published a report after the war which was highly critical of the government's management of logistics, medical care and sanitation during the war.
British foreign relations	Britain remained an ally of France but relations between the two countries were uneasy until the Entente Cordiale in 1904. Britain adopted an isolationist approach to Europe until the early 20th century and maintained a small professional army, unlike other European countries which had conscription.
The Treaty of Paris, 1856	The self-government of Wallachia and Moldavia was agreed; the Danube was declared a free waterway for all nations; the Black Sea was made a demilitarised zone with free access to all and the Christian citizens of Turkey had their rights safeguarded. Sebastapol was returned to Russian control. The rights and integrity of the Ottoman Empire were guaranteed. The peace was short lived as a new Russo-Turkish War broke out in 1877.
Other consequences	
Technological	The use of the telegraph ensured that the public and politicians were quickly updated on the progress of the war. The public and the press exerted more influence than before. The Balaclava Railway was acknowledged to have played a key role in providing supplies in the second Crimean winter.
Organisation and administration	Administration was streamlined so that there was one Minister for War, a politician, and one Commander-in-chief, a soldier. A Medical Staff Corps and Military Train were set up. A Staff College was established at Camberley in 1862 to improve organisation and leadership.

Information taken from Hastings and Jenkins (1983), Anderson (2002) and Middlebrook (2001)

 © HODDER EDUCATION

Investigation B

Plenary study: the Falklands War

In the evocative *Forgotten Voices of the Falklands*, Robert Fox, a BBC correspondent, describes sitting on board ship in the hours before British troops were landed at Goose Green to attack the Argentinians. He speaks of the grating sound that echoed around the decks; a rasping sound of metal on stone. It was an ancient sound of war which might have been heard on the eve of Agincourt or Balaclava. The marines were sharpening their bayonets. Nor was it just an empty ritual, even in those days of Exocet missiles and harrier jets. On the hills above Port Stanley there was hand-to-hand fighting and men died in this 'old-fashioned' way. Some have argued, most evocatively in the film *Tumbledown*, that it was this aspect of the Falklands War which left the deepest psychological scar. However, many died without ever seeing the men who killed them. Sailors on the *Belgrano*, the *Coventry* and the *Sheffield* were hit by guided missiles using modern weapon systems. Port Stanley airfield was attacked by that supreme achievement of military engineering: the Vulcan bomber. Freedman has stated that this war was the 'last war of a past imperial era' while also now recognised as 'one of the first of the coming post-cold war era' (Freedman, 2005, Vol. II: 747). It is this blend which makes the Falklands an ideal plenary study for evaluating change and continuity.

By this stage in their learning your class should feel fairly confident about the terminology and techniques of war so you should keep direct teaching to a minimum and hand over the learning to them. After their map work, provide them only with a basic introduction to the war so that they understand its causes and context. With the aid of DVD, PowerPoint exposition and note taking, ensure they have a timeline of key events and an understanding of the contemporary British and Argentinian situations. Hindsight tempts young people to consider British success inevitable, so present them with this extract to clarify the difficulty of the operation:

> This was an operation to be conducted 8000 miles from the United Kingdom when Britain was supposed to have shrugged off its global pretensions. This was to be the first 'missile age' naval encounter. It was intended to be directed by a Task Force Commander situated in a bunker in north London. Operation Corporate* required a Royal Navy, intended to be used to fight a submarine war in the Eastern Atlantic, to project and support two brigades of troops onto a hostile shore and in a hostile air environment. It was opposed by a modern, numerous airforce when much of the equipment to accomplish such missions – such as conventional aircraft carriers and helicopter carriers – had disappeared in the wake of numerous Defence Reviews since the mid-1960s. The South Atlantic winter was fast approaching. There was the ever-present wind and the difficult terrain with which to contend but with little of the supporting infrastructure one might have expected in a European conflict. Few vehicles were taken; there were no roads on which to drive. Helicopters were always in short supply, necessitating the famous 'yomps' and 'tabs' (forced marches in Royal Marine and Parachute regiment terminology). The Argentine defenders outnumbered the British and were, in many cases, better equipped, and had been dug in for some time.
>
> * The code name for the Falklands expedition
>
> *Badsey, Havers and Grove (2005: xiv–xv)*

In Woodward's words, British victory should be judged as a 'fairly close run thing in matters of timing, land forces and air forces' (Woodward, 2003: xix).

When the students have this basis, launch your *Apprentice*-style competition (see Figures 1.6 and 1.7).

Figure 1.6 *Using the TV show* The Apprentice *as a classroom activity*

The Apprentice is a reality show where young businessmen and women try to win a top job with leading entrepreneur Sir Alan Sugar. It involves setting the teams of applicants a series of challenging tasks and eliminating the least competent member of the losing team at the end of each episode. After each task the teams have to face the boardroom when the evidence of their achievements is analysed and they are grilled about their performance. Two advisers observe the teams at work and report back to Sugar, chipping in during the assessment process with their views. There is an American version with Donald Trump which preceded the UK series. It is hugely popular and offers a very familiar format for students.

It is up to you how religiously you follow the original idea. It is certainly helpful for the teacher to adopt the role of a rigorous, no-nonsense interrogator in the boardroom. You can go further and project Sugar's image on your whiteboard and put on a business suit. Two external advisers are also a great asset. If you can involve parents, trainee teachers or even military personnel, then they will add a lot of value to the activity. If they are not known to your students they will make the process a little more formal and scary, which encourages them to put in maximum effort. You could, of course, film the final session and make it available on your intranet too.

The TV show is quite brutal and focuses on the mistakes and failures of individuals. This, you should make clear, is a feature not being replicated in your classroom enactment. Teams will be held to account and be made to justify the quality of their history but attempts to attack particular team members will not be accepted. The teacher will have to set a tone of robust group review without any name-calling or personal attacks.

Activity 1

Mini question:

Which factors determined the conduct and outcome of the Falklands War?

Organise your class into teams, focusing on the key themes studied in the enquiry: leadership, technology, tactics, and other factors. Of course, this last category is large and will require a broader brush approach. Keeping it to four teams will make the activity manageable. Make the focus of the competition to produce the best quality historical evaluation rather than arguing for the importance of each factor. The trouble with competitions over questions of relative historical importance is that they can encourage poor historical practices such as distortion or omission of evidence. It is a strange feature of our history courses that we rarely make explicit what a good historian actually is although it is often implicit in lesson objectives and assessment criteria. Make this clear in this task and ensure a healthy respect for evidence by telling the class that they are being assessed as historians and that poor history will result in penalty points. Guide them to the key issues with a few bullet points for each theme and recommended sources. Providing reading tips undermines the independence of the project but is probably worth it for cutting down time wastage and improving the quality of the outcome. Such reading tips will just be a selection of useful pages and articles from a range of books at hand.

Figure 1.7 *Adaptation of* The Apprentice *format for Falklands War evaluations*

1. Organise your class into teams. I would recommend random, mixed-ability grouping to encourage healthy and balanced competition.
2. Before you get going, tell your students that they are going to enter a team competition and ask them to select what they consider to be a worthwhile prize. You could offer letters home to parents, being excused a homework exercise, watching a DVD, a voucher, a chocolate bar or get them to nominate something else you consider appropriate. Have a class vote on the most popular prize and tell them all members of the winning team will be awarded it. This will prove motivational and help to create a team spirit.
3. Summon them all to the boardroom. If you want a bit of drama, play the introductory music from the TV series as you enter the room in your business suit. Explain the key task and borrow these adapted words from Sugar to set the tone: *One of the teams is going to end up winning* (state the agreed prize) *but I tell you what, the prize does not mean anything. I've been in the business of history for over* (state the right number!) *years. Your prize is being the best historians in* (name your school or college). *This is a history boot camp. Mary Poppins I am not. I'm not going to hold your hand. I'm not going to tell you what to do. You're on your own two feet. You might think you're going off now to relax. Well, you're not. History starts now.* (www.bbc.co.uk/apprentice/about/general.shtml)
4. Give out the task sheet with information about the rules, deadlines and assessment criteria. (Resource 1L). If you are lucky enough to have advisers for two lessons, warn the students that they will be observed and feedback will be given about how well they work as teams of historians. If you are on your own, make them aware that you will be on hand, taking notes of their performance. Their first task is to select a project manager, who should then allocate roles and responsibilities.
5. Provide access to a full range of resources with the guidance sheets (Resources 1M–1P) to help students focus on the essential. Draw their attention to the fact that the Internet is not the most useful source for this topic and should be used with discrimination. Aimless trawling of Google and Wikipedia will waste time and may attract penalty points.
6. Each team should produce a PowerPoint presentation and a written report of no more than four sides of A4. Point out the advice on the task sheet and remind them that the two products have different purposes.
7. Once all the presentations have been heard, summon all the teams to the boardroom, recreating the drama of the first occasion if you wish. Bring in the advisers and hear their recommendations. Prepare thoroughly so that you have challenging questions to ask each team, focusing on their work as historians rather than the importance of their factor.
8. Fire the weakest team first, making explicit the reasons why. (In this version whole teams are fired rather than individuals.) It may be best not to be as blunt and negative as Sugar here, by recognising some of the team achievements, but some plain speaking will not do lasting harm.
9. Move on to your second bank of questions, drawing in your advisers and allowing other students to chip in and defend themselves. Fire your runner-up teams until you have two left. Allow the surviving teams to retire and prepare their final piece of evidence (of any kind) which will throw light on their factor (Outcome 3 on the task sheet). While they are out of the room, instruct the 'fired' teams to prepare for the critical evaluation of this 'Exocet' evidence.
10. Invite the surviving teams back into the boardroom to present their evidence. This should be done orally, on the spot. Students from the unsuccessful groups should lead the interrogation of the two remaining teams and their presented evidence.
11. Retire with your advisers for your final verdict. Return to the boardroom and announce the winner with a clear explanation of the reasons for your choice.

RESOURCE 1L *Falklands task sheet*

How did .... affect the conduct and outcome of the Falklands War?

FACTOR: ....

Focus

The purpose of this assignment is to evaluate and communicate the key points about how your factor (a) affected the conduct of the war and (b) affected the outcome of the war.

Outcome

1. You must produce a PowerPoint presentation of no more than four slides. The purpose of this is to communicate the key points to your audience, clearly, fluently and accurately. You need to summarise and explain the most important points.
2. You must produce a written evaluation of no more than four sides of A4. The purpose of this is to show that you have considered a range of relevant evidence to reach your developed conclusion.
3. You must find an 'Exocet', i.e. a weighty piece of evidence to hold in reserve in case you reach the last two teams in the competition. This must be a piece of evidence which you have found for yourselves and has not been given in your resources list or pack. You should be prepared to present this in the boardroom, explaining how it elucidates the role played by your factor and why you consider it such a valuable piece of evidence. Make sure you are confident about its strengths and weaknesses as evidence because you may be cross-examined on these.

Deadlines

The two tasks must be completed by

....

Method

1. Appoint your project manager.
2. Allocate roles and responsibilities for your team.
3. Decide on a timetable of realistic internal deadlines for each task.

Assessment

This competition will be won by the best team of historians, not by the most important factor in the Falklands conflict. As historians you will be assessed on how well you demonstrate the following:

1. Analysis supported by well selected information
2. Information used from a range of sources
3. Discriminating use of reading and other material, i.e. it is considered critically and not at face value
4. Cogent and lucid exposition.

Based on exam board's list of qualities of high level work (Edexcel Specifications 2007: 65)

The following checklist will help you to ensure you score highly:

- Have you considered (in depth) the role played by your factor – strengths and weaknesses and how it worked in conjunction with other factors?
- Have you included at least two different forms of primary evidence?
- Have you considered the views of at least two historians?
- Have you checked the quality of your communication in terms of clarity and accuracy?
- Have you reached a clear conclusion?
- Have you referenced all your sources correctly?

Remember penalty points will be awarded for failure to do the above. Your team work will be observed to see if you are working as good historians.

RESOURCE 1M Resources and content guidance

Leadership

Key issues you might consider

- How much co-operation and clarity was there in relationships at senior level (e.g. between land and sea forces, between political and military leaders)?
- How strong were relationships at lower levels?
- How effectively were resources managed?
- How good was the quality of decision making?

Key people you might consider

- Higher levels: Admiral Fieldhouse (Commander of the Task Force) and under him Rear Admiral Woodward (in charge of the carrier battle group), Commodore Clapp (in charge of Amphibious Operations) and Brigadier Thompson (in charge of the Landing Force) and his relief, General Jeremy Moore
- Lower levels: Colonel H. Jones (Commander of 2nd Battalion the Parachute Regiment), David Hart-Dyke (Captain of HMS *Coventry*)

Reading and research tips

These whole articles are very useful:

Prince, S. (2002) 'British command and control in the Falklands Campaign', *Defense and Security Analysis*, 18: 4, 333–49. (This whole article is very useful but you will need to access it through JSTOR or equivalent.)

Band, J. (2005) 'British High Command during and after the Falklands Conflict' in Badsey, S., Havers, R. and Grove, M. (eds) (2005) *The Falklands Conflict Twenty Years on: Lessons for the Future,* London: Routledge, pp. 30–39.

Key leaders

Leadership at the top:

Leach, H. (2005) 'Crisis Management and the Assembly of the Task Force' in Badsey, S. Havers, R. and Grove, M. (eds) (2005) *The Falklands Conflict Twenty Years on: Lessons for the Future,* London: Routledge, pp. 69–72.

Hastings, M. and Jenkins, S. (1983) *The Battle for the Falklands,* London: Pan Books, pp. 377–84.

The leadership of Admiral Woodward:

Hastings, M. and Jenkins, S. (1983) *The Battle for the Falklands,* London: Pan Books, p. 359.

The leadership of the Admiral of the Fleet, Fieldhouse:

Hastings, M. and Jenkins, S. (1983) *The Battle for the Falklands,* London: Pan Books, pp. 211–12.

The leadership of Colonel H. Jones:

Hastings, M. and Jenkins, S. (1983) *The Battle for the Falklands,* London: Pan Books, pp. 269–81

Anderson, D. (2002) *The Falklands War 1982*, Oxford: Osprey Publishing, pp. 49–50.

National Army Museum online exhibition:

www.national-army-museum.ac.uk/exhibitions/falklands/page5.shtml

Key decisions

The decision to sink the Belgrano:

McManners, H. (2007) *Forgotten Voices of the Falklands,* Ebury Press, pp. 150–51.

Hart-Dyke, D (2007) *Four Weeks in May*, Atlantic Books, pp. 85–86.

The decision to land at Bluff Cove:

Anderson, D. (2002) *The Falklands War 1982,* Oxford: Osprey Publishing, pp. 58–60.

Woodward, S. (with Robinson, P.) (2003) *One Hundred Days: The Memoirs of the Falklands Battle Group Commander,* London: Harper Collins, pp. 454–57.

Efficacy of teamwork

Hart-Dyke, D. (2007) *Four Weeks in May*, Atlantic Books, pp. 85–86.

McManners, H. (2007) *Forgotten Voices of the Falklands War,* Ebury Press, pp. xii–xiii.

Middlebrook, M. (2001) *The Falklands War 1982*, London: Penguin, pp. 92–96.

Woodward, S. (with Robinson, P.) (2003) *One Hundred Days: The Memoirs of the Falklands Battle Group Commander*, London: Harper Collins, pp. xxvii–xxxii.

RESOURCE 1N Resources and content guidance

Technology

Key issues you might consider

- How far did British technology suit the tasks it faced?
- How well did the weapons perform?
- How did Argentine and British weapons compare?
- How well was the technology deployed in battle?
- How much wastage was there?

Advice: Beware of preparing lists of weapons and their relative merits and defects. You need to consider the role that technology played in (a) the conduct and (b) the outcome of the campaign. To help here are some significant incidents you might look at:

- The strategic use of aircraft: the 'Black Buck' raids by Vulcan bombers
- The use of helicopters in the capture of South Georgia
- The use of submarine and torpedo to sink the *Belgrano*
- The strengths and weaknesses of offensive and defensive systems in the sinking of *Sheffield* and *Coventry*
- The deployment of Super Etendard guided missiles (Exocet) by the Argentine airforce
- The role of naval bombardment in the capture of Mt Harriet and Mt Longdon.

Technology you might consider

- Ships: Aircraft carriers (*Hermes* and *Invincible*), destroyers and frigates, submarines, amphibious warfare vessels
- Aircraft: Harrier GR3, Sea Harrier, Pucara, Mirage 111-E, Vulcan bomber, Skyhawk, Lear jet
- Artillery and missiles: Sidewinder AIM-L missiles, Super Etendard with Exocet missiles, Sea Dart, Sea Cat, Sea Slug, Rapier L 118 Light Gun, Blowpipe missile
- Defensive and warning systems: defensive radar decoys (chaff), satellite communications systems (SCOT), Airborne Early Warning (AEW)
- Rifles and machine guns: GPMG (British machine gun) or FN MAG (Argentine machine gun), SLRs, Sterling, MILAN anti-tank guided weapon.

Reading and research tips

These whole sections or articles are very useful:

Zakheim, D. S. (1985) 'The South Atlantic Conflict: Strategic, Military and Technological Lessons' in Coll, A. E. and Arend, A. C. (eds) (1985) *The Falklands War*, Unwin Hyman, pp. 180–83.

Anderson, D. (2002) *The Falklands War 1982,* Oxford: Osprey Publishing, pp. 35–69.

Cooksey, J. (2004) *3 Para Mount Longdon: The Bloodiest Battle*, Barnsley: Pen and Sword Books, chapter on weapons, pp. 52–60.

Kiszely, J. P. (2005) 'The Land Campaign: A Company Commander's Perspective' in Badsey, S., Havers, R. and Grove, M. *The Falklands Conflict Twenty Years On: Lessons for the Future,* London: Routledge, pp. 105–06.

The role of aircraft

Philip, D. (2002) 'Falklands Conflict 1982 – The Air War: A New Appraisal', in Badsey, S., Havers, R. and Grove, M., *The Falklands Conflict Twenty Years On: Lessons for the Future* (Sandhurst Conference Series), London: Routledge.

The role of ships

Hastings, M. and Jenkins, S. (1983) *The Battle for the Falklands,* London: Pan Books, state of ships p. 103, destroyers p. 179, aircraft carriers p. 209.

Operational strengths and weaknesses

Hart-Dyke, D. (2007) *Four Weeks in May*, London: Atlantic Books, p. 148.

Hastings, M. and Jenkins, S. (1983) *The Battle for the Falklands,* London: Pan Books, pp. 357–58.

Middlebrook, M. (2001) *The Falklands War 1982*, London: Penguin, pp. 382–85.

The Exocet threat

Hart-Dyke, D. (2007) *Four Weeks in May*, London: Atlantic Books, pp. 87–88, *Sheffield*'s response to the threat pp. 90–92.

RESOURCE  Resources and content guidance

Tactics

Key issues you might consider

- How effective was the planning of the Falklands operation?
- How effective were the tactics employed to capture South Georgia?
- How effective were the following operations:
  - the recapture of South Georgia
  - the landing at San Carlos Water
  - the Battle of Goose Green
  - Special Forces operations on Mount Kent, on Pebble Island and Rio Grande
  - the events at Bluff Cove and Fitzroy
  - the capture of the mountains above Port Stanley.

Aspects you might consider

- Timing: the pace of the operations, the times and dates of landing, the constraints of the South Atlantic winter
- Location: the decision to land at San Carlos Water, the decision to attack Darwin and Goose Green, the positioning of naval vessels such as *Hermes*, the positioning of frigates as 'picket ships'
- Force deployment: the use of special forces in the operation in Chile and at Pebble Island; the nature of air and sea support for the land battle at Goose Green and on Mount Longdon.

Reading and research tips

The whole of the following is useful:

Zakheim, D. S. (1985) 'The South Atlantic Conflict: Strategic, Military and Technological Lessons' in Coll, A. E. and Arend, A. C. (eds) (1985) *The Falklands War*, Unwin Hyman, pp. 174–79.

Kiszely, J. P. (2005) 'The Land Campaign: A Company Commander's Perspective' in Badsey, S. Havers, R. and Grove, M. *The Falklands Conflict Twenty Years On: Lessons for the Future,* London: Routledge.

Gray, P. W. (2005) 'Air Power: Strategic Lessons from an Idiosyncratic Operation' in Badsey, S., Havers, R. and Grove, M. (2005) *The Falklands Conflict Twenty Years on: Lessons for the Future,* London: Routledge.

Plans and preparations

Hastings, M. and Jenkins, S. (1983) *The Battle for the Falklands,* London: Pan Books, pp. 213–15.

Middlebrook, M. (2001) *The Falklands War 1982*, London: Penguin, Chapter 13 Plans and Preparations. pp. 195–205.

The recapture of South Georgia

Hastings, M. and Jenkins, S. (1983) *The Battle for the Falklands,* London: Pan Books pp. 150–55.

The decision to land at San Carlos

Hastings, M. and Jenkins, S. (1983) *The Battle for the Falklands*, London: Pan Books, pp. 213–16.

Woodward, S. (with Robinson, P.) (2003) *One Hundred Days: The Memoirs of the Falklands Battle Group Commander*, London; Harper Collins, pp. 256–63.

The decision to land at Bluff Cove

Anderson, D. (2002) *The Falklands War 1982*, Oxford: Osprey Publishing, pp. 58–60.

Woodward, S. (with Robinson, P.) (2003) *One Hundred Days: The Memoirs of the Falklands Battle Group Commander*, London: Harper Collins, pp. 454–57.

The operation at Goose Green

Middlebrook, M. (2001) *The Falklands War 1982*, London: Penguin, Chapter 16, pp. 248–73.

The use of warships to support land forces

Thompson, J. (2005) 'Force Projection and the Falklands Conflict' in Badsey, S., Havers, R. and Grove, M., *The Falklands Conflict Twenty Years On: Lessons for the Future*, London: Routledge, pp. 95–96.

The use of special forces

Middlebrook, M. (2001) *The Falklands War 1982*, London: Penguin, pp. 192–93 (in Chile).

Woodward, S. (with Robinson, P.) (2003) *One Hundred Days: The Memoirs of the Falklands Battle Group Commander*, London: Harper Collins, pp. 274–78, 302–06 (Pebble Island).

The use of 'picket ships'

Woodward, S. (with Robinson, P.) (2003) *One Hundred Days: The Memoirs of the Falklands Battle Group Commander*, London: Harper Collins, pp. 7–8.

Intelligence

Keegan, J. (2004) *Intelligence in War,* London: Pimlico, pp. 343–53.

 © HODDER EDUCATION

RESOURCE 1P *Resources and content guidance*

Other factors

Key issues you might consider

- The contrasting armies: organisation, training, age and experience and special forces
- Logistics: the role of aircraft carriers, troop carriers and the *Atlantic Conveyor*, the importance of Ascension Island, Argentinian problems with supplies after the bombing of Stanley airfield
- Terrain and climate: the South Atlantic winter and the problems of timing, the cold and wet conditions, the mountainous landscape near Stanley, the lack of metalled roads.

Reminder: You have a much larger scope than the other groups so your assessment will not be expected to cover each factor in so much depth.

Resources

Armies

Anderson, D. (2002) *The Falklands War 1982*, Oxford: Osprey Publishing, pp. 29–30, 69–71.

Cooksey, J. (2004) *3 Para Mount Longdon: The Bloodiest Battle*, Barnsley: Pen and Sword Books, pp. 51–55.

Gonzalez, H. M. (2002) 'An Argentinian Airman in the South Atlantic', in Badsey, S., Havers, R. and Grove, M. (eds) (2005), *The Falklands Conflict Twenty Years On: Lessons for the Future,* London: Routledge, pp. 75–80.

Hastings, M. and Jenkins, S. (1983) *The Battle for the Falklands*, London: Pan Books, pp. 364–67, 361–64.

Logistics

Anderson, D. (2002) *The Falklands War 1982*, Oxford: Osprey Publishing, pp. 26–28.

Hastings, M. and Jenkins, S. (1983) *The Battle for the Falklands*, London: Pan Books, pp. 324–25, 209–10, 359–60.

McManners, H. (2008) *Forgotten Voices of the Falklands*, Ebury Press, pp. 311–12.

Woodward, S. (with Robinson, P.) (2003) *One Hundred Days: The Memoirs of the Falklands Battle Group Commander*, London: Harper Collins, pp. 415–22.

Middlebrook, M. (2001) *The Falklands War 1982*, London: Penguin, pp. 90–91.

Zakheim, D. S. (1985) 'The South Atlantic Conflict: Strategic, Military and Technological Lessons' in Coll, A. E. and Arend, A. C. (eds) (1985) *The Falklands* War, Unwin Hyman, pp. 176–78.

National Army Museum online exhibition:

www.national-army-museum.ac.uk/exhibitions/falklands/page8.shtml#logistics

Terrain and climate

Bramley, V. (2006) *Forward into Hell*, London: John Blake Publishing, pp. 65–75.

Woodward, S. (with Robinson, P.) (2003), *One Hundred Days: The Memoirs of the Falklands Battle Group Commander*, London: Harper Collins, pp. 473.

Middlebrook, M. (2001) *The Falklands War 1982*, London: Penguin, pp. 321.

Activity 2

Mini question:

How far did the Falklands conflict change the nature of warfare?

The Falklands campaign has been called an 'idiosyncratic operation' (Gray, 2005: 253) and a 'freak of history' (Hastings and Jenkins, 1983: 357); an aberration when the British government resumed the guise of a colonial power in the Cold War age. Writing shortly after the war, Hastings and Jenkins (1983) commented:

> Very few of the conclusions that can be drawn from the Falklands experience have a wider application than to this conflict.
>
> *Hastings and Jenkins (1983: 357)*

Yet, 25 years later, it is the Cold War concentration on the Soviet threat, the emphasis on deterrence and the exercises in Eastern Europe which seem irrelevant. The Falklands task force, reacting to a localised emergency caused by an aggressive military dictator, in some ways has more in common with the British military actions over recent years in the Gulf, Kuwait and Sierra Leone.

To put together a quick overview, set up a dartboard card sort (see Figure 1.8 and Resources 1Q and IR) as the basis for the evaluation of how the war affected future conflicts, with the aim of teasing out the longer and shorter term military significance of the conflict.

Figure 1.8 *Activity: dartboard card sort*

This is a familiar card sort activity.

1. Give each group of students an envelope with the cards inside (Resource 1R). Ask students to categorise the cards and to divide the diagram (Resource 1Q, enlarged to A3) into the appropriate number of segments for each category. Make sure they do the sorting first as some categories might be much larger, needing more space, than others.
2. Ask them to place their cards on the diagram in the segment and circle zone they consider to be best.
3. Ask them to highlight in pink longer term significance, and shorter term significance in yellow.
4. Ask them to summarise the military significance of the war using their diagrams.
5. Discuss with your students the view that most people considered the war was an unusual 'one off' at the time but that in the post-Cold War era it has appeared more noteworthy.

Activity 3

Mini question:

Do we remember what is most significant about the Falklands War?

Stage 1

Start with Pink Floyd and 'The Fletcher Memorial Home'. Give your students the lyrics (from www.azlyrics.com) and see how many of the references they can work out for themselves. Ask them to speculate about who Fletcher could be. Then reveal that the song is written in memory of the writer's father, Eric Fletcher Waters, who died in the Second World War at Anzio. The song was released in 1983, less than a year after the end of the Falklands War. For Roger Waters, the war seems a betrayal of the values that his father died for.

David Tinker was 25 years old, had been married for two years and was creating a home from a tumbledown old cottage in the country. He loved poetry, had a history degree and was fascinated by the First World War. He was having doubts about his military career, writing in one of his letters: 'they really should not send people in the Services to study history at university' (Tinker, 1982: 190).

When the Falklands war broke out, he had already put in his notice to quit but he still had to serve out his notice. On 12 June, his ship, the HMS *Glamorgan*, was hit by an Exocet missile and he was killed instantly. Two days later the Argentinians surrendered.

Stage 2

Both Tinker and Waters focus on the human cost of the war – for them, its most significant aspect. To put these personal and military views of the war in a broader perspective, provide your students with the information sheet about the costs and consequences of the war (Resource 1U). Balance out the earlier negative views with the extracts from Bramley and Mrs Thatcher's speech (Resource 1T).

Stage 3

Mini question:

Do we remember what is most significant about the war?

In your final enquiry, draw out the threads that have run through this study:

- The military significance of the Falklands conflict; particularly the changing role of leadership, technology and tactics
- The high costs of the war, both human and otherwise
- The features of the war that have been remembered as significant afterwards, using the parental questionnaires

Discuss with your class the conflicting needs to commemorate those who have died and to judge the significance of war in retrospect. Finally, ask them to write down what they consider to be the most significant aspects of the Falklands conflict as a military historian and as a general historian; and then how they, as individuals, will remember the war.

Provide further evidence for this view with the extract from Tinker's *Message from the Falklands* (Resource 1S).

RESOURCE 1Q *Dartboard card sort diagram*

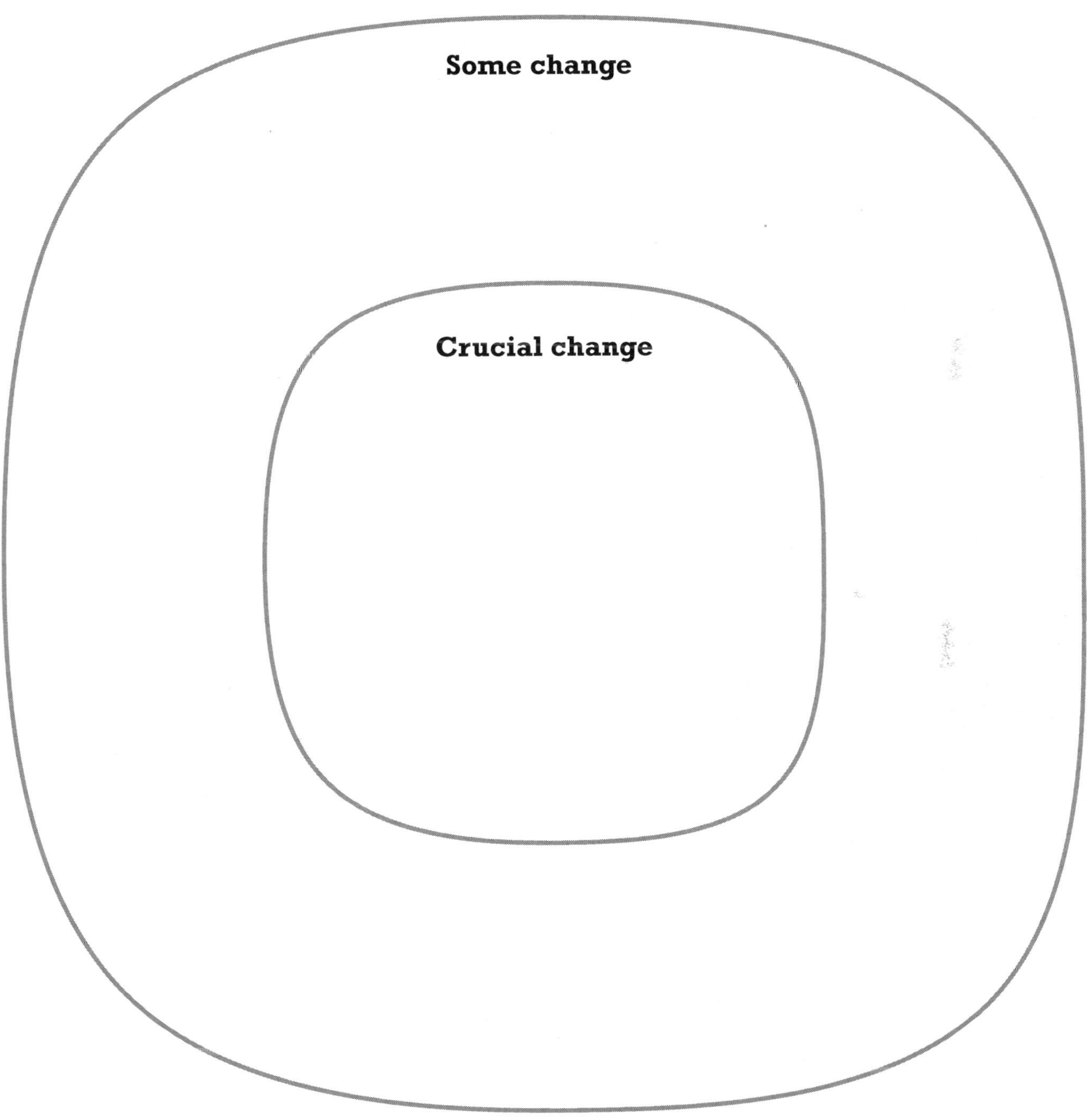

RESOURCE  Dartboard card sort cards

In the 15 years after the war, there was considerable investment in new Sea Harriers equipped with improved weapons and radar.

The decision not to invest in Airborne Early Warning radar was reversed after the war.

The importance of helicopters was recognised with investment in new radar and better air transport in the 15 years after.

In the longer term, the importance of stress-related illness amongst servicemen has become apparent.

In the immediate years following, inflammable material on ships was reduced as a result of the terrible burns sustained.

The war exposed the vulnerability of ships but the Royal Navy still has not invested in modern radar-guided guns to fight air attacks.

Military leadership has become more unified with organisation of joint doctrine and joint command in times of conflict put in place.

The MOD admitted in 2003 that British ships had had nuclear depth charges in 1982 but there was never any intention to use them.

After the war public attitudes towards the armed services became more positive and more confident.

Many weapons used were old-fashioned, e.g. a conventional torpedo sank the *Belgrano*, bayonets were used on Mt Longdon.

After 1982 it was decided to retain the three aircraft carriers due to the vital role they played in the conflict.

Flaws in computer weapon systems were exposed in the war, e.g. Sea Wolf would not lock on when faced with two adjacent targets.

The war confirmed the need to invest in the training and equipping of specialist forces such as the SAS and SBS, which has been ongoing since.

It was decided in 2006 to remove the AMRAAM Sea Harrier FA2 from front line service although this aircraft was crucial to success in 1982.

In the 1980s Soviet analysts concluded that they had underestimated the capability of the British military.

The British Strategic Defence Review (1998) decided to procure and design new carriers and amphibious vessels, remembering their value in 1982.

In the first Gulf War, the organisation of the Joint Forces Headquarters, with one overall commander, was influenced by lessons learnt from 1982.

Naval defence cuts continued, with the size of the surface fleet declining from 59 to around 30 in the years 1982–2002.

© HODDER EDUCATION

RESOURCE 1S *Extract from Tinker's Message from the Falklands*

David Tinker, a lieutenant in the Royal Navy serving on HMS *Glamorgan*, writing to an old friend who had served in the navy in the Second World War:

> Of course, what is happening here must feel familiar to you from the Second World War: the bravery and courage of our own pilots, flying an aircraft which was designed simply to intercept Soviet reconnaissance aircraft and which is now being pitted against supersonic fighters and used for bombing with gear little more advanced than the Lancaster. And the bravery and tragic waste of life of the Argentinian pilots, sent against overwhelming anti-aircraft missiles by heartless superiors. The devotion to duty of our frigates in the Falklands Sound, who were sitting ducks for the Argentinian aircraft and which were all hit by bombs. And, above all, the tragedy, anguish, and horror of the British lives that have been lost: which have been spent quite willingly by Mrs Thatcher and Mr Nott to make up for the political ineptitude and pig headedness of the Government. When one considers the total of sorrow, financial loss, loss of ships for Britain (which I doubt will ever be replaced) and destruction to the Falklands – now dotted with war graves – all balanced against a 'principle', a flag, and the ousting of two dozen islanders (those expelled) it does seem to me personally the most pointless of wars ever fought by Britain.
>
> I had hoped that our Government would compromise, to bring a peaceful settlement: but now the only way to end this, for the time being, will be to defeat the Argentinians, and I hope that they surrender soon. They have proved their bravery, honourably, already. Of course, once we regain the islands we will still have to talk to the Argentinians, unless we want to provide a garrison of three soldiers for every inhabitant. The Falklands will end up much better defended than the UK!

Tinker (1982) A Message from the Falklands: The Life and Gallant Death of David Tinker Lieut. R.N. From his Letters and Poems, *p. 187*

RESOURCE 1T *Different views of the Falklands War*

I fully believe that we, as a nation, performed the most excellent of tasks. I am fully behind the decision to send the task force and I wouldn't hesitate to fight again for our country and its beliefs. People who whinge about the decisions taken in a war they weren't involved in are to me the most misguided of all. Take the sinking of the *Belgrano*. Nobody at home has the right to say it was wrong, when thousands of British lives could have been at stake. I believe the sinking saved more lives than it claimed. Nobody, but nobody, will change my view on that. Also, we should remember that the Argentine regime of that time showed scant regard for human life. What if the boot had been on the other foot? No, we British had been kicked once too often.

Bramley, V. (2006) Forward into Hell*, p. 285*

Twenty five years ago British forces secured a great victory in a noble cause. The whole nation rejoiced at the success; and we should still rejoice. Aggression was defeated and reversed. The wishes of local people were upheld as paramount. Britain's honour and interests prevailed. Sending troops into battle is the gravest decision that any Prime Minister has to take. To fight 8,000 miles away from home, in perilous conditions, against a well armed, if badly led, enemy was bound to be an awesome challenge. Moreover, at such times there is no lack of people, at home and abroad, to foretell disaster. Then, when things go well, they are just as quick to press some hopeless compromise.

Mrs Thatcher's Speech on the Anniversary of the Falklands War, BBC News Online, 13 June 2007. To play the recording directly: http://news.bbc.co.uk/player/nol/newsid_6740000/newsid_6748800/6748807.stm?bw=nb&mp=wm&news=1&bbcws=1wm&news=1&bbcws=1

 © HODDER EDUCATION

RESOURCE  *The costs and consequences of the Falklands War*

The human cost	
British servicemen killed	255
British servicemen wounded	777
British servicemen who have committed suicide since (SAMA* estimate)	264
comparisons with other wars	The death rate was not as high as Korea (537), Malaya (525) or Northern Ireland (352 up to 1982) but more than that suffered in Palestine, Cyprus, Aden or the Oman. However, the fighting was more intense, as the war lasted only six weeks.
Argentine dead	746 (but 652 was the later official figure provided by the Argentine government)
Argentine wounded	1,105
Military losses	
British ships	6 sunk and 10 badly damaged
British aircraft	10 planes and 24 helicopters
Argentine ships	*Belgrano* and several smaller ships
Argentine aircraft (British claims)	109
The financial cost	
cost of the operation	£700 million plus £900 million in lost planes and ships
cost of holding and keeping the Falklands 1982–86 (estimated)	£2 billion
approximate annual cost of garrisoning the Falklands (2002)	£70 million (0.3% of defence budget)
The political consequences	
Britain	From a low point before the war, Mrs Thatcher won an emphatic election victory in 1983, the start of a further 15 years of Conservative government. The Franks Report, published in January 1983, stated that the government was not to blame for failing to anticipate the war.
Argentina	The military dictatorship of General Galtieri fell from power almost immediately the war finished. The Radical Party took office after elections in October 1983. Galtieri was put on trial for crimes committed during his rule and sentenced to imprisonment.
The consequences for the islands	
From a small, neglected, sheep-farming community, the islands have been transformed. The total population was 1800 people with a density of less than 0.4 per square mile compared to the UK average of 100 per square mile. After the war the population swelled, new roads were constructed and better radio and television services installed. A systematic plan to explore for oil has been initiated and the islands have become a popular tourist destination.	
* South Atlantic Medal Association	
Information taken from Hastings and Jenkins (1983), Anderson (2002) and Middlebrook (2001)	

Concluding study

Activity

Has technology changed the nature of warfare more than anything else?

Stage 1
One of the key themes for the above sequence of lessons is the development of military technology, so make this the key focus of your concluding lessons. Return to your Duplo timeline and the students' hypotheses about the relationship between war and technology. Start off with the technological determinist view and complete the two tasks suggested in Figure 1.9.

Figure 1.9 *The technological determinist case*

Task one
Add to the Duplo timeline with more detailed annotations of key technological developments from 1850 to 1990.

Task two
Find evidence to support each of the following assertions:

- Civilian innovations in communications and transport have had a big influence on the conduct of war.
- New technology has had a huge effect on casualty rates.
- Mass production of weapons has had a massive impact.
- The development of nuclear weapons has transformed the nature of warfare.
- Computer technology has caused huge changes in modern conflict.
- Military technology has improved at a rapid but regular pace.

Use the final chapter of Stewart, N. (2001) *The Changing Nature of Warfare* as a basis for your research.

Stage 2
Now provide students with a conflicting view (Resource 1V) from a leading military historian and ask them to find evidence for the assertions in Figure 1.10. Encourage them to use knowledge from the full scope of their studies of war.

Figure 1.10 *The attack on technological determinism*

Find evidence to support the following assertions:
- Other aspects of warfare such as leadership and tactics have been more influential in changing the nature of warfare than technology.
- There has been considerable continuity as well as change in weaponry.
- New defensive systems have mirrored offensive innovations, minimising their impact.
- New weapons have had more impact on prestige and deterrence than actual fighting on the ground.
- Supposedly 'war-winning' weapons have often proved disappointing in their impact.

Stage 3
Now make your students decide which view they support and prepare their case for a final structured debate. Dust down the comparison studies, especially those on technology, and remind students to use them as evidence for the debate. In order to provide a sharp focus on the nature of change, inform them of the stages of the debate. To facilitate full participation, divide the teams so that different members of the class take a lead in chosen phases of the debate. Figure 1.11 suggests the possible sequence for your discussion.

Figure 1.11 *Structured debate on the impact of military technology*

Debate one
Has military technology followed a path of even progress?

Debate two
Has military technology been an independent factor in changing warfare?

Debate three
Has military technology been the most decisive factor in changing warfare?

RESOURCE 1V *A military historian's view*

There is little evidence to show that casualties proportional to soldiers engaged have been much influenced by technological change; they have gone up and down with the numbers of combatants rather than the volume of firepower. Even one of the most popular examples of technological war, Blitzkrieg, fails to support the decisiveness of weapons. Blitzkrieg experts seem to disagree about everything except the idea that superior tanks and planes had little to do with its definition or its impact. Even where weapons superiority seems indisputable, as in cases where one side had a monopoly of improved armaments, the degree of technological impact is ill defined. This is the case in examples from European colonial conquests and from experiences with 'secret' weapons such as British tanks at Cambrai or German rockets in 1944. If there is indeed insufficient evidence to demonstrate that improved military technology has increased casualties or won battles, then this marginality of impact seems remarkably different from the impact of civilian technology on society in peacetime.

Raudzens (1990: 404)

Sample lesson sequence

Rationale

The aim of this module plan is to suggest ways to blend overview and depth into your 100-year study. The two parallel themes of continuity and change and historical significance are threaded through the enquiry, while there are also opportunities to pursue independent studies and to evaluate sources.

Prior learning

There is no expectation of any prior learning for this study.

Enquiry question

Three questions are asked in sequence for each of the conflicts studied in depth.

1. How important was one factor compared to others in the conduct and outcome of the war?
2. How far did the war result in changes in the nature of warfare?
3. Do we remember what is most significant about this war?

Outline of learning flow

As a scheme of work this can be allocated one term's teaching or about 12 weeks. In this model, the teacher could directly teach the Crimean War introduction and the Falklands War finale, while allowing students to work their way through the intervening material on their own with the teacher providing initial context and guidance. This approach might be particularly suitable for coursework modules or where a large part of the learning needs to take place independently.

An outline of timings is provided in the plan in Figure 1.12 below.

Figure 1.12 *The changing nature of warfare, 1845–1991*

What were the most significant changes in the nature of warfare in the years 1845–1991? 12-week module (each week has 3 x 90-minute lessons)	
War on land and sea in the 19th century Depth study: the Crimean War Focus on leadership 3 weeks	Cover the introduction, the investigation into Balaclava and the broader study of leadership in your initial four lessons. Then give the students lesson time and homework to complete the comparison study, supporting them with contextual knowledge and understanding which they will lack in this first study. Use the last two lessons to examine the nature and extent of change and then how the war has been remembered.
The First World War Depth study: the Western Front Focus on technology 2½ weeks	In the first lesson, use a video such as *The Killing Fields* (People's Century) to provide the main framework for the enquiry. Next, divide the class into teams to look at the impact of four named new weapons: gas, tanks, machine guns and aircraft, requiring students to evaluate the role they played. In the second week, put their judgements alongside other factors in the war such as leadership (the 'Lions led by Donkeys' debate), tactics and armies. Make some time for the comparison study and then finish with your plenary discussion. Use the song 'Hanging on the Old Barbed Wire' as the focus for your review of the significance of the war, how it is remembered and commemorated, bringing in the parental responses.
The Second World War Depth study: the Allied Invasions Focus on tactics 2½ weeks	To provide the class with a basic framework, give each student a key event of the war to research (assuming about 20 in the class; if smaller, then double up). Then play an elimination game until you end up with the 12 most important events and make sure they record them. After this, use computer-based resources (both the Imperial War Museum and National Archives have good material) for individual research into the role of planning, intelligence and strategy in the invasions of Italy and France. In the second week, bring in other factors such as leadership and technology and guide students in their comparison study. Finish off with the opening sequence to *Dad's Army*, which sums up many common memories of the war: Britain alone, Dunkirk spirit and courageous amateurism. Ask students to judge how well this equates with their own view of the significance of the war and their parents' views.

Warfare in the nuclear age Depth study: the Falklands conflict Focus on other factors 3 weeks	In the first lesson, provide students with the contextual background and explain the difficulties of the campaign using the text provided. Then allow four lessons and homework for the *Apprentice* activity, insisting on the first lesson being entirely devoted to reading and allocating lesson 4 for your boardroom finale. Follow this up by studying the military significance of the war in the dartboard activity and then the final evaluation of its broader significance using the Fletcher Memorial song, parental questionnaires and the other sources.
Plenary session The nature and extent of change brought about by technology 1 week	In the first lesson, return to the Duplo timeline and the students' original ideas and add more detail to that overview. Follow this with the technological determinist argument, with homework to find the supporting evidence. In the next lesson, produce the counter-arguments and the associated task. In your final lesson, set up the structured debate and follow this with a summative assignment.

● **Figure 1.13** *The Edexcel Module on The Changing Nature of Warfare, 1845–1991*

Teachers who use the Edexcel board and are planning to do this A2 coursework module will notice that the above plan deviates in many ways from the board's suggestions. In fact one of the advantages of this coursework option is that only the top four bullet points in the specification are prescriptive and the rest can be interpreted by each centre as they wish. In my case, a British army focus had so much local resonance that I have modelled our teaching around this. The Edexcel module also has a source-based enquiry included but I have not addressed this, as the purpose of this chapter is to address the problems of planning a long-term development study.

Useful sources and resources for teachers

The Crimean War

The Crimean War was the first war to be photographed and there are some real gems to share with your classes:

The Crimean War Research Society has a useful online collection and links:
www.crimeanwar.org/cwrsentry.html

Roger Fenton Crimean War Photographs, Library of Congress, Prints and Photographs Reading Room:
www.loc.gov/rr/print/coll/251_fen.html

Royal Archives, Windsor Collection, available through the Imperial War Museum Website:
www.iwm.org.uk/server/show/conMediaFile.38049

Original maps and plans from the National Archives:
http://yourarchives.nationalarchives.gov.uk/index.php?title=Maps%2C_plans_and_pictures_of_the_Crimean_and_Baltic_War_1854–56

Film *The Charge of the Light Brigade* (1969) from Budget DVD

The National Army Museum (www.national-army-museum.ac.uk/) has a wealth of resources. Visit it if you can. The online resources are under reconstruction at the time of writing but should prove invaluable when ready for public release.

The Falklands War

National Army Museum: Task Force Falklands: A War that defined the Eighties:
www.national-army-museum.ac.uk/exhibitions/falklands/

The Imperial War Museum has a wealth of material including remarkable photographs:
www.iwm.org.uk

The South Atlantic Medal Association has pages of information about the war:
www.sama82.org/

The BBC information pages for the 20th Anniversary of the War:
http://news.bbc.co.uk/hi/english/static/in_depth/uk/2002/falklands/

There are many veterans of the war willing to come and talk about their experiences. Contact your local Royal British Legion office or the South Atlantic Medal Association to see if there are any volunteers living close to your school or college.

CHAPTER 2 Exploring the historicity of evidence

Chapter summary

- This chapter considers the role and purpose of evidential work at post-16 level. There is discussion of the problems associated with source work and an assessment of the skills expected in the exams.
- The activities suggest ways in which sources can be used as part of a meaningful historical enquiry. They encourage students to speculate and ask questions of the evidence and to use sources to challenge their own preconceptions.
- In the first activity students select from a range of sources in order to debate a key issue. This provides them with the material to reassess the views they had reached from studying secondary evidence. This is then the basis for an extended essay.
- The second activity introduces students to a complex text. As they gain more information about the text, they develop the skills of 'weighing up' the value of evidence.
- The sequence of lessons is based on a broad enquiry: How much change was there in English religion in the reign of Henry VIII?

Context

Why sources matter

A few years ago a kind lecturer from a local university came to give a talk to my students. While I drove him back to the station he put forward the view, not an uncommon one amongst the HE fraternity, that where school history had gone wrong was by introducing sources. Stick with knowledge and understanding, he said, and give them a sound chronological overview. They have time to engage with sources at university when they have the maturity to understand them. It was only by exerting considerable self control that I delivered him to the station in one piece.

For me, sources are at the heart of history. You may as well watch *The Last Tango in Paris* without the sex scenes as study history without the sources. No history, at whatever level, is worth learning without them. But, of course, the lecturer has a point. Anyone who has had to prepare students for any public examination questions which ask 'How useful' or 'How reliable' is this source can say that these types of task enthuse their students. Studied in a stale vacuum of formulaic questions, sources are enough to put anyone off history, as many commentators have observed (Husbands, 2003; Luff, 2003; Historical Association, 2005; Howells, 2007). Sources, even in advanced study, are too often fish fingers, when they should be Dover sole. They are packaged and processed, presented in standardised shapes for easy consumption with teacher ketchup. Real fish are smelly and slimy and flavoursome. By the time students have reached this level, they should be experiencing the real thing.

In 2008 in England and Wales new specifications were introduced with the promise that this kind of exercise would be a thing of the past and all source work in examinations at this level would be part of a meaningful enquiry. In the end, however, there will always be some gulf between what we believe to be the best historical practice in the use of sources and the way they are addressed in examinations. Perhaps the only exception to this is the personal study.

Sources connect students to the past

> Using source material and tackling the problems of evidence gives a feeling of reality which second hand history can rarely give. To handle evidence from the time gives an insight into the many aspects of that time, and helps us to feel for the topic we are studying. Material given at second hand does not readily attach our emotions, our imagination or our commitment; first hand, primary sources do, if they are handled with care.
>
> *Fines (1994: 125)*

The simplistic and occasionally crude focus on empathy of the 1970s and 1980s has sometimes led to a view that emotion and imagination should somehow be excluded from history, and this is particularly true in the post-16 years. However, experiences which enable students to make genuine connections with the past help them to understand both its familiarity and its strangeness. Counsell (2000: 2) has argued that the word 'empathy' has been much misunderstood and, in particular, mischievously misrepresented in the press. She argues that true empathetic understanding is vital at all levels, including and especially at university.

Dawson and Banham (2002) have described how effective role play can be at all levels when it is firmly based on evidence and placed within a critical enquiry. Luff (2003: 35) has argued convincingly that AS/A2 students are still 'young and fun loving' and this applies as much to a 'hands-on' approach to source work as it does to the use of role play. Yet there is still an assumption that, at 16, you have grown out of getting your hands dirty, moving out of your seat or putting on a crown. Connection with the past should persist throughout the years of history study, something modern telly historians recognise with their effective use of artefacts, buildings and pictures. My students have tried on Tudor hats at Hampton Court and constructed wattle and daub walls at the Weald and Downland Museum. At the Imperial War Museum they attended a session on the Holocaust called 'Handling the Past', which started with the examination of a shoe. This direct contact with the past is even more important now when, for so many young people, not only the past but the countryside is a 'foreign country'. At the Weald and Downland Museum a group of my students stood in Pendean farmhouse and used their noses. They could smell the pigs in the sty outside, the smoke from the fire and the onions hanging over a beam in the loft upstairs. That was a moment of true connection with the sixteenth century.

This is why our choice of sources should not be dictated by exam papers or even textbooks. At a stroke this would exclude music, artefacts and, for more than one awarding body, pictures. It would also make our use of text restricted and often unimaginative. Howells (2007) has provided powerful examples of how well chosen extracts from both historians and contemporary writers can engage students in the details of working-class lives, bringing an apparently dry subject, such as the Poor Law, to life. Although many textbooks are good, their use of visual evidence is severely restricted by copyright costs. Why use a postcard sized, black and white reproduction of a Bolshevik poster when you can project a colour version on your whiteboard? Why use a photo of a classical coin when your students can handle the real thing for relatively low cost? Sources used as initial stimulus material (Phillips, 2002) can help to challenge or stimulate your students as you start your lesson. Sources provide a feel for period by involving the senses and it is this which needs to underpin the thinking, reading and writing of our students.

Sources *should* make students think like historians

Students who have chosen history at AS/A2 level might be expected to come with a secure basis in evidential reasoning. Lee and Shemilt (2003) have suggested ways in which students' ideas about evidence might progress. At level 5 (the second highest level on this scale) students might be expected to understand that the role and value of evidence depends on the questions asked of it. At the highest level, Lee and Shemilt suggest that students will understand that:

> A source only yields evidence when it is understood in its historical context: we must know what a source meant to those by and for whom it was produced.
>
> *Lee and Shemilt (2003: 21)*

It might be reasonable to expect that students starting an AS course would already be, at least partially, at level 5. However, the assumption that students are already at this stage would be a dangerous one. In my first term at the sixth form college, I set my class a practice paper on Boom and Bust America in preparation for their January exam. Figure 2.1 shows how John responded.

Figure 2.1

How reliable is this source? *[5 marks]*

The source was a short extract from an academic textbook by an American history professor.

William Leuchtenburg's source may be considered unreliable because it may be biased. He is a History Professor at an American University.

Why do Sources A and B disagree? *[5 marks]*

The two sources were the extract from Leuchtenburg and a speech by a US senator in the 1920s.

The two sources disagree because they are both going to be biased. A senator is not going to criticise the people of America for making derogatory statements.

There is no need to list what is wrong with this and it is the kind of answer which is sickeningly familiar at earlier stages in school history. The problem was that John was not a lone student with special needs in an otherwise high-achieving class. He achieved a B standard in his GCSE examination in history and was competent at English. Notice the word 'derogatory' in his response, a clue to his intelligence that was confirmed by useful oral comments in class. He probably would not have been in an A-level class before 2000 and his real passion in life was football, but he certainly had the capability to gain a creditable pass. Although his answers to the practice questions were particularly poor, John was not an unusual student in my large mixed-ability classes of that year. His response was an extreme example of what Byrom (1998) has called 'lazy cynicism', dismissing all sources as unreliable and therefore not useful. It might be hoped that John had progressed way beyond this at the start of AS but in the end there he was and in the same class as students wanting to do history degrees at Oxbridge.

It took me a while to realise that the problem was not John but the exam paper. Even a professional tennis player will not perform well against a clumsy novice and John had no motivation to raise his game when faced with the repetitive, formulaic questions he had already endured at GCSE. Furthermore, John's response is limited by his present-day assumptions about the role and attitudes of academics and politicians. Wineburg (2001) has shown how even highly intelligent students misunderstand sources because of the modern preconceptions they bring to bear on them. The way to help John to 'understand the historian's method' was to give him tasks that made him work more like a historian. There have been several examples of how this might be achieved in articles in *Teaching History*, most notably Howells' work (2000) on using documents to develop understanding of Gladstone's relationship with the working class. Howells noted that his model lesson, based on reading and discussion of a range of documents, helped students to feel involved and engaged in a genuine historical enquiry.

Of course, the end point must be exam preparation but the current specifications offer hope that genuine historical skills are what are needed at the higher levels. For most examination boards, the source-based units occur in the AS year and focus primarily on source comparison and on use of sources and knowledge to reach a conclusion. Examination of the three leading boards at the time of writing shows some consensus about what skills are required (see Figure 2.2).

● **Figure 2.2** *Generic level descriptors for Assessment Objective AO2a from the leading examination boards*

Question	Edexcel	AQA	OCR (A)	OCR (B)
Style of question (comparison)	Unit 2 (a) *How far do sources 1 and 2 confirm the evidence in source 3 that …?*	AS Unit 2 1 (a) *Use sources A and B and your own knowledge. Explain how far the views in Source A differ from those in Source B about …*	AS Unit F 963 (a) *Study sources A and B. Compare these sources as evidence for …*	AS Unit F983 The question is preceded by a hypothesis. *Using your knowledge of the period to interpret and evaluate the sources, explain how far Sources 1–8 support this view.*
Highest level in mark scheme	'Reaches a judgement in relation to the issue posed by the question supported by careful examination of the evidence of the sources. The sources are cross-referenced and the elements of challenge and corroboration are analysed. The issues raised by the process of comparison are used to address the specific enquiry. The attributes of the source are taken into account in order to establish what weight the content will bear in relation to the specific enquiry. In addressing 'how far', the sources are used in combination.'	'Responses will show secure and developed understanding of the extent of difference between the two sources and will use this in conjunction with own knowledge to demonstrate good understanding of the issue in context. Evaluation and differentiated judgement will be effectively supported by reference to both sources and own knowledge.'	'Response provides a focused comparison and/or contrast of both content and provenance. Evaluates qualities such as reliability, completeness, consistency, typicality, and especially utility, in relation to the question.'	'Evaluates sources of evidence in their historical context: makes sophisticated inferences from the sources, makes an informed use of the provenance of the sources and cross-references the sources to reach a reasoned and supported conclusion.'
Style of question (judgement using sources and knowledge)	Unit 2 (b) *Use sources 4 and 5 and your own knowledge. How far do you agree with the view that …?*	Unit 2 1 (b) *Use sources A, B and C and your own knowledge. How far do you agree that …?*	Unit F963 (b) *Study all the sources. Use your own knowledge to assess how far …*	For this specification the skills of comparison and judgement are merged into one question.
Highest level in mark scheme	'A response which relates well to the focus of the question and which shows some understanding of the key issues contained in it. The analysis will be supported by accurate factual material which will be mostly relevant to the question asked. Candidates are able to provide some integration between what they know and the evidence gleaned from the source material.'	'Answers will be focused and closely argued. Arguments will be supported by precisely selected evidence from sources and own knowledge, incorporating well developed understanding of historical interpretations and debate.'	'Excellent analysis and evaluation of *all* sources with high levels of discrimination. Analyses and evaluates the limitations of the sources and what is required to add to their completeness as a set.'	

All examination boards currently require the following skills at AS level:

- To combine and contrast sources with discrimination, using skills of inference and cross reference
- In response to a specific enquiry, weigh up the value of sources in terms of content and provenance and use them, in conjunction with knowledge, to reach a judgement.

In my experience, most students have gained reasonable competence in making comparisons and deductions, considering provenance and combining sources and knowledge from GCSE, although many need a rigorous refresher course to reawaken their skills. The biggest hurdle is to develop the skills of 'weighing up' that a top-quality AS answer requires. Frequently teenagers write about sources in the same way they drive a car: a worrying mix of timidity and foolhardiness. They need to acquire the assertive caution of the good driver, based on a secure grasp of history's highway code. At this level, we should be aiming for a developed and nuanced understanding of the relationship between a source and its context in order to judge how it may be used to answer the questions posed.

Activities

Rationale for the activities

In a talk to the Reading branch of the Historical Association in March 2005, George Barnard raised the interesting question of when, if ever, England became a Protestant country. He made a good case for the argument that, in some ways, England has always remained 'Catholic' if not 'Roman Catholic'. Although modern students have not gone through the Protestant Whig indoctrination that I experienced in my Presbyterian school in Glasgow, they come as AS students with the general perception that Henry VIII made England Protestant. Despite most teenagers' secularism, there is still a persistent feeling that Sellar and Yeatman (1930) were basically right – 'England is bound to be C of E' – and that Henry set the ball rolling. This can be a serious barrier to their understanding of religion in early modern England. It is one that real engagement with sources can help to overcome.

In my experience, enquiry questions are just as important at advanced level study as they are for younger pupils. The importance of framing a meaningful question around which to build your historical investigation has been clearly expounded by Riley (2000). This is important, both to stimulate interest around a genuine puzzle and to make the learning creative and ambitious. However, there is always a problem that pursuing one line of enquiry will be problematic when weaker students may be confronted by a question from a very difficult angle in their exam. This means that you have to find broad questions that will allow you to twist and turn within them to help your students gain the skills to mould the answers to fit the questions. The following sequence of lessons therefore has a series of mini questions within the broader enquiry. Setting students an 'unexpected' question at the end of a topic, rather than the one which naturally leads from the enquiry, often helps them to develop this confidence. In my Tudor course, students have to study and understand the religious views and practices of early sixteenth-century England and how these were changed by the actions of King Henry VIII and other factors such as the European Reformation. Within this topic they might face a range of questions such as the relative strength of the Catholic Church on the eve of the Reformation, the effects of King Henry's marriage problems or the extent of Lutheranism. In order to encompass this range of possibilities, I have chosen a broad question:

How much change was there in English religion in the reign of Henry VIII?

The two activities form the basis of a sequence of eight lessons on the religious aspects of the reign of Henry VIII. The students have completed work on the pre-Reformation Church in England, and have already covered the main points through reading and discussion based on textbooks and supplementary reading. They have not yet encountered any contemporary sources.

Activity 1

Putting the Catholic Church on trial to test the validity of historical interpretations

Mini question:

What was the state of the Church in England in the 1520s?

The activity uses the format of a trial to develop source skills to assess the condition of the pre-Reformation English Church.

Rationale for Activity 1

When students are asked to write a judgement essay at the completion of a topic, they can often produce competent and balanced answers. They use textbooks and articles with some skill to support their case but it is disappointing how little they use primary sources and it is a real rarity for them to use any kind of visual material. Even in their extended essays for their Tudor architecture coursework, only a minority exploit the rich resources of photographs, plans and drawings which could support their views.

What are the deeper reasons for these common weaknesses? In students' minds, there is a hierarchy of evidence with articles by historians at the apex and artefacts and pictures at the base. This problem is often apparent when confronting a collection of sources in their A2 essays. Students reverentially repeat the words of a historian while dismissing the words of a contemporary observer as subjective. The sequence of stages outlined below aims to raise the status of primary evidence and to encourage students in using it to reach genuinely independent judgements. The final essay requires them to use the primary evidence to challenge the views they have already assumed from their study of textbooks and articles.

Activity procedure

Stage 1: Preparation

A clip from Simon Schama's BBC film *Whatever happened to Catholic England?* will set the scene nicely and give students a sense of the power and beauty of the Church at the time.

To prepare for the activity, give your students a range of secondary sources to study for homework. Set them the question: '"The Catholic Church was weak and divided by 1529." Do you agree?' and ask them to come to the lesson with an answer and at least five reasons why. This is a well rehearsed old chestnut for which A. G. Dickens (1964) can be dusted down to do battle with Eamon Duffy (1992). The clarity of the arguments help give the students confidence and assume strong views of their own.

Stage 2: Lining up

At the start of the lesson, students have to form a viewpoint line, with those with the most entrenched opinions at either end. Make them record their position on a large line on sugar paper or by writing their names on an electronic whiteboard and saving it. The top two on each side are the barristers. Usually these are the most opinionated people in the class who enjoy the cut and thrust of debate. The twist is that they will have to lead the case from the opposite viewpoint in court. They will not like it but it will be a much more stretching test of their skills. The remainder of the students will play the part of talking sources.

Stage 3: Organising the sources

If you can include pictures and extracts from your local area, this will give the activity extra interest and relevance. Using a photo of a local church tower or, if possible, from a church warden's account book, for example, will help to engage your students with it.

Lay out the sources on a large table and allow the students to adopt a source. They have to be prepared to set out a market stall or poster which promotes their source in terms of both content and context. Provide a bit of guidance as to how the students might choose to pitch their source, either targeting one side (the defence or the prosecution) or selling to a broad market (both defence and prosecution). Allow them a bit of freedom in how they do this. The idea of the market is that it should be boisterous and noisy with a strong element of competition between 'traders'.

Stage 4: The sources market

Declare the market open by ringing a bell and give it no more than 6–7 minutes, strictly timed. I use the pizza timer on the whiteboard but any device which provides some sense of urgency can be used. The barristers from both teams have to select three pieces of evidence to support their case, of which one must be visual.

Stage 5: The court case

To ensure full involvement of the class, the leftover 'sources' play the roles of jury and cross-examiners. The two barristers on each side have to prepare a short opening statement and the final summing up, as well as organising the talking sources that they are going to summon to the witness box to support their case. Talking sources need to study their source very carefully and be prepared to defend themselves in terms of both content and context. The jurors are allocated one source each to cross-examine, focusing on the strengths and weaknesses of evidence. At the end, ask the jurors to retire to reach a verdict and elect a foreman to report their verdict and why they reached it.

Stage 6: The follow-up

Return to the line that was recorded in stage 2. Ask students to look at their positions on the original line and say whether they have changed their minds and, if so, which evidence persuaded them to do so. This makes explicit the ways in which primary material can be used to confirm or confront the judgements made through the students' factual work.

Stage 7: The concluding essay

To pull the learning together, provide a bit of a twist in order to ensure that students are able to adapt and reconstruct their ideas. Asking 'How much was the Catholic Church threatened by the religious changes in England in the 1520s?' will require them to select their evidence with more care and rethink the position they assumed at the end of the class. In my mixed-ability groups, a bit of discussion and guidance such as paired essay planning will be needed to get students on the right track. Make all the primary evidence available to them – online on your intranet if possible – and insist that they use and correctly reference at least four from the collection.

Activity 2

Weighing up Anne Askew

Rationale

Mini question:

How much can one text tell us about how religious beliefs changed?

The idea behind the tasks is to investigate the extent of change in religious views through the exploration of one text. The activity focuses particularly on the skills of 'weighing up' a piece of evidence through in-depth study of both its context and its content.

In the previous activity, when the purpose was to use a range of sources to make a judgement, generous amounts of explanation were given. However, when studying one source in depth, the common problem is too little text and too much explanation. Much has been written about how the traditional 'gobbet' can make the history more rather than less difficult.

Another associated problem is that the background information above (or below) a source can end up as a text in itself and one that encourages students to prejudge. Shemilt commented that this kind of information can lead to students becoming swamped with 'background noise' which 'degrades the pupil's capacity to know what he is doing' (McAleavy, 1998). Giving the students a long piece of text without information about its origin can encourage real engagement with it. (This principle lies behind the imaginative OCR (B) specification Units F985 and F986.) Allowing students to speculate, even to explore blind alleys, helps them to develop as historians. One attribute of good historians is caution, an attribute gained sometimes through risk taking and mistakes rather than through plentiful guidance and information.

In the context of this enquiry, the students are confronted with a text coming from the end of Henry's reign, written by someone most students have never heard of: Anne Askew. My students will already have studied the state of the Church in the 1520s and the legal and organisational changes brought by Henry VIII. The focus of this exercise is to examine how much one text could reveal about the extent of change in religious beliefs.

Anne Askew is a religious femme fatale, and bound to fascinate. Not only does her life story include sex and violence, at its centre is a feisty feminist who is as witty as she is brave. But for the purposes of this activity, you cannot let the character and the narrative dominate over the text. Letting Anne's words speak first is essential for this task to work well.

Activity procedure

Stage 1: Factual reminder

Although this text-based exercise should be approached fresh, students do need to be confident about the key Catholic beliefs, especially regarding the sacraments, the role of the clergy and belief in purgatory. To ensure this common foundation knowledge, give pairs of students these different aspects and ask them to come up with three or four key statements for each topic which can then be incorporated into a summary sheet. This sheet can be saved electronically and used during and at the end of the study. Figure 2.3 is an example of what you might expect.

Stage 2: Weighing up in terms of content

(a) Set up a silent conversation (see Figure 2.4). Give students the extract (Resource 2A), having first prepared it as explained in point 5 of Figure 2.4, with no explanation of its origin. Tell them that the extract is to be used to find out how much religious beliefs had changed by the end of Henry VIII's reign. Start your silent conversation. In this first round, ask the students to focus on what the text is saying and how it might help to answer the question. Tell them to think about not only what is said but how the argument is put forward. There will be quite a lot of words and phrases they do not understand and they should be encouraged to pose questions about the meanings of words, to admit things they do not understand and to request clarification or more information. Pass the sheet on.

Figure 2.3 *Overview of key Catholic beliefs*

What was the role of the clergy?	• The monasteries were run by 'regular clergy' who lived there and provided services such as education and care for the sick. • The celibate clergy had special authority in the Church as the only people who could deliver the sacraments. • The clergy had the role of interpreting the scriptures for the people. It was not expected that people would read the Bible for themselves.
What were the sacraments?	• There were seven sacraments which were important to salvation and which could be received from a priest. These included Eucharist, penance (confession) and the last rites. • During the mass, the bread and wine were transformed into the body and blood of Christ.
How could you get to Heaven?	• After death, souls spent time in Purgatory to make up for their sins before they could be admitted to Heaven. It was possible to reduce time in Purgatory by having prayers said for your soul and by making donations to the Church. • People believed that you got to Heaven by leading a good life, receiving the sacraments and confessing your sins.

RESOURCE  *Foxe's account of Anne Askew's interrogation*

Text 1

To satisfy your expectation, good people ..., this was my first examination in the year of our Lord 1545, and in the month of March. First Christopher Dare examined me at *Saddlers' Hall* being one of the *quest*, and asked if I did not believe that the *sacrament hanging over the altar* was the very body of Christ really. Then I demanded this question of him: wherefore Saint Stephen was stoned to death. And he said he could not tell. Then I answered that no more would I *assoil* his vain question.

Secondly, he said that there was a woman which did testify that I *should read* how God was not in temples made with hands. Then I showed him the seventh and the seventeenth chapters of the Acts of the Apostles, what Stephen and Paul had said therein. Whereupon he asked me how I *took* those sentences. I answered that I would not throw *pearls among swine*, for acorns were good enough.

Thirdly, he asked me wherefore I said that I had rather to read five lines in the Bible, than to hear five masses in the temple. I confessed that I said no less. Not for the dispraise of either the Epistle or Gospel, but because the one did greatly edify me, and the other nothing at all. As Saint Paul doth witness in the 14th chapter of his first Epistle to the Corinthians, where as he doth say: "If the trumpet giveth an uncertain sound, who will prepare himself to the battle?"

Fourthly, he laid unto my charge that I should say: "If an *ill* priest ministered, it was the Devil and not God." My answer was that I never spake such thing. But this was my saying: "That whatsoever he were which ministered unto me, his ill conditions could not hurt my faith, but in spirit I received nevertheless the body and blood of Christ." He asked me what I said concerning confession. I answered him my meaning, which was as Saint James sayeth, that every man ought to *knowledge* his faults to other, and the one to pray for the other.

Sixthly [sic], he asked me what I said to the *King's book*. And I answered him that I could say nothing to it, because I never saw it.

Seventhly, he asked me if I had the spirit of God in me. I answered if I had not, I was but reprobate or cast away. Then he said he had sent for a priest to examine me, which was there at hand. The priest asked me what I said to the *sacrament of the altar*. And required much to know therein my meaning. But I desired him again to hold me excused concerning that matter. None other answer would I make him, because I perceived him a *papist*.

Eighthly, he asked me if I did not think that private masses did *help souls departed*. And [I] said it was great idolatry to believe more in them than in the death which Christ died for us. Then they had me thence unto my Lord Mayor and he examined me, as they had before, and I answered him directly in all things as I answered the quest afore. Besides this my Lord Mayor laid one thing unto my charge which was never spoken of me but of them. And that was whether a mouse eating the host received God or no. This question did I never ask, but indeed they asked it of me, whereunto I made them no answer but smiled. Then the Bishop's Chancellor rebuked me and said that I was much to blame for uttering the scriptures. For Saint Paul (he said) forbade women to speak or to talk of the word of God. I answered him that I knew Paul's meaning as well as he, which is, 1 Corinthians 14, that a woman ought not to speak in the congregation by the way of teaching. And then I asked him how many women he had seen go into the pulpit and preach? He said he never saw none. Then I said, he ought to find no fault in poor women, except they had offended the law. Then my Lord Mayor commanded me to *ward.*

Source: www.wwnorton.com/college/english/nael/16century/topic_3/askwexam.htm

Text 2

They said to me there that I was a heretic, and condemned by the law if I would stand in my opinion. I answered that I was no heretic, neither yet deserved I any death by the law of God. But as concerning the faith which I uttered and wrote to the council, I would not, I said, deny it, because I knew it true. Then they would needs know if I would deny the sacrament to be Christ's body and blood. I said, "Yea, for the same son of God that was born of the Virgin Mary, is now glorious in heaven, and will come again from thence at *the latter day*, like as he went up (Acts 1). And as for that ye call your God, is but a piece of *bread*. For a more proof of thereof (mark it when ye list) yet it lie in the *box* but three months, and it will be mould and so turn to nothing that is good. Whereupon I am persuaded that it cannot be good."

'The First Examination of Anne Askew' included in John Foxe's Acts and Monuments *(1563), better known as Foxe's* Book of Martyrs. *Beilin, E. V. (ed.) (1996)* The Examinations of Anne Askew, *pp. 110–11*

 © HODDER EDUCATION

RESOURCE  *Notes and additional information for Anne Askew task*

Source 1: Notes

Saddlers' Hall: belonging to the guild of saddle-makers

quest: inquest, in this case, interrogation

sacrament hanging over the altar: the holy wafers were sometimes held in a hanging vessel in the shape of a dove, symbolising the Holy Ghost

assoil: resolve

should read: would teach

took: interpreted

pearls among swine: quoted from the Gospel of St Matthew

ill: wicked

knowledge: acknowledge

King's book: *A Necessary Doctrine and Erudition for Any Christian Man* (1543) sought to put a brake on reformers' 'sinister understanding of scripture, presumption, arrogancy, carnal liberty, and contention', by affirming a number of basically Catholic positions

sacrament of the altar: Eucharist

Papist: follower of the Pope, i.e., Roman Catholic

help souls departed: by shortening their time in Purgatory

ward: prison

Source 2: Notes

the latter day: Day of Judgement

bread in the box: the communion bread or wafer

Extra notes

Catholic doctrine held that sacraments properly performed were independent of the spiritual condition either of the priest or of the worshipper. Hence, for example, if the formula of consecration of the bread and wine was correctly spoken by a properly ordained priest, the miraculous transubstantiation of the Host into the body and blood of Christ would occur, whether or not the priest or the communicant (person receiving the sacrament) was in a state of grace. Indeed, some Catholic theologians argued, since the bread had objectively been transformed into the body of God, even a mouse, nibbling on a consecrated host, would be receiving Christ's flesh.

Notes provided by the Norton Anthology of English Literature. www.wwnorton.com/college/english/nael/16century/topic_3/askwexam.htm

Access to dictionaries in old English

The following online version is recommended:

Old English Made Easy: http://home.comcast.net/~modean52/oeme_dictionaries.htm

RESOURCE 2C *Religious change*

Summarise the main ways this text suggests religious beliefs had changed.

What does the source suggest about how beliefs changed?		
Beliefs about the clergy	Beliefs about the sacraments	Beliefs about getting to Heaven

 © HODDER EDUCATION

RESOURCE 
Changes in religious ideas suggested by Anne Askew's confession

Complete this chart by studying the text (Resource 2A) carefully and adding to the points and quotes already given.

Aspect	Main beliefs in 1509	This is challenged by the text in this way	Quote from text
What was the role of the clergy?	• The monasteries were run by 'regular clergy' who lived there and provided services such as education and care for the sick. • The celibate clergy had special authority in the Church as the only people who could deliver the sacraments. • The clergy had the role of interpreting the scriptures for the people. It was not expected that people would read the Bible for themselves.	The writer states that reading the Bible for herself is better than attending mass.	*'I had rather to read five lines in the Bible, than to hear five masses in the temple.'*
What were the sacraments?	• There were seven sacraments which were important to salvation and which could be received from a priest. These included Eucharist, penance (confession) and the last rites. • During the mass, the bread and wine were transformed into the body and blood of Christ.		
How could you get to Heaven?	• After death, souls spent time in Purgatory to make up for their sins before they could be admitted to heaven. It was possible to reduce time in Purgatory by having prayers said for your soul and by making donations to the Church. • People believed that you got to Heaven by leading a good life, receiving the sacraments and confessing your sins.	The writer denies that saying prayers for the dead can help them reach heaven.	*'it was great idolatry to believe more in them than in the death which Christ died for us'.*

Figure 2.4 *How to organise a silent conversation*

1. Introduce the enquiry question that the conversation is about. From the start, the students need to know *why* they are studying the text to give their conversation a focus.
2. Organise the students into groups. Three is the best number to ensure that all students have a good enough view of the text to read it easily and have enough opportunity to 'discuss' it with their peers. Remove everything else from the worktops so they are uncluttered.
3. Insist on complete silence. The teacher needs to be silent too or the spell will be broken. If you need to communicate, write a note. Make sure the students know their work will be shared with other students and their teacher to discourage any silliness.
4. Arm each student with a medium-tip felt-tip pen. The ink needs to be dark enough and the writing thick enough for everyone in a small group to be able to read it easily.
5. Stick the text in the middle of a large sheet, e.g. light coloured sugar paper. Allow generous amounts of space.
6. Allow students at least 5 minutes' initial reading time, especially if the text is challenging. Then give them an additional 5 minutes for 'conversation time'. This means underlining, highlighting or annotating points in the text which they wish to comment on, challenge or request further information about. Make the timing very clear and inflexible as this helps the students to focus – the pizza timer on a whiteboard or an egg timer can be useful.
7. Pass the annotated sheets to the next group and so on. The subsequent stages can take a variety of forms, for instance, carrying on the same conversation, introducing different questions or more information.

The idea of the silent conversation comes from Feinberg, K. (2002) Facing History and Ourselves.

(b) Provide dictionaries and the notes and additional information sheet (Resource 2B), still not revealing the context, and ask the students to respond to the queries and comments of the first group. Pass the sheets on one last time.

Stage 3

Give students time to read over the previous conversations.

Lift the silence bar and ask each group to write at least one point in one of the columns in Resource 2C, either on paper or on the board. Discuss their ideas and help them to find points they have missed. This should give them the confidence to complete the chart in Resource 2D individually.

Stage 4

As a final review, summarise the areas of belief that are not mentioned in the text and those areas where there are strong points made. Record a judgement about the completeness of the text regarding religious beliefs.

Stage 5: Weighing up in terms of context

(a) Typicality

Now is the moment to introduce Anne Askew as a character. Ask your students to build up a basic CV for Anne as you take them through a short but lively PowerPoint presentation (see Figure 2.5). Include a snippet of her poetry, woodcut pictures and Foxe's description of her death to capture student interest. Build on this with some student research to judge how representative Anne was as a spokesperson for religious views. Give some general headings to help: gender, class, region. Follow this up by providing the class with a summary of Protestantism at this time in terms of numbers, background and beliefs (Resource 2E will help with this). Ask students to record careful notes, as they will need to come back to them later.

(b) Reliability

Start by putting an extract up on the board (see Resource 2F). It is an interchange recorded in Anne's *Examinacyon*.

This should get across the idea that Anne's writing was edited and manipulated by the Protestant propagandists who published her scripts. Provide the information sheets about Protestant attitudes to women and about how Anne's works were recorded and published (Resources 2G and 2H). Ask students to complete the worksheet (Resource 2I) by recording their suggestions about why Foxe made the changes he did. Follow this up with a discussion about how far this affects the text's reliability as evidence for religious belief at this time.

Stage 6: Final weighing up of Anne Askew

Now is the time for the final weighing up. Ask the students to complete the chart (Resource 2J) in pairs, using the information in Resource 2E. The depth and detail of their study means that not only can they easily list all the problems with the text in terms of reliability, typicality and completeness, they can also recognise its value as evidence of religious belief.

A useful final exercise is to require students to answer the question: 'How much can this source tell us about changes in religious belief?' Allow them no more than 500 words. They should have lots to say but the requirement for brevity will encourage precision and focus.

Stage 7: Final review

Place the analysis of the Askew text in the broader context of religious change by allocating pairs of students different aspects of religious change to assess and setting up a class seminar on the main features of religious change in Henry VIII's reign.

Figure 2.5 *Information for teacher's PowerPoint presentation*

Anne's background and career

- Anne was born in 1521, the daughter of a knight, Sir William Askew, who was a landowner in Lincolnshire.
- It is thought that she was made to marry the Catholic Thomas Kyme, at the age of 15, as a substitute for her sister who had died.
- Anne quarrelled with her husband, particularly over religion, and left for London. Here she preached sermons and distributed Protestant books. She was arrested and interrogated by the authorities. Although she was pardoned the first time and sent back to Lincolnshire, Anne returned to London only a year later and was re-arrested.
- Anne refused to take her husband's surname and there is some evidence that she tried to gain an annulment on scriptural grounds using verses in 1 Corinthians which suggest it was possible to end a marriage to an unbeliever.
- Anne had some contact with Henry VIII's sixth wife, Katherine Parr, who was sympathetic to reform.
- Unusually for a woman, Anne was tortured on the rack in the hope that she would reveal the names of other heretics. Her response was so brave that it is said the Constable of the Tower refused to continue with the torture.
- Anne was too weak to walk to the scaffold but this did not prevent her suffering the penalty of being burnt at the stake in 1546.

Anne's ballad

(The first verse provides a good flavour. Anne apparently sang this while in prison in Newgate.)

Like as the armed knight
Appointed to the field,
With this world will I fight
And Faith shall be my shield.

Foxe's description of her death

> Wherefore the day of her execution was appointed, and she brought into Smithfield in a chair, because she could not go on her feet, by means of her great torments. When she was brought unto the stake she was tied by the middle with a chain that held up her body. When all things were thus prepared to the fire, the King's letters of pardon were brought, whereby to offer her safeguard of her life if she would recant, which she would neither receive, neither yet vouchsafe once to look upon. Shaxton also was there present who, openly that day recanting his opinions, went about with a long oration to cause her also to turn, against whom she stoutly resisted. Thus she being troubled so many manner of ways, and having passed through so many torments, having now ended the long course of her agonies, being compassed in with flames of fire, as a blessed sacrifice unto God, she slept in the Lord, in anno 1546, leaving behind her a singular example of Christian constancy for all men to follow.

RESOURCE 

Protestantism at the end of Henry VIII's reign

Protestants were still a small group in England in the 1540s. Within the Church the overwhelming majority were traditional Catholics, although there were some churchmen sympathetic to reform, such as Archbishop Cranmer and Bishop Latimer. At court, Queen Catherine Parr encouraged the study and translation of texts which challenged Catholic teaching. Both Catherine Parr and Thomas Cranmer were able to resist plots to remove them from power in the 1540s, suggesting the declining influence of the conservatives. A reforming faction, dominated by the Seymour and Dudley families, gained more influence in the last few years of Henry's reign, although Protestants still remained a minority. In London, the university towns and some commercial centres, there were groups of reformers who met to read and discuss the Bible in English. Few of the peasantry or the noble class were Protestant but there is evidence of more support among the artisans, yeoman, merchants and gentry.

Although Protestants celebrated the royal injunctions of 1538 which required each church to provide a Bible in English, in 1543 Bible reading was restricted to those of higher social class. The Six Articles of 1539 had reaffirmed the King's support for traditional doctrine: denial of transubstantiation was punishable by death. The *King's Book*, which was published in 1543, supported prayers for the dead and attacked Lutheran ideas such as justification by faith. It seems therefore that while court, Church and people accepted the organisational changes to the Church and the use of the vernacular, they also held on to Catholic doctrine.

Opponents of the Catholic Church at this time were divided and Protestant theology was still evolving. Most English reformers held Lutheran views, influenced by the writings of William Tyndale. They were clearest on what they opposed: the authority of the Pope, the power of the saints, prayers for the dead, the seven sacraments and, most important of all, transubstantiation. They strongly promoted the authority of the scripture and the belief that salvation could be found through faith alone. Reformers viewed clergymen as leaders and teachers and did not think they had a special authority to interpret the scriptures.

The number of Protestant martyrs in these years was relatively small. Some of the better known are listed in the table.

 © HODDER EDUCATION

Name	Date	Class/job	Where from	Main offence
Thomas Bilney	1531	Cambridge graduate, preacher	Norwich	preaching; distributing illegal literature
John Lambert	1538	Cambridge graduate, preacher and writer	Norwich	attacks on worship of saints; publication of denial of transubstantiation
John Harridaunce		Bricklayer	London	preaching; Protestant views
Robert Barnes William Jerome Thomas Gerrard	1539	Scholars and theologians	Based in Cambridge	denial of the Six Articles
Robert Testwood Henry Filmer Anthony Pierson (Two others were accused but granted a royal pardon)	1543	Musician Tailor Priest	Windsor	possession of illegal Protestant tracts; denial of the Six Articles
John Lascells [Lascelles] (Burnt with Anne Askew and two others)	1546	Courtier and lawyer, of gentry class The two others appear to have been of lowly birth	Nottinghamshire	a leader of a Protestant group in London; wrote a radical Protestant tract denying the Six Articles and promoting radical views
Kerby (first name unknown)	1546	Unknown	Ipswich	denial of the Six Articles

RESOURCE 2F *Extract from Anne's* Examinacyon

Bishop Stephen Gardiner: A woman has no more business with Scripture than a sow has wearing a saddle.

Anne Askew: My lord, a sow has as much business wearing a saddle as an ass does wearing a bishop's miter [hat].

This exchange is included in a Dutch translation of Anne's *Examinacyon*, but is not included in either of the two English versions. It is thought that it is likely to be a true record because the Dutch version shows little evidence of alteration or addition.

Why do you think the two English editors missed it out?

Think about this and then write down your idea on your mini whiteboard.

© HODDER EDUCATION

RESOURCE  *Protestant attitudes to women*

Protestants believed in the scriptural authority of the Bible and many were influenced by two extracts from St Paul:

> Wives, submit yourselves unto your own husbands, as unto the Lord. For the husband is the head of the wife, even as Christ is the head of the church: and he is the saviour of the body. Therefore, as the church is subject unto Christ, so let the wives be to their own husbands in everything.
>
> *St Paul's Letter to the Ephesians*

> Let your women keep silence in the churches: for it is not permitted unto them to speak; but they are commanded to be under obedience, as also saith the law. And if they will learn anything, let them ask their husbands at home: for it is a shame for women to speak in the church.
>
> *St Paul's Letter to the Corinthians*

In general, Protestant theologians believed that a good woman was quiet, obedient and modest. Few would go as far as John Knox, who wrote *The First Blast of the Trumpet Against the Monstrous Regiment of Women* in 1558, attacking female rulers, but there was general discomfort at the idea of women in authority.

RESOURCE  *Information about the text*

The version of the text you have studied is that included in Foxe's *Book of Martyrs*, published in 1563, seventeen years after Anne's death.

What did Anne write?

Anne wrote two accounts of her trials and interrogations: *The First Examinacyon of the Worthy Servant of God Mistresse Anne Askew* and *The Lattre Examinacyon of the Worthy Servant of God Mistresse Anne Askewe*. She also wrote a poem: 'The Balade which Anne Askewe Made and Sange When She Was in Newgate'.

How did Anne's work come to be published?

Anne's writings were smuggled out of England and reached the hands of John Bale, a Protestant bishop in exile in Germany. He edited her writing, adding long commentaries of his own, which are interspersed with Anne's text, and this was published just a year after her death. Bale's account was very popular and was reprinted at least four times by 1560.

Who was John Foxe?

Born in Lincolnshire in 1516, Foxe was a Protestant scholar who went into exile abroad on the accession of the Catholic Queen Mary in 1553. While in exile, he collected information about religious persecution, especially the burnings of Protestants in England. When he returned to England, on the accession of Queen Elizabeth, Foxe published an English version of this work.

How did Anne's work come to be included in Foxe's *Book of Martyrs*?

John Foxe published a Latin translation of Anne's examination in his *Rerum in Ecclesia Gestarum ... Commentarii* of 1559 and an English version in his *Actes and Monuments* (Book of Martyrs) of 1563. The evidence suggests that Foxe based his version on a translation of Askew's text which was printed by William Copland in 1550. However, he also appears to have read and used Bale's version of Anne's writing. Foxe also includes additional information in his book, which suggests he had access to oral informants.

How can we know that these versions of the text are actually Anne's words?

We can't. There are no autographed or authenticated versions of Anne Askew's text. The only versions we have are those that have been edited and produced by Bale and Foxe. There is some compelling evidence that these texts are mostly reproductions of her words but it is impossible to know with certainty how much has been cut or amended.

How much did Foxe change Anne's text?

Again, it is hard to know for sure but recent research suggests he did the following:

1. He put the text into paragraphs.
2. He sometimes added extra adjectives or phrases.
3. He sometimes missed out parts of the text.
4. He sometimes added extra bits.

These notes are all based on the article by Freeman, T.S. and Wall, S. E. (2001) 'Racking the body, shaping the text: The account of Anne Askew in Foxe's "Book of Martyrs"', Renaissance Quarterly, Vol. 54

 © HODDER EDUCATION

RESOURCE 21 *How and why did Foxe edit Askew?*

Read and complete this sheet.

Aspect	Change	Possible reason why
Anne's family background	Foxe introduced Anne's words with an introductory paragraph about her family background and virtuous upbringing in the 1559 (*Rerum*) version. This was dropped in all his subsequent accounts.	Foxe may not have known that Anne had left her husband in 1559 and when he found out he wanted to cover it up. He was known to disapprove of wives leaving their husbands and would not have wanted to give Catholic critics an easy way of attacking Anne.
Anne's lack of theological argument	Foxe added a letter, written by John Lascelles, her fellow martyr, to the 1563 version of the text. In this, Lascelles puts forward the Protestant view of the Eucharist.	Foxe wanted to persuade his readers of the strength of Protestant beliefs. Anne's refusal to engage in any detailed scriptural debate was a weakness from his point of view. He added the Lascelles letter to compensate for Anne's evasiveness.
Anne's plain writing style	Foxe added extra words such as 'certain and sure' instead of 'sure' and 'friends and well-wishers' rather than simply 'friends'.	Foxe liked alliteration and rhythm in his writing and this was part of the emerging Protestant style (e.g. Cranmer's marriage service: 'for better or worse, for richer or poorer'). He probably made these changes for stylistic reasons.
Anne's torture on the rack	Foxe put this in a separate paragraph rather than in the middle of a continuous section about Anne's interrogation.	
Anne's attack on the mass	Earlier versions have Anne saying: 'The mass was idolatry' but Foxe's version states: 'The mass was superstitious, wicked and no better than idolatry'.	

How does Foxe's editing affect the reliability of this text as evidence for religious beliefs in the 1540s?

RESOURCE  *The final weighing up*

How much does Anne Askew's *Examinacyon* tell us about how religious views changed?

Weighting	Content	Typicality	Reliability	Completeness
Featherweight				
		Anne was a very unusual character and not representative, even of Protestant martyrs.		*Little is said about what Protestants did believe, e.g. justification by faith.*
			Foxe's amendments of the text seem unlikely to have altered Anne's religious statements.	
Heavyweight	*The denials of transubstantiation and attack on prayers for the dead show the ways Catholic doctrine were being opposed.*			

 © HODDER EDUCATION

Sample lesson sequence

Rationale

The aim of this enquiry is to put sources at the heart of lessons and develop evidential skills without repetitious completion of exam-style questions. Both activities practise those skills the exam boards target and will enable students to handle evidence with more confidence and care.

Prior learning

Students should have studied religion in the reign of Henry VIII and be familiar with the key features of the Church at this time, such as its relationship with the monarchy, the attitudes of the people and the main beliefs and practices.

Enquiry question

How much change was there in English religion in the reign of Henry VIII?

Outline of learning flow

Eight lessons over three weeks, as shown in Figure 2.6. This enquiry represents about a third of a module.

Figure 2.6 *Eight lessons over three weeks*

How much change was there in English religion in the reign of Henry VIII?	
Lesson 1 *Mini question:* What was the state of the Church in England in the 1520s?	Kick off with a clip from Simon Schama's BBC video *Whatever happened to Catholic England?* to give students a sense of the power and the beauty of the Church at that time. Then students work individually to assess the evidence for the strengths and weaknesses of the Church using a range of books. As homework, get them reading and tell them to come to the next lesson with a clear opinion and supporting reasons for it.
Lessons 2 and 3 *Mini question:* What was the state of the Church in England in the 1520s?	Set off **Activity 1** with the line-up, auction and court case. Ensure you have enough time for the re-evaluation of views, which will probably take up your second lesson on this theme. Set the essay: 'How much was the Catholic Church threatened by the religious changes in England in the 1520s?' Set the factual reminder exercise for **Activity 2** as homework.
Lessons 4–6 *Mini question:* How much does Askew's *Examinacyon* tell us about how religious beliefs changed?	Introduce **Activity 2** by completing the overview table of key beliefs. Review the factual reminder work and ensure students understand it. Then get going with the silent conversation and complete the 'weighing up' in terms of content. Begin the next lesson with the PowerPoint presentation and examine the context, before doing the final weighing up. Set the written task to check their understanding.
Lessons 7 and 8 *Review:* How much change was there in English religion in the reign of Henry VIII?	Run a class seminar on this issue by allocating pairs of students different aspects of religious change to assess. This is an opportunity to fill in gaps and improve knowledge where it might be a little thin.

CHAPTER 3 Dissecting a happy marriage: the relationship between knowledge and interpretation

Chapter summary

- This chapter addresses several interlinked problems in student learning at AS/A2. Students' approach to historical knowledge is often simplistic, they see the tasks of gaining knowledge and interpreting it as separate, and they often perceive historical debate as a two-sided battle.
- The suggested activities aim to address these problems by making students more aware of the different kinds of historical knowledge they encounter and the relationship between historical knowledge and its interpretation. As students are directly engaged in the process of acquiring knowledge, they gain a better understanding of the nature of that knowledge.
- The practical activities include production of a reference guide, in-depth analysis of extracts from a historian and the creation of wiki pages which reflect developing knowledge and interpretation of a historical issue.
- The exercises form the basis for two forms of traditional AS/A2 assessment for public examinations: an extended research essay and an answer to a question based on sources and knowledge.
- The sequence of lessons is based on a broad enquiry: **What was the nature of Nazi society?** with a series of mini questions within this wider framework.

Context

Just give us the facts: student perceptions of historical knowledge

It is a sad fact that most university students starting a history degree apparently perceive learning history to be the 'acquisition of a large body of uncontested knowledge' (Hibbert, 2006). Both Hibbert and Booth (Booth, 2005) have shown that one of the biggest hurdles in the transition to university study is to move students on from a view of history as a collection of facts to what Booth calls a 'contested discourse' (Booth, 2005). Reflecting on the exciting work which has been done on interpretations, especially at Key Stage 3, and the existence of demanding interpretation work in A2 history papers, this seems a disappointing admission of failure. Even if we accept that only a minority of our A-level students will become history graduates, this is a problem we cannot ignore because it reveals a serious failure to communicate the very nature of our subject.

With all the pressures sixth-form teachers are under – modular exams, content-heavy syllabi, league tables and performance management to name a few – it is perhaps not surprising that students focus on the detailed handouts, accessible textbooks and judgement essays which can predominate in their experience of post-16 history. Of course, they learn about sources and about interpretations, but their perception is often that these are extras added on by the whims of examination boards, the hors d'oeuvres and desserts which may precede or follow the main course of factual nourishment (Hibbert, 2006; Booth, 2005). The idea that learning history involves separate, if sometimes sequential, processes – knowledge acquisition (the most important), analysing evidence and working with interpretations – leads students to this wonky view of their own subject and harms all aspects of their learning. This chapter aims to show how knowledge acquisition and the use of historical interpretations can be successfully interwoven.

Knowledge 'transforming not transferring'

Surveys of my own students show that they consider 'learning the facts' to be the biggest and most important challenge of their courses. Lomas' research (2005) confirms that history is thought to be difficult not because of the analytical demands but because of the sheer volume of learning required. In my own action research project (Laffin, 2006), students stated that it was the amount of precise learning of names, dates and events which caused them the greatest difficulty.

This is a serious problem: modular exams and unpredictable exam questions mean that teachers are sensibly anxious to ensure breadth and depth of coverage with adequate time for revision. In the days of the old A levels, a good portion of lessons were spent taking notes either through some form of dictation or from old-fashioned textbooks. Now this has been replaced, in many cases, with teacher handouts or sets of factual notes provided online. These methods have the advantage that they provide both teachers and learners with a comfortable security blanket. The regular transference of knowledge from one vessel to another, with minimal engagement or understanding, can create a superficial view of the nature of historical knowledge, which is damaging. It is an example of the more superficial 'knowledge telling' identified by Bereiter and Scardamalia (1987) rather than the more mature forms of historical writing which emerge from 'knowledge transforming', when students have had to engage with the knowledge in some form of problem-solving task. It also encourages students to think that acquiring a knowledge base is the responsibility of the teacher, rather than themselves.

Several articles in *Teaching History* have suggested models of how to make 'learning the facts' a meaningful part of a historical enquiry. LeCocq (1999) demonstrated how the process of note taking requires sound historical thinking and can be used to develop pupil understanding of a topic. Harris (2001) has described how a reading sheet can be used by students to highlight the purpose, nature and difficulties of gaining knowledge from an article or book and Hammond (2002) has shown how Year 10 can be taught to use knowledge to develop a powerful argument. In all these cases, the acquisition of knowledge has been part of the historical process; where factual knowledge has been found and used for a clear historical purpose.

From labelling to learning: some problems with interpretations

Since the setting up of the National Curriculum in England in 1991, the interpretation of history has been accepted as a central aspect of historical study. The agreed assessment objective for AS and A2 History is below.

> Analyse and evaluate, in relation to the historical context, how aspects of the past have been interpreted and represented in different ways.
>
> *QCA, AS and A2 Assessment Objectives, 2008*

Chapman (2006) has rightly highlighted the weaknesses of 'interpretations' work at A level, something I can confirm from a depressing stint as examiner for the Edexcel synoptic paper. Students often repeat a rehearsed summary of a historian's view and then affix a few worthy points from their own knowledge. Their answers frequently fall into one of two worrying extremes. Either they think that a quote from a historian is the final proof that their view is right, even if that historian died 50 years ago, or, armed with a pertinent fact or two, they cheerfully disprove the theory of a professor who has spent five years researching the archives. Hammond (2007) has shown how students, even before they start public examination courses, can be introduced to historical methods and make valuable assessments of them. However, even with older students, it is unusual for answers to lie in the rich middle ground which appreciates the process which has led the historian to that view and evaluates its contribution to historical understanding.

Another associated problem with historiographical work at this level is the tendency to see historians at polarised extremes. Students feel comfortable with oppositional labels: intentionalist vs structuralist or traditionalist vs revisionist. Sometimes the way debates are presented in textbooks and exam papers encourages the idea that most historical debates consist of sets of warring historians obstinately dug into opposing trenches. Although this can be an attractive way of engaging student interest and making the issue accessible, it is actually a simplistic caricature of most historical debate. The truth is that historians build on each other's foundations, adding their own corrections, amendments and additions, and sometimes, it is true, demolishing a little of what was laid before, but working together in an act of historical construction.

Furthermore, students who only encounter historians through edited and selected gobbets (Historical Association, 2005; Hibbert, 2006) will struggle to write with the cogency, coherence and style which is expected at the highest levels. The extracts can appear all the more daunting in those final A2 papers when students find the sentence construction, use of vocabulary and written expression alien. Ward (2006) has shown how detailed study of historians' text progresses student understanding of the interweaving of factual knowledge and personal expression. Although many teachers encourage detailed study of primary source material, searching for tone, omission and inference, a much more generalised approach is often used for secondary sources. Yet, applying the same rigorous approach to language and style in historians' writing can help students to achieve a deeper appreciation of historiography and to respond to it with greater sophistication.

Handling interpretations is probably the biggest challenge for teachers and students in their A-level history courses and one that can be helped by planning carefully and providing some structure or support. There are many different methods that can be used here, such as the card sorts described by Rudham (2001) or the structured questioning used by Chapman (2006) to assess the work of Gellately (2001). Sometimes teachers are hesitant to use the kinds of effective thinking tools they employed at earlier key stages with their post-16 students, perhaps for fear of the accusation of 'dumbing down'. My experience is that the planned use of these tools is often a necessary scaffold to enable students to climb higher.

Activities

Rationale for the activities

The big enquiry question

What was the nature of Nazi society?

To be successful in tackling such a question, students need to be able to answer questions on youth, race, women and the degree of support shown for the regime. I have made this enquiry question deliberately broad in order to enable a series of mini questions within it and to embrace possible aspects of the topic.

Knowing and interpreting Nazi society

Putting aside the sterile debate about whether so many young people should study Nazi Germany so much and so often, it is a truism that many students will be returning to this topic at AS or A2. Curriculum changes may reduce this trend but it is still probable that when they encounter the Nazis at sixth-form level, students will already have a baseline knowledge. This is as much a problem as an asset. In my context, with students from over 30 different schools and some who do not have History GCSE, there will be huge variations in the amount and quality of knowledge and understanding. Avoiding boredom or bewilderment is difficult. Yet without the basic factual toolkit, it is hard to achieve any higher-level thinking. It is no use planning a challenging seminar if the students do not know the key dramatis personae, the basic concepts and vocabulary or the main events. How often is an exciting activity let down by an often sizeable minority of students who have failed to do the basic preparation set? All too often, in my experience. And yet teachers can encourage this laziness by using class time to go over material set for homework or by providing handouts which compensate for student omissions. My colleague at Farnborough, Martin Thomas, has been an excellent role model in making students take responsibility for their own factual learning. This first activity is based on his idea.

Activity 1

A guide to Nazi society

Mini question:

What do we need to know in order to analyse Nazi society?

Rationale and procedure

It is surprising how even bright students lack an appreciation of the different forms of knowledge they encounter (Hibbert, 2006). I remember having a rather awkward conversation with an Oxbridge candidate over the personal statement on his UCAS form. His personal tutor had advised him to include more about what he read and he had responded by including the sentence 'I am an avid reader of Wikipedia'. He found it hard to understand why an admissions tutor would be unimpressed. You won't be surprised to learn that he was not offered a place!

So it is worth starting out by having a short discussion about the different forms of knowledge to give students a critical framework to start from. Ask them at this initial point to write down their own definition of historical knowledge and to keep it somewhere safe – it will prove useful at the end of the enquiry. Wikipedia is a wonderful tool to use here, not least because it is so familiar to most teenagers. The founders of Wikipedia are very clear about what it is for:

> It is an encyclopedia. Its goals go no further.
>
> *Rosenzwieg (2006)*

It is worth spending a bit of time here exploring what kind of knowledge is presented in an encyclopedia and what an encyclopedia is for. Wikipedia's own set of rules is helpful (Figure 3.1).

Despite Wikipedia's commitment to neutrality there are still degrees of contentiousness within its pages. Address that word 'contentious' with your students and then do a little experiment with Wikipedia. Go to the pages on the Armenian Genocide. Give your students a very quick summary of what it was and why it still causes debate. Over 300,000 words have been contributed to this topic in Wikipedia and the main factual articles are often locked because of the degree of online dispute it arouses. Using the editing history, you can find the pages which are most contentious and those that are not. Print out a selection, from the innocuous list of Armenian patriarchs to the disputed role played by the Turkish government, and ask your students to make a line from least to most contentious. Usually they get this right and it is a helpful reminder that even 'neutral, factual knowledge' varies in its supposed objectivity.

Figure 3.1 *The four key policies for Wikipedia writers*

- Articles should summarise and report conventional and accepted wisdom. There is no place for original research, critical reviews, propaganda or personal essays.
- Articles should be written from a neutral point of view. Disputes should be described without taking sides.
- Copyright must not be infringed.
- Respect other contributors.

Adapted from Rosenzwieg (2006: 5–8)

Building on this basis, ask your students to create their own basic reference guide to Nazi society. Introduce this with some discussion of what knowledge they need before they can make judgements about Nazi society. This will usually produce a quick checklist of people, concepts and key events or developments, which you can add to if need be. Explain that the guide is to be on the bottom of the contentiousness scale. Provide clear guidance on readability and word limits and remind them of the Wikipedia rules. On the copyright front, it is sensible to allow quite a bit of attributed pasting to speed up the process. Encourage peer editing and checking to develop a shared ownership of the guide, as competition and bullying is generally unhelpful. Your end product could be electronic or on paper or both.

The task has a second agenda, however, and that is to pass responsibility for the completion of the guide firmly onto the class's shoulders. How far you get involved in the organisation depends a little on how well you know the class and how well they know each other, but the more you can delegate the better. Cohen (1994) has described how the most effective group work results from teachers who are prepared to 'let go':

> It is of critical importance to let them make decisions on their own. They even need to make some mistakes on their own. They are accountable to you for their work. You must let go and allow the groups to work things through without you overseeing every step. They must learn to solve some problems for themselves.
>
> *Cohen (1994: 107)*

It is vital to insist that the guide is only available when all sections are complete. Peer pressure can be very powerful. Allowing the class to manage the omissions and delays can be hard but in the end sends clear messages about shared responsibility for learning and helps the class to work together as a group. Keep the activity short and focused; one lesson plus homework time and a deadline the students set themselves. Of course, the resulting guides are always a little uneven in quality and never fully comprehensive, but these blemishes are made up for by the learning in the process and the pride taken in the final product.

Activity 2

Transforming Claudia Koonz

Mini question:

In what ways did women change in the Third Reich?

One of main objectives in this module is to get students to read a range of kinds of texts and to use them to support a developed argument in an extended essay. In the past, students have been overly dependent on the standard textbooks and only the more able have dipped into the impressive array of articles and books provided in the college library. It was a key aim for my department this year to get students to use more challenging material.

Focusing on the role of women in Nazi society, students completed data capture sheets and then watched and discussed a video clip. At this point, the predominant view was that most German women were domestic doormats with the odd exceptions such as Leni Riefenstahl and Sophie Scholl. Further reading and discussion introduced the concepts of social reaction and social revolution, exploring the contrasting views of Schoenbaum and Mason. With the help of the case histories from Owings' (1995) book *Frauen* (Kitson, 2003), students began to formulate their own views. In previous years, this is where we left it. However, the resultant essays tended to be oversimplistic, with students arguing for one side or the other with the underlying assumption that German women were pliable clay moulded by the hands of Nazi men. This year I felt it was time to bring in a bit of feminism. It was time to introduce Claudia Koonz.

Koonz (1987) breathed fresh air into the debate in the 1980s by challenging many of the assumptions made by the (mostly male) historians writing before. She writes from the viewpoint of an American feminist in the 1980s, but it is very important you do not introduce this fact until the students have got to grips with her writing.

Activity procedure

Stage 1: Using Koonz – what do her words mean?
Koonz's writing poses considerable difficulty for many students but teachers have shown how challenging prose can be used successfully with pupils of different abilities and ages, and it certainly should not be avoided in the sixth form (Counsell, 2004; Woolley, 2003). A little peer editing can go a long way to make a passage more accessible for students and they are more likely to admit problems to each other than they are in a whole-class situation.

Organise your students into pairs to work on the text (Resource 3A). This can be best done online. Get each of them to highlight words, phrases or even whole sentences which they don't understand. They then exchange their highlighted text with their partner student and ask the partner to insert footnotes which explain the problematic writing they have highlighted. You can be on hand as an expert, as well as providing dictionaries and other reference books. Students then merge the two documents together at the end and print them off so that each student has the text with some explanatory notes. As an alternative to the computer-based exercise described here, copy Resource 3A onto A3 paper and ask your students to work as pairs of editors, highlighting difficult words in the text, using dictionaries to add definitions and working out tricky sections together.

An able pair of students in one of my classes felt the need to explain the following words and phrases: 'obviate their complicity' (para 1); 'misogynist' and 'latitude' (para 2); 'élan' and 'ersatz gloss of idealism' (para 3); '*Weltanschauung*' and 'immutable' (para 4); 'hierarchy' and '*Reichsfrauenfuhrerin*' (para 5).

Set students the homework task described in stage 2 below.

Stage 2: Using Koonz – what are her ideas?
The second task requires students simply to summarise Koonz's ideas. Their homework was to produce a diagram which summarised Koonz's views on one page of A4. We had some discussion of different forms of diagrams which could be used but students were allowed freedom to choose. Predictably mind maps and flow charts abounded – the least satisfactory being a series of copied statements joined by arrows. Even so, I regarded this as a better outcome than many 'read-and-take-notes' tasks I had set before. Some students went much further than this and showed intelligent understanding of how Koonz developed her thinking.

One student's work (Figure 3.2) shows that he is able to discern different threads in Koonz's argument and understand the sophistication of her conclusion – that there were unintended outcomes to Nazi policy, that in some ways women gained status and even power but that power was always to some degree a 'façade'. Although the line of thinking here is all Koonz, the words are completely the student's own. He has transformed the text into something accessible and clear but also subtle and accurate.

RESOURCE  *Editing Koonz*

Every woman Nazi in Germany did not 'adore' a brute hearted fascist. The women who followed Hitler, like the men, did so from conviction, opportunism, and active choice. Far from being helpless or even innocent, women made possible a murderous state in the name of concerns they defined as motherly. The fact that women bore no responsibility for issuing orders from Berlin does not obviate their complicity in carrying them out. Electoral statistics charted their enthusiasm, and Party propaganda depicts swooning women as well as marching men. But women did more than faint and vote for the only violently anti-feminist party in Weimar politics. And they received more than a 'boot in the face'.

What did this overtly misogynist movement offer to women? Nazi men inadvertently gave women Nazis a unique opportunity because they cared so little about the women in their ranks. Men allowed women considerable latitude to interpret Hitler's ideas as they wished, recruit followers, write their own rules, and raise funds. In other parties male leaders welcomed women officially, but then curtailed women leaders' independence and chastised them at the slightest sign of separatism. In the service of womanly ideals, Nazi women sometimes behaved in most 'unladylike' ways: managing the funds they raised, marching, facing down hecklers, making soapbox speeches, and organising mass meetings, marches and rallies. While espousing women's special nature and a reactionary view of the family, these women never thought they would retreat to the household. True, they crusaded to take women out of politics, but they did so in order to open up other areas of public life to women. Before 1933 Nazi women viewed the world around them in pessimistic terms, actively working in the public but not the political arena to preserve their nostalgic vision of the world that never was.

What, then, did women do for the men who ignored them? Before 1933, they provided men with an ambience they took for granted, complementing the stridently masculine élan of the Nazi movement and cultivating a homey domestic sphere for Hitler's motley and marginal band. They gave men Nazis the feeling of belonging not just to a party but to a total subculture that prefigured the ideals of the Nazi state for which they fought. Women kept folk traditions alive, gave charity to poor Nazi families, cared for SA men, sewed brown shirts, and prepared food at rallies. While Nazi men preached race hate and virulent nationalism that threatened to destroy the morality upon which civilization rested, women's participation in the movement created an ersatz gloss of idealism. The image did not, of course, deceive the victims, but it helped the Nazis to preserve their self esteem and to continue their work under the illusion they remained decent.

To a degree unique in Western history, Nazi doctrine created a society structured around 'natural' biological poles. In addition to serving specific needs of the state, this radical division vindicated a more general and thoroughgoing biological *Weltanschauung* based on race and sex as the immutable categories of human nature. The habit of taking psychological differences between men and women for granted reinforced assumptions about irrevocable divisions between Jew and 'Aryan'. In place of class, cultural, religious divisions, race and sex became the predominant social markers. To people disoriented by a stagnant economy, humiliated by military defeat, and confused by new social norms among the urban young, these social categories provided a sense of safety. The Jew and the New Woman, conservatives believed, had become too powerful in progressive Weimar society. The Nazi state drove both groups, as metaphors and as real individuals, out of the 'Aryan' man's world.

For women, belonging to the 'master race' opened the option of collaboration in the very Nazi state that exploited them, that denied them access to political status, deprived them of birth control, underpaid them as wage workers, indoctrinated their children, and finally took their husbands and sons to the front. The separation of masculine and feminine spheres, which followed logically and psychologically from Nazi leaders' misogyny, relegated women to their own space – both beneath and beyond the dominant world of men. The Nazi system rested on a female hierarchy as well as a male chain of command. Of course, women occupied a less exalted place in Nazi government than the men, and *Reichsfrauenfuhrerin* Gertrud Scholtz-Klink, who stood at the pinnacle of the women's hierarchy, wielded less real power than, say, a male district chief or deputy minister. Standing at the apex of her own sphere, the woman leader minimised her lack of status vis-à-vis Nazi male leaders above her and instead directed her attention to the battalions of women under her command. As in wartime, women believed their sacrifices played a vital role in a greater cause. Scholtz-Klink saw herself as the chief of a lobby for women's concerns and as the leader of women missionaries who would bring Nazi doctrine 'home' to every family in the Reich. Far from remaining untouched by Nazi evil, women operated at its very centre.

Koonz, C. (1987) Mothers in the Fatherland: Women, the Family and Nazi Politics

 © HODDER EDUCATION

● **Figure 3.2** *One student's homework exercise summarising the ideas of Claudia Koonz*

Main Points of 'Mothers in the Fatherland' (Claudia Koonz, 1987)

• Women were just as guilty of bringing about the Nazi Reich as men, not just through voting for them, but during the regime as "women missionaries" and collaborators in their own piece of the society the Nazis gave them.

They did this because they had freedom in the Nazi Reich, as long as they did it 'in service of womanly ideals' of which they were trying to achieve anyway.

Women made the Nazis seem homely and drew away from the race hate in their policy. They made the Nazis seem more human and gave the Nazi men support. They also convinced the members themselves they were part of a culture – making them fight harder for it.

Women had this freedom because the Nazis looked at the world as biologically as they could, whereas before the major divisions were mainly between men and women, now they were between different races – so the women felt part of the society and equal (obviously Jewish women and other anti-Nazi women wouldn't be equal).

✓ Excellent!

Women had a special place in the Nazi Reich – which enabled them to have the freedom, because they weren't always compared to men. Women had a special role under the Nazis which made them feel special and valued when compared to men – it gave them a façade of power.

Stage 3: Using Koonz – what does she bring to the debate?

The next stage is to understand a little more about Koonz and her contribution to the historical debate. Once more, rather than providing a label for the students to stick on, it is better to turn to Koonz's own words and help them to deduce her 'world view'. Resource 3B is an extract from the preface to her book. To engage the students with her words, students use the 'language bag' technique (Figure 3.3) to decide what tones underpin the writing. My students are used to doing this and so I let them choose their own adjective rather than giving them a selection to choose from.

Students should provide at least two good reasons for selecting their adjective and this forces them to look closely at the text. Expect the discussion which follows to focus a lot on Koonz's repeated use of the first person and of inverted commas: grammatical clues to a strong message. Her use of emotive language such as 'evil', 'decent', 'distrust' and 'perverted' will be picked out by students, leading to useful discussion of Koonz's approach.

● **Figure 3.3** The language bag

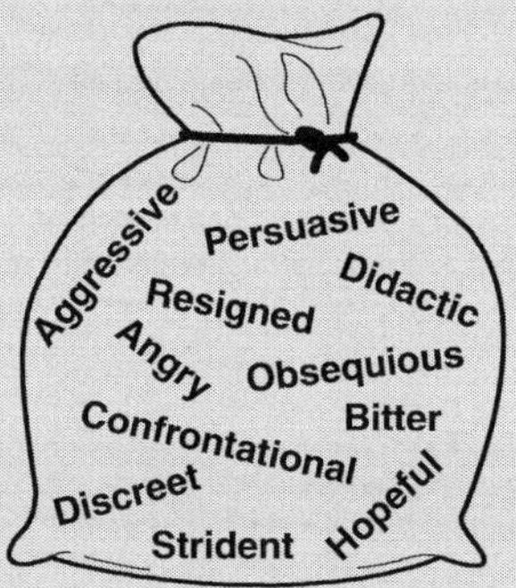

This idea is based on the fact that students can grasp the meaning of sources better by reading them out loud. Reading for an audience requires them to think about the meaning of words, the significance of punctuation and, more generally, the tone and emphasis of the writer. The technique works best in small groups. Give students a generous 5 minutes to read over the source and think about its meaning. They then need to agree its dominant tone, either from a provided 'language bag' (which would be much larger than this example) or by thinking of an adjective of their own.

If reading out loud is an issue, let students choose a volunteer from the group to read the text in the appropriate tone. The rest of the class have to guess the word the volunteer has chosen.

Using the same source with several groups makes the point that most texts include varying tones and may change tone within a paragraph.

It is worth ensuring you have enough time at the end of this process to look carefully at the final sentence. First of all, ask your students to work out the assumptions which lie behind the word 'although', which starts the sentence off, and then get them to critically appraise these assumptions. Is it really true that academic readers are uninterested in social issues of today or the past? What about the view that the broader audience may not be receptive to work based on archival research? Is Koonz right to see a tension between raising contemporary issues and writing academic history? What is Koonz implying about the purpose of her book when she directs it at this audience? (see Figure 3.4.)

Stage 4

The final part of the jigsaw is to put Koonz in the broader span of student knowledge, assessing the significance of her feminist 1980s context. At this stage you can provide some information about her background and a short review of her book. Students should already have studied historians who have promoted the social reaction and social revolution view.

Ask students, working in small groups, to complete a Venn diagram with assertions about women in Nazi Germany placed within it (Resource 3C). Enlarge or redraw the diagram as necessary. Then ask students to add at least five more of their own points. This will help them to see the overlaps and differences between the viewpoints and set them up nicely for their extended research essay.

● **Figure 3.4** *Assumptions behind the word 'although'*

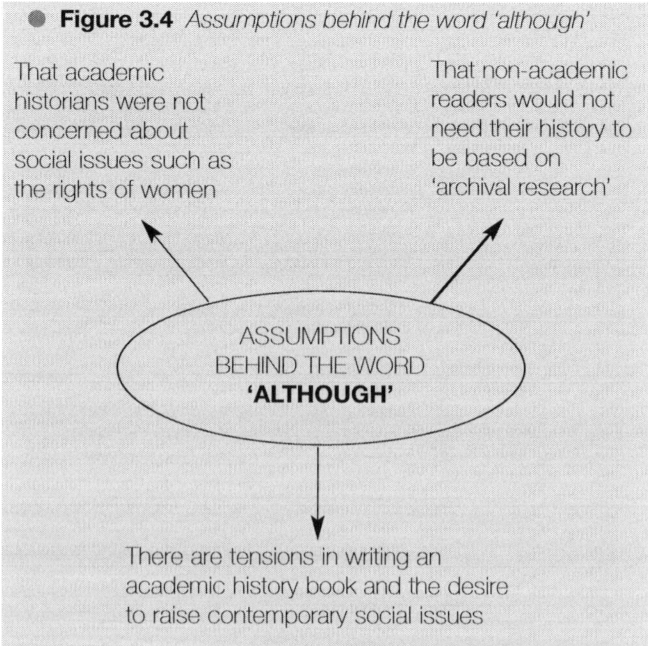

RESOURCE 3B *Extract from the preface of Claudia Koonz's book*

In the preface to her book, Claudia Koonz describes an in-depth interview with Gertrude Scholtz-Klink, the leader of the Nazi women's organisations, and how it influenced her decision to write the book. This paragraph is towards the end of the preface.

> As I faced her that day – in a posh editorial office, with tea growing cold on the table – this book began to take shape. In it, I would bring to light the contribution to evil made by Scholtz-Klink and other women leaders, find out what they had done, what they believed they were doing and why. I would ask how 'normal' people (women, in this case) brought Nazi beliefs home in everyday thought and action. Above all I would record the history of average people without normalizing life in Nazi society. This would mean examining the lives of Nazism's victims and opponents to recapture the picture of how Scholtz-Klink's women looked from outside their womanly sphere. How did 'decent' people adapt to a state that inverted morality, perverted civilized traditions and imposed distrust on all forms of social life? At what points did Hitler's charisma wear thin? When did Nazi policy contradict loyalty to religion and family? As I formulated these questions, I made a second decision. Although my book would depend upon archival research, I resolved to frame that material in a broad context and to write for an audience beyond academe, for people concerned about women's status in modern society, social history, and the impact of misogyny and anti-Semitism on public life.
>
> *Koonz, C. (1987)* Mothers in the Fatherland: Women, the Family and Nazi Politics

RESOURCE  *Views on the position of women in Nazi Germany*

Cut out the assertions and place them in the correct position on the Venn diagram. Add five points of your own.

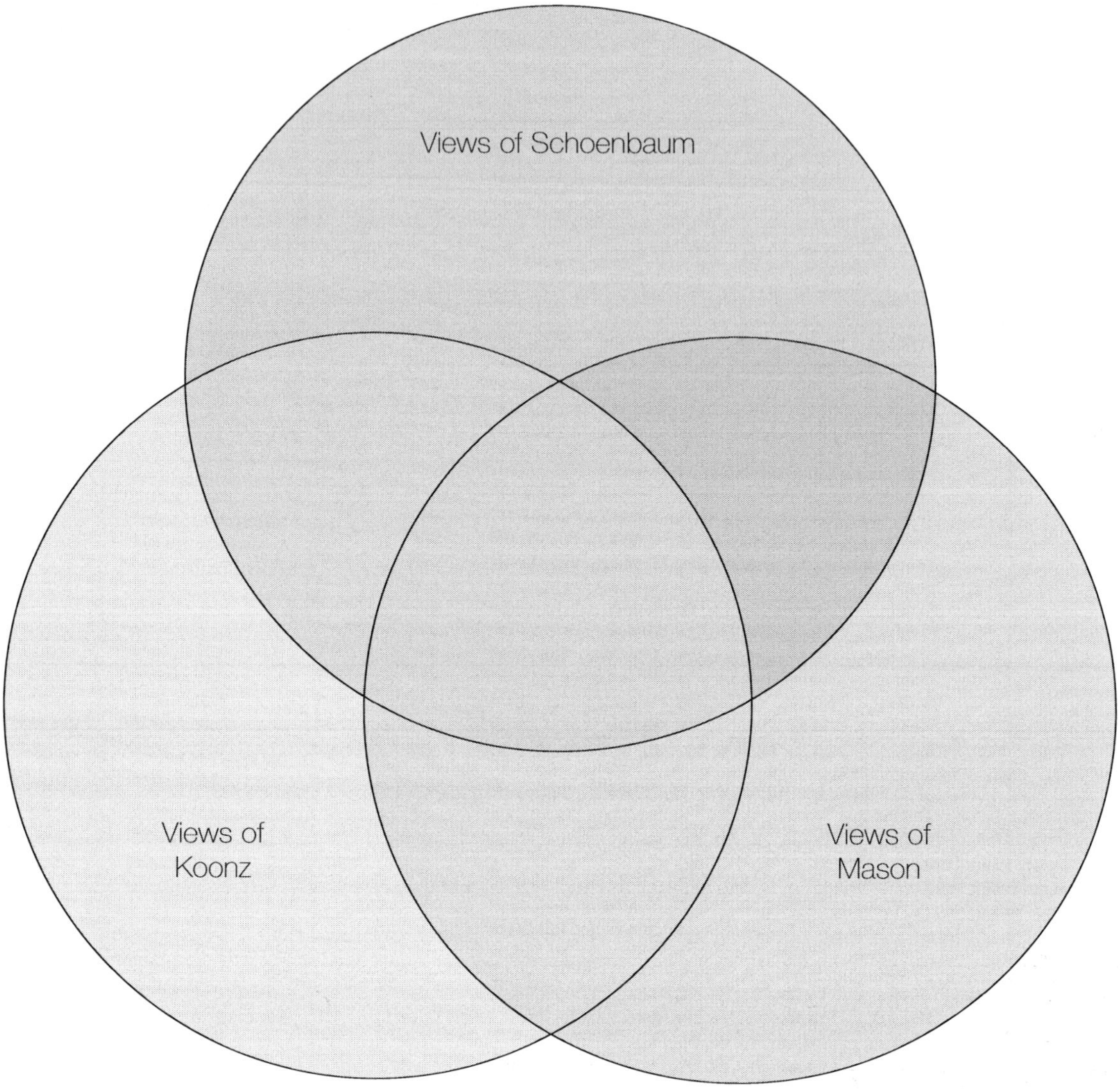

Women were willing collaborators of the Nazi state.	Women had access to a greater range of leisure activities.	Women's educational opportunities were reduced by the Nazis.	Women's health and welfare improved.	Women did not cooperate with the Nazi agenda.
Women's employment opportunities were reduced.	Class divisions became stronger under the Nazis.	Women gained more social status.	Women's political influence was reduced.	Women were more sexually liberated.

 © HODDER EDUCATION

Activity 3

Using wikis to widen minds

Mini question:

Was Nazi society ruled by fear?

Rationale

One of the central and most controversial issues in the study of Nazi society is the role of terror in the state. Did German people conform out of fear or were they genuinely won over by Hitler? In their responses to this complex question students are expected to understand the views of the leading historians and to be able to comment intelligently on the context of those interpretations.

The quality of their responses has not been helped by the predominance of judgement-style essay questions which encourage an either/or answer. This type of analytical task predominates much of the AS/A2 programme (in the 2008 Edexcel specifications, for instance) and is well liked by both students and examiners because it lends itself to clear planning and argument. However, it can encourage the confrontational view of historians suggested above and an oversimplified understanding of their writing. Lang (2003) has suggested that we need to rethink the predominance of analysis as a superior form of writing and learn to appreciate the skills which go into the construction of a successful narrative. This task aims to blend the two together by requiring students to create wiki pages.

There are many gulfs between students and teachers but few as dramatic as their contrasting views of Wikipedia. Teachers loathe it as the source of so much unthinking copying and pasting, the bland material behind pretty handouts and PowerPoints which students cheerfully present as their 'research'. Students treasure Wikipedia almost as much as their mobile phones. It is quick, reliable and accessible. What's not to like?

Wikipedia has around 15,000 hits per second. It is growing at a rate of 1700 articles per day and has 7.5 million pages. It is probably worth more than £2 billion. Its aim, according to its founder, Jimmy Wales, is to 'bring the sum of human knowledge to every single person on the planet, free, in their own language' (Adams, 2007). It is as much a phenomenon of the modern world as e-mail or electric toothbrushes. Teachers, you may as well join the student love affair.

Activity 1 established the fact that Wikipedia provides a particular form of knowledge. At this stage, it is worth exploring the nature of this knowledge in more depth. Wales was inspired by the views of political philosopher von Hayek, who stated that 'all knowledge is partial and the closest you can get to truth comes from the aggregation of as many partial understandings as possible'. Most students are familiar with how wiki pages work and find the collaborative and open nature of the site attractive. The constructive nature of Wikipedia is a powerful antidote to the view that knowledge emerges from cyclical academic warfare.

Figure 3.5 *Page from Wikipedia*

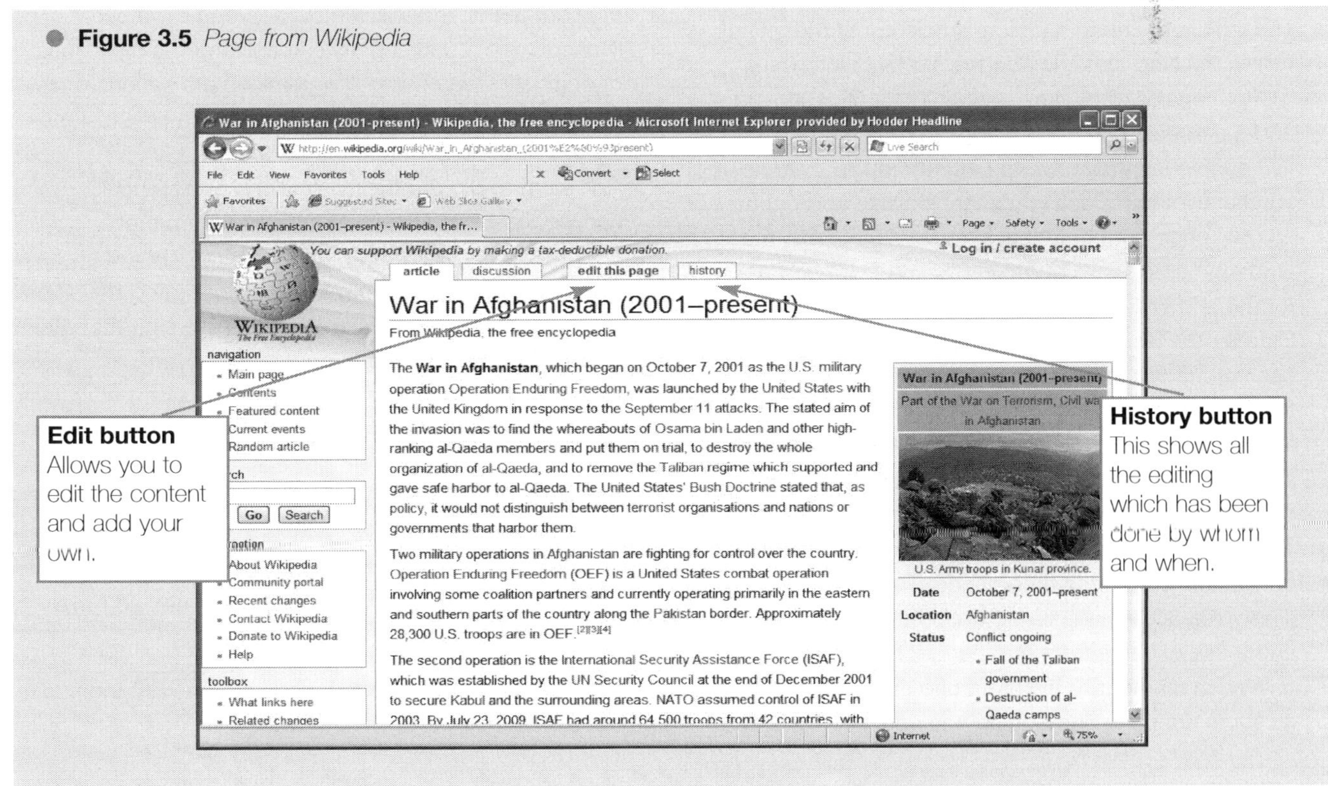

I put up a wiki page on my whiteboard of a controversial event in the news. For a start it was much more detailed than the single article I had from the previous week's Sunday paper. It had over 90 references at the bottom from more than fifteen different sources. The bar at the top enables us to read assessments of the article's reliability and overall rating and also to see how it had been edited. This article had already been substantially worked on by three different editors and the diary of their changes and reasons for them were faithfully and accurately recorded. The clear principles of constructive dialogue, honest criticism and justified editing provide powerful lessons for trainee historians. This point has been made forcibly by Rosenzweig:

> Professional historians have things to learn not only from the open and democratic distribution model of *Wikipedia* but also from its open and democratic production model. Although *Wikipedia* as a *product* is problematic as a sole source of information, the *process* of creating *Wikipedia* fosters an appreciation of the very skills that historians try to teach.
>
> *Rosenzweig (2006: 25)*

This activity uses the facility to add, edit and remove content to help students re-create the development of knowledge of Nazi society. It is inspired partly by the wonderful presentation by Belshaw and Dennis at the Schools History Project Conference in 2007, in which they demonstrated the motivational effect of allowing students to make their own wiki pages.

Activity procedure

1. The task is to create a factual article about the role of fear in the Nazi state. Divide the students into three groups organised by time period: 1945–65, 1965–89 and the 1990s. Make the first group a larger one – up to five people, as they have to write the original article. If you have a large class you might want to add another '2000s' page but I hold this in reserve for use in the students' practice exam task. Remind them of the format and style of wiki pages.
2. Stagger the task over a week, with tight deadlines for each group to complete their stage. Be very strict on this and do not allow the odd absence or technical hitch to be used as an excuse. It may be useful to remind students that they will all need the material for the practice exam task which follows.
3. The first group should write the original article using only material from the time period. The task sheet (Resource 3D) includes a bit of contextual information and a few extracts from that period. It can be helpful to give each member of the team one extract to work with, as some are quite challenging and you may be able to allocate texts according to what each student can cope with. Encourage students to add to this evidence bank but remind them they can only use material available before 1965. Clear rules about referencing and word limits help to avoid waffle or copying. A reminder to write according to wiki rules is also important – students should be describing the prevailing consensus, not arguing a case.
4. The subsequent teams now need to add, amend and edit the first article. Allow them an extra 200 words each. (Resources 3E and 3F.)
5. Make sure you build in some time for review of the final product. If you have more than one class doing this, peer review by class is very successful and, of course, a normal part of the wiki experience. Add to the richness of your classroom discussion by introducing your students to the Peukert quote from the preface to his book *Inside Nazi Germany*:

   > Since history is in its true sense a twofold dialogue, a hermeneutic engagement with the testimony of the past and a public discourse in the present, each generation confronts history in a new way and writes history in a new way.
   >
   > *Peukert (1989: 17)*

   Once you have overcome the hurdle of 'hermeneutic', the wiki-writing students appreciate the strength of this statement about the nature of history and can join in a meaningful discussion about its implications.
   It is time to be a bit more critical of Wikipedia by exploring the students' frustrations at having to write a neutral summary and not being able to express an opinion. In the end wiki writing's 'broad synthetic' (Rosenzweig, 2006: 11) style is dull and the omissions of original research and new thinking are serious ones for historians. If the students reach these conclusions for themselves, so much the better.
   Ask them to dig out their definitions of historical knowledge (from Activity 1) and give them the opportunity to review and rewrite them if they wish. They will probably find it hard to write a good definition in a sentence and this is an encouraging sign that their understanding has moved on.
6. The final part of this activity is to set an exam-style task (Resource 3G). I deliberately pick a text which brings the debate up to date and put this alongside more familiar views to remind students that research is still moving on from the 1990s where they left it. At this point, the students are free to make their own judgements, which the wiki-writing task should have given them an appetite for.

This sequence of activities is greedy on time but the end product is usually worth waiting for.

RESOURCE 3D *Task sheet for Group 1*

Wiki writers from 1945 to 1965

Your article has the title: **The role of fear in Nazi society**. You should consider three key areas in your article: the nature and extent of terror and its impact on the German people. The article must be no more than 800 words long. Include references where possible. Write in clear and correct English. Remember you are writing a neutral summary, using the evidence in front of you.

Political background

The Allied victors in Western Europe were keen not to repeat the mistakes of the 1919 peace settlements. Although there was a strong view that the perpetrators of atrocities should be brought to justice, with the resultant Nuremberg Trials, there was also a desire not to blame the mass of German citizens for the Nazi regime. The division in Europe between the Communist East and the democratic West was soon apparent, with Churchill making his Iron Curtain speech in 1946 and NATO being set up in 1949. West Germany was strongly supported by the Western Allies after the war, for example in the Berlin air lift and over the Berlin Wall. In Germany itself, there was a strong desire to move on and build a new country rather than dwell on a painful past.

The evidence base

In the years immediately after the war, the bulk of evidence was provided by victims, opponents and perpetrators of Nazism. A large proportion of Nazi records were either deliberately or accidentally destroyed in the last year of the war. In its aftermath, the evidence of the Nuremberg Trials was highly influential, as were the willing testimonies of freedom fighters and captives. As the Russians had invaded all of Eastern Germany and reached Berlin first, a great deal of evidence was removed and inaccessible for Western historians. Most of the historians writing at this time were from the Allied countries, some of whom had been directly involved in the war.

Source 1

In this interview used as evidence at the Nuremberg Trials, a witness described the so-called 'elections' in Austria after the Anschluss *in 1938. Austrians were required to vote on whether Austria should be united with Germany.*

> The whole thing took place in a rather large hall. There was an entrance, and when you came in there was a round table at which sat several officials, and they registered you. They would hand you an envelope which had a sheet of paper in it; and there were two circles in it, a large circle and a small circle, and you were supposed to make a cross in one of the circles, the larger circle meaning 'Yes', and the smaller circle meaning 'No'. Then at the other end of this hall was a telephone booth, and you were supposed to go in there, and make your cross, put the ballot in the envelope, return, and drop it into a box which was provided at the end of the table. It was handled in this manner. However, when somebody came in, the officials would greet him with 'Heil Hitler', and then give him the ballot and they said, 'You are voting "yes", there is no reason to go to the booth at the end of the hall'; and everybody would make a cross in the larger circle. Then they would give the ballot to the official, and he would put it in the envelope, and put it in the box. Nobody dared to go to the booth in order to vote secretly. Well, I came into this place, and I was the only one among hundreds of people who dared to go into this booth.

Overy, R. (2001) Interrogations: The Nazi Elite in Allied Hands, *p. 313*

Source 2

From The History of the Gestapo *by J. Delarue, published in 1962. The author was a member of the French resistance who was captured by the Gestapo and who interrogated Gestapo agents at the end of the war.*

> The Gestapo acted on its own account by secretly installing microphones and tape recorders in the homes of suspects. In the absence of the victim, or in the pretext of making repairs or of checking the telephone or the electrical installations, a few microphones were discreetly installed, allowing the individual to be spied upon even in the bosom of his family. No one was safe from this type of practice … Spying became so universal that nobody could feel safe.

Quoted in Edexcel Revision Guide, p. 56

Source 3

A message to all Gestapo offices and to the Political Police of the State No 33590, Berlin, 22 April 1936.

> A list must be sent by return of post of those people in your area who were prominent in opposing and slandering the National Socialist movement before the take over of power. The following details are requested concerning the prominent leaders in politics and business from the camp of the former DNVP, DVP, and Democratic Party (*Staatspartei*): the first name and surname, the date and place of birth, whether or not a Jew, present domicile, profession, including all the offices held by the person concerned, whether the person had his citizenship revoked or whether an application has been made for the revocation of his citizenship. Furthermore, his present occupation must be reported. At the same time, a detailed report must be made about the incidents in which the individual was involved, particularly hostile activity towards the NSDAP, and whether or not the person in question is still a clandestine opponent of the National Socialist State or has drawn attention to himself by acting in a hostile way towards the State and the Party.

Noakes, J. and Pridham, G. (1984), Nazism 1919–1945, *p. 517*

Source 4

William Shirer was an American radio journalist who reported from Germany until 1940. His book was the first account of the Third Reich in English.

> Under the expert hand of Heydrich … the SD soon spread its net over the country, employing some 100 000 part time informers who were directed to snoop on every citizen in the land and report the slightest remark or activity which was deemed inimical to Nazi rule. No one – if he were not foolish – said or did anything that might be interpreted as 'anti-Nazi' without first taking precautions that it was not being recorded by hidden SD microphones or overheard by an SD agent. Your son or your father or your wife or your cousin or your best friend or your boss or your secretary might be an informer for Heydrich's organization; you never knew, and if you were wise nothing was taken for granted.

Shirer, W. (1960) The Rise and Fall of the Third Reich, *p. 273*

RESOURCE 3E *Task sheet for Group 2*

Wiki writers from 1966 to 1989

Your task is to edit and amend the wiki article on **The role of fear in Nazi society**. It must be no more than 900 words long. You should consider three key areas in your article: the nature and extent of terror and its impact on the German people. Any amendments or additions you make must be correctly referenced. Write in clear and correct English.

Political background

In these years, West Germany became an economically strong and politically stable country which played a major role in Europe. The Cold War persisted with the Soviet invasion of Afghanistan and the Vietnam War, and Germany was still divided between the Communist East and capitalist West. However, in the 1980s, relations began to thaw with the signing of détente treaties and the emergence of Gorbachev as Soviet leader in 1985. Those directly involved in the war were becoming older and less influential and memories were dimming.

The evidence base

In these years, new approaches to researching and writing history were developed. In Germany, the study of *Alltagsgeschichte* (the history of everyday life) emerged with in-depth, often regional, research into the ordinary experiences of German people. This challenged the view that general judgements about how the Nazi state worked could be applied across all classes, age groups and regions of Germany. At the same time, writers with a Marxist perspective, such as Tim Mason, or a sociological one, such as Ralf Dahrendorf, began to contribute to the debate. While evidence in Eastern Germany was still not available to Western historians, regional research was unearthing a wealth of information about the lives of German families and workers.

Source 1

SPD report from South West Germany in the spring of 1937.

> The number of those who consciously criticise the political objectives of the regime is very small, quite apart from the fact that they cannot give expression to this criticism. … Conversations with workers and with members of Church circles demonstrate how varied are the causes of the anti-National Socialist mood. Some were and still are very much up in arms about the development of National Socialist Church policy and look at everything in terms of that. However, in conversations with workers the reply to the question of what they thought about the Church dispute was almost invariably 'That doesn't interest us'... In other sections of society, e.g. among the self employed and the peasantry, things are not very different. Their discontent focuses superficially on matters they find unpleasant and it can sometimes go as far as open sabotage of official measures … It becomes increasingly evident that the majority of people have two faces; one which they show to their good and reliable acquaintances; and the other for the authorities, the Party offices, keen Nazis and for strangers. The private face shows the sharpest criticism of everything that is going on now; the official one beams optimism and contentment.

Noakes, J. and Pridham, G. (1984), Nazism 1919–1945, *p. 580-81*

Source 2

Extract from a sermon preached by Friedrich Dibelius on the re-opening on the Reichstag in March 1933.

A new beginning in the history of the state is always marked, in one or another way, by the use of force. For the state is power. New decisions, new attitudes, transformations and upheavals always signify victory on one side and defeat on another. And if the life and death of a nation are at stake, then the power of the state must be employed effectively and with vigour whether internally or externally…

If the state carries out its duties against those who undermine the foundations of state order – against those, in particular, whose coarse and corrosive words destroy marriage, expose faith to contempt, and slander all who lay down their lives for the fatherland – then let the state carry out its duties, in God's name!

Quoted in Peukert, D. J. K. (1989) Inside Nazi Germany: Conformity, Opposition and Racism in Everyday Life, *p. 198*

Source 3

Extract from A Social History of the Third Reich.

Anti-Nazi humour was both a low keyed expression of resistance (or at least disapproval) and a form of therapy. None the less, for many Germans the circulation of political jokes represented a comfortable (or even socially admired) substitute for thinking – let alone acting – about evils which existed on a plane extraneous to word-play and punch lines. Defeatist jokes could occasionally cancel out the regime's efforts at morale boosting, but the average joker prefacing his sotto voce delivery with 'Preamble – this one carries three years' hard labour' was actuated less by political awareness (let alone anger) than by the raconteur's perennial craving for an audience.

Grunberger, R. (1971) A Social History of the Third Reich, *p. 419*

Source 4

Extract from Inside Nazi Germany.

The thesis that the Hitler Youth successfully mobilised young people fits only one side of the social reality of the Third Reich. The more the Hitler Youth arrogated state powers to itself, and the more completely young people were assimilated into the organisation, the more clearly visible became an emergent pattern of youth nonconformity. By the end of the 1930s thousands of young people were declining to take part in the leisure activities of the Hitler Youth and were discovering their own unregimented styles in spontaneous groups and gangs. Indeed, they defended their autonomous space all the more insistently as the Hitler Youth *Streifendienst* and the Gestapo applied ever more massive pressure.

Peukert, D. J. K. (1989) Inside Nazi Germany: Conformity, Opposition and Racism in Everyday Life, *p. 153*

RESOURCE 3F *Task sheet for Group 3*

Wiki writers, 1990s

Your task is to edit and amend the wiki article on **The role of fear in Nazi society**. It must be no more than 1000 words long. You should consider three key areas in your article: the nature and extent of terror and its impact on the German people. Any amendments or additions you make must be correctly referenced. Write in clear and correct English.

Political background

The Berlin Wall came down in 1989 and the collapse of Communism in Eastern Europe followed. Germany became one country once again and new archives became accessible. Those involved in the Nazi regime were now elderly or dead and a new openness resulted.

The evidence base

Historians from a wide range of backgrounds and nationalities undertook research into the Third Reich, raising issues and questions which might have been considered too sensitive in earlier times. In particular, research into records of the military and security aspects of the Nazi state led historians to consider the degree of collaboration and complicity of the German people.

Source 1

'Omniscient, Omnipotent, Omnipresent? Gestapo, society and resistance', by Klaus Michael Mallman and Gerhard Paul. This paper, based on research into the Gestapo archive at Wurzburg, reveals the role played by German civilians in voluntarily providing information for the secret police.

Although the Gestapo was certainly the final authority, in most cases, it was not the driving force. It interrogated, selected, made decisions, deported or delivered cautions: but it was scarcely able to engage in investigations by itself. The widespread collaboration with the regime, the acceptance of terror by society, cancelled this deficit and provided the Gestapo with many ears, in the immediate vicinity of the regime's political opponents. The concept of 'mass crime' therefore has a double meaning; these were the crimes that affected masses of Germans, but a large part of the German population had also participated in these crimes.

At the same time the structural intelligence deficiencies of the Gestapo and its dependence upon denunciations, informers and spies whose statements were often unusable in a proper court of law, encouraged the police increasingly to take the administration of 'justice' into their own hands….

Mallman, K. M. and Paul, G. (1994) 'Omniscient, Omnipotent, Omnipresent? Gestapo, society and resistance' in Crew, D. (ed.) Nazism and German Society 1933–1945, *p. 185*

Source 2

Extract from Christopher R. Browning, (1992) Ordinary Men. *Browning researched Reserve Police Battalion 101, which was directly involved in the killings of Jews during the occupation of Poland in 1939. He noted that only 12 out of 500 men asked not to take part in the first massacre at Jozefow when given the opportunity to opt out by their commanding officer. In this passage, he describes the composition of the battalion.*

> The men of reserve Police Battalion 101 were from the lower orders of German society. They had experienced neither social nor geographic mobility. Very few were economically independent. Except for apprenticeship or vocational training, virtually none had any education after leaving *Volkschule* (terminal secondary school) at age fourteen or fifteen. ... By virtue of their age, of course, all went through their formative period in the pre-Nazi era. These were men who had known political standards and moral norms other than those of the Nazis. Most came from Hamburg, by reputation one of the least nazified cities in Germany, and the majority came from a social class that had been anti-Nazi in its political culture.

Browning, C. R. (2001) Ordinary Men: Reserve Police Battalion 101 and the Final Solution in Poland, *p. 48*

Source 3

Extract from Backing Hitler.

> Beginning in early 1933, the police and the Nazi Storm Troopers started cracking heads, and new concentration camps were established, but not much more than a mini-wave of terror swept Germany. By and large, terror was not needed to force the majority or even significant minorities into line. By mid 1933, or the end of that year at the latest, power was already secured, and the brutalities and violence that are identified with the so-called Nazi 'seizure of power', began to wane. Terror itself does not adequately explain how the Third Reich came to be, nor account for its considerable staying power. As I will show, the regime continued to elicit popular support well into the war years.

Gellately, R. (2001) Backing Hitler: Consent and Coercion in Nazi Germany, *p. 2*

Source 4

Extract from 'I will bear witness', the diary of Victor Klemperer, 16 May 1936. Klemperer was a Jewish linguistics professor who recorded a detailed diary of his experiences.

> The majority of the people is content, a small group accepts Hitler as the lesser evil, no one really wants rid of him, all see in him the liberator in foreign affairs, fear Russian conditions, as a child fears the bogeyman, believe, insofar as they are not honestly carried away that it is inopportune, in terms of Realpolitik, to be outraged at such details as the suppression of civil liberties, the persecution of the Jews, the falsification of all scholarly truths, the systematic destruction of all morality. And all are afraid for their livelihood, their life, all are such terrible cowards. (Can I reproach them with it? During my last year in my post I swore an oath to Hitler, I have remained in the country – I am no better than my Aryan fellow creatures.)

Klemperer, V. (1999) I Will Bear Witness 1933–1941: A Diary of the Nazi Years, p. 165

 © HODDER EDUCATION

RESOURCE  *Exam-style question as summative assessment*

Read the sources carefully and then answer the question at the end.

Source 1

Sebastian Haffner, *Defying Hitler*, a memoir published in English in 2002, p.125. This memoir was written by a young man who opposed the Nazis and left the country.

> It is typical of the early years of the Nazi regime that the whole façade of everyday life remained virtually unchanged. The cinemas, theatres and cafes were full. Couples danced in the open air and in the dance halls. People strolled down the streets. The Nazis used this to great effect in their propaganda. 'Come and see our normal, peaceful, quiet country. Come and see how well even the Jews are doing here.' The secret vein of madness, fear and tension, of living by the day, and dancing a dance of death: those one could not see.

Source 2

Robert Gellately, (2001) *Backing Hitler: Consent and Coercion in Nazi Germany*, p. 188.

> The study of police practices shows that especially by the war years, the Gestapo side of Hitler's dictatorship was driven forward by ordinary citizens who reported their suspicions and allegations. If we add to this picture the important role of denunciations in the enforcement of measures aimed to isolate both the Jews and the Poles … then there are grounds to call into question many of the images of how the Gestapo operated. In fact, the Gestapo tended to be reactive and waited for information to come from the outside. Most of it came from 'ordinary' Germans, that is, civilians who were not even members of the Nazi Party.

Source 3

Extract from Michael Burleigh, (2001) *The Third Reich: A New History*, p. 182.

> These organisations may have been relatively small, and thinly distributed outside the capital, but it is important to remember that the intelligence agents of the SD could rely on the Gestapo, while the latter could deploy larger numbers of police or paramilitary auxiliaries whenever it needed to cordon off an area searching for weapons or Communist literature. In Berlin, in 1935, Gestapo raids on allotments in the north of the city involved two hundred regular policemen, a hundred auxiliaries and three mobile units consisting of armed motorcycle police. The noise of their engines was sometimes broadcast live on the radio to maximise the impression of a drastic crackdown on crime. Total omniscience may have been in the eye of the beholder, but localised dominance was not illusory. Terror both neutralised political opponents and repressed the wider population through a more pervasive insecurity.

Using these three sources and your own knowledge, how far would you agree that most German people were repressed by terror? *[40 marks]*

Sample lesson sequence

Rationale

This suggested enquiry moves away from the view that all aspects are covered in the same depth. The idea behind the initial activity is to give all students a basic reference guide as a safety blanket. After this it is suggested that some topics, such as race and youth, are covered fairly broadly to allow time for the in-depth enquiries into women and the role of fear. Of course, this poses the risk that lazy students with poor attendance will not have thorough notes on all aspects for the exam. In my view it is a risk that is worth taking for the broader rewards of making time for challenging investigations.

There is also a heavy reliance on homework. Again, it is hard but if you can set the pattern that homework provides the foundations of lessons and that the teacher is not going to compensate for failure to do it, it pays off in the end.

Prior learning

Students should have some basic knowledge of the Third Reich, such as the key tenets of Nazi ideology, a factual outline of Nazi rule and the roles of the main characters in the Nazi state. It is not expected that they have studied Nazi society in any depth.

Enquiry question

What was the nature of Nazi society?

Outline of learning flow

Nine lessons over three weeks, as shown in Figure 3.6. This enquiry represents about a third of a module.

Figure 3.6 *Nine lessons over three weeks*

What was the nature of Nazi society?	
Lesson 1 *Mini question:* What do we need to know in order to analyse Nazi society?	At the start of the lesson introduce your enquiry question and tell the students that it has a dual goal: understanding Nazi society and coming to some conclusions about the nature of historical knowledge. Get them to write down a sentence defining what historical knowledge is and to save it somewhere safe until the end of this enquiry. Start **Activity 1** with a quick discussion of kinds of knowledge by using the Wikipedia extracts and lining them up by degrees of contentiousness. In your discussion tease out the meaning of the word 'contentious' and briefly raise the issue of objectivity of knowledge. Then go on to the second stage of the activity: the guide to Nazi society. Remember to delegate most of this task while keeping expectations high and the pace of work brisk. The factual guide should be finished for homework with the students taking responsibility for its completion by their set deadline.
Lessons 2, 3 and 4 *Mini question:* Did the Nazis unite German society?	These lessons explore the main features of German society and how Nazi policy changed them. There are many ways teachers could tackle different aspects of Nazi society. Students could work in groups and use a range of texts to complete data capture sheets to examine class divisions and the impact of Nazi policies on them. Subsequent lessons could look at racial policy, using a video for note taking and discussion, and the effectiveness of Nazi youth initiatives.
Lessons 5 and 6 *Mini question:* In what ways did women change in the Third Reich?	Start by giving the class a sound overview of women's policy by using a video (Channel 4's *Hitler's Brides* is recommended) and some routine textbook work. Then introduce **Activity 2** with the online editing of Koonz. Set the second task, the diagram work, for homework. The next lesson can begin with sharing and discussing their responses to Koonz to warm the students up for the third task. The language bag activity can follow, with a structured discussion of the issues raised. Follow this with the small-group work completing the Venn diagram and set the extended essay.
Lessons 7 and 8 *Mini question:* Was Nazi society ruled by fear?	Introduce **Activity 3**. A whole-class discussion of Wikipedia centred on a whiteboard demonstration is a good starting point. Ask if students have contributed to it and if they have ever found any errors. There is usually a range of experiences to draw on. Then start the first group off in their writing exercise while the rest of the class complete factual work on the structure, roles and activities of Himmler's empire. Follow this up in the next lesson to allow the other groups to finish off.
Lesson 9 *Mini question:* Was Nazi society ruled by fear?	Do stage 5 of **Activity 3**, the peer review, and make time for a discussion of Peukert's statement about historical knowledge. Ask students to dig out their initial sentences about what knowledge is and give them time to rewrite or amend their view. With this in mind, set the exam practice task, highlighting the need for meaningful engagement with the texts as interpretations of history.

CHAPTER 4 Slow cooking: independent learning in a coursework module

Chapter summary

- This chapter outlines an effective way of developing student responsibility for learning through a coursework study. It suggests that students need to be given the time to listen, reflect and question, to become competent historians. This is the ideal module for this.
- The first activity describes a teacher introduction which requires active listening and critical thinking. It advocates the use of two unfashionable methods of enriching student learning: the PowerPoint presentation and teacher talk.
- The second activity involves the creation of an effective learning community using an online message board. This encourages reading and debate outside the classroom using modes of communication and review which are already familiar to many students.
- In the third activity, students take responsibility for their own learning through a peer tutorial and management system organised on the message board. This enables them to set staged deadlines, consider assessment criteria and agree the form of tutorials.
- Concluding the teaching sequence, students return to the initial thesis in the first teacher presentation, to reassess and reflect on their learning.
- The sequence of lessons is based on the big enquiry question:
  Did Chamberlain follow the only realistic policy at Munich?

Context

Casseroling classroom conversation

Teaching for examinations requires us to put historical learning in the pressure cooker. In the end, all the subject matter must be on the plates in digestible portions in time for the set meal. However hard we try, compromises have to be made in order to cover content. We often talk of knowledge and understanding as if the two are inextricably wedded. They are not. Sadly, students can quite often acquire knowledge without much understanding. Gardner has explained this perhaps better than anyone else:

> The greatest enemy of understanding is coverage – I can't repeat that often enough. If you're determined to cover a lot of things, you are guaranteeing that most kids will not understand, because they haven't had time enough to go into things in depth, to figure out what the requisite understanding is, and be able to perform that understanding in different situations.
>
> *Gardner (1993: 24)*

Gardner's concept of 'performance of understanding', where students engage with their knowledge by explaining it and applying it in a range of ways, is one that history teachers can instantly recognise and subscribe to. Yet content-heavy syllabi means that this level of understanding is not always achieved.

Research evidence confirms my own experience that the desire for fast-paced coverage of material squeezes out the time to absorb and understand. The influential paper 'Inside the Black Box' (Black and Wiliam, 2001) demonstrated that classroom discussion is very often 'pressure cooked' with minimal time for reflection or development of understanding. Husbands (1996) described how many practitioners continue to adopt a 'transmission model of teaching' where teachers prompt students towards pre-ordained outcomes. Frequently its purpose is factual recap with a fast pace set by teachers, nervous, perhaps, of students losing interest while an enthusiastic few dominate the classroom.

It took a lesson observation of a young teacher in my team at college to remind me of how quality classroom dialogue could move students on (see Figure 4.1).

In the lesson described in Figure 4.1, the teacher talk was used to draw out the thinking of the students and to challenge their intellectual sloth. With the teacher as guide, the students moved from simplistic assertions towards more sophisticated and tentative conclusions. The role of teacher talk is to 'generate meaning and relevance, to support the ways in which pupils construct interpretive understandings of the past' (Husbands, 1996). While the fast pace of much teacher discussion is driven by the fear of student disengagement, the slow rhythm of good quality discussion arises from the knowledge that students are genuinely involved in it.

It is no coincidence that this lesson was within a coursework module. In the 2008 specifications, a coursework assignment is to be compulsory in England and Wales and all are based on the principle that students should develop independent learning. Coursework provides us all with the opportunity to bring out the slow cooker and to plan for understanding and reflection rather than content coverage. In coursework, at least, the teacher can refuse to allow 'coverage' to be the driving force and ensure all students take responsibility for their own knowledge acquisition. It is also the territory which is best suited to fulfil one of the more neglected purposes of AS and A2 history: 'to develop the ability to ask relevant and significant questions about the past and to research them' (QCA, 2006). Wineburg (2007) argues that

Figure 4.1 *Why did the class groan?*

Observation of Chris teaching an A2 class about the reasons for the decline in British cinema after the Second World War

As homework the students had had to put the key reasons (from a provided list of ten) in a priority pyramid and come to the lesson prepared to justify their choices. They had also had to read a few pages about cinema in Britain in the post-war era.

Chris started the lesson by asking each student to say which reason was the most important and why. There was almost total classroom consensus that the increase in television ownership was the obvious overriding factor (reason F). Of course, people would prefer to watch films in the comfort of their own homes with the benefit that it was cheap and convenient. A few students argued that it was the diversification of leisure and rising living standards that were crucial (reason C). And then Laura piped up. Actually it was none of these. Cinemas had suffered from wartime bombing and had never recovered from this setback because it would be so expensive and difficult to rebuild them (reason E). Chris recorded their points on the pyramid on the board, occasionally asking for a little development and clarification. He could easily have finished the discussion at this point. After all, the students could explain two or three reasons why cinema declined with some sort of justification for their views.

Chris was rightly not satisfied with this. They were a bright group of second-year students and their judgements were based more on their own experience of leisure and a desire for an easy answer than any reflection on the reading they had been given. So they were challenged to develop their views using a range of questioning methods:

- So, if television had not become available, would cinema have remained strong? (counterfactual)
- You have television in your homes, with a huge number of channels to choose from. Why do you still go to the cinema? (relating it to their own experience)
- If only the cinemas in London had been badly affected by bombing, would that still be such an important reason? (challenging the significance)
- The post-war British films were mostly popular escapism, so why did not more people go to see them? (challenging a student assertion that the films were too dull and serious)

After 25 minutes of discussion, Chris went round the class asking each student to re-assess their original judgement. Some changed their views, some stuck with the first view, while many now hedged their bets, saying: 'I now think it was a mix of C and F because ...'. There was some discussion as to whether it was valid to put forward dual reasons as this did not fit the pyramid, but the class accepted that this must be allowed because several reasons worked together to cause the change. The proponents of reason C put forward a good case that reason F should be subsumed into reason C as television was a symptom of higher incomes and changing leisure rather than a cause of change in itself. And then Chris reached Laura. Had she changed her mind about the impact of bombing? No, she hadn't. Why? The same reason as before. And then the best moment of the lesson happened. It was a class groan.

Why did the class groan? Not because Laura had stayed with her original view; other students had done that. It was the fact that she had not moved on in her thinking with the rest of the class which caused disappointment – even indignation.

Chris's discussion was unsophisticated and free of gimmicks. It was simply well planned. But that groan was audible proof of the level of historical understanding the class had reached.

questioning before judging is one of the key features of mature historical thinking:

> Faced with an unfamiliar document, the historian's goal is not merely to issue a judgement about it, but to use it to stimulate new questions, to identify gaps in knowledge that prevent them from understanding the fullness of the historical moment. Students typically encountered this document and issued judgements. By painstakingly specifying what they did not know, historians positioned themselves not only to judge. They positioned themselves to learn.
>
> *Wineburg (2007: 11)*

In lessons I have observed, students more frequently answer questions than pose them. According to Wood (1992), most teachers ask two questions a minute while students rarely ask more than two questions an hour. It is an unsatisfactory ratio, particularly in the post-16 classroom.

It is a common criticism of teachers that they talk too much. In my view it is not the quantity of teacher talk which is the problem, it is more often the quality. Fearful of talking too much, some teachers retreat into the role of facilitators; filling their lessons with lots of group work and activities. Yet if we remember some of the teachers who really inspired us at school, it is rarely this sort of teacher who stands out: it is the charismatic talkers we remember. Many teachers are natural communicators and should not be shy of using one of their key assets. Planning a lesson where the teacher makes assertions and the students ask the questions can lead to high-quality classroom talk. PowerPoint presentations have also come in for a lot of criticism on the grounds that they are usually lectures thinly disguised with pretty pictures. The underlying assumption behind both these views is that listening is a passive activity. This need not be so.

In the series of activities presented in this chapter, the teacher takes the lead in the oral work, creating a model of effective talking and listening for students to follow. This acts as a valuable template to help students prepare for and participate in their own tutorials in the activities which come later.

● **Figure 4.2** *Individual assignment or coursework module?*

Under the 2008 specifications in England and Wales, all A-level courses have to include some form of coursework. For some boards (such as AQA or OCR) this means an individual study of an issue which the student has chosen entirely for themselves. This has to be completed independently under the general supervision of the teacher and will often require some form of research log followed by an extended essay.

Other boards (Edexcel and WJEC) have set coursework assignments which usually include an extended essay and, in some cases, a source investigation as well. This might be set by the examination board or be devised by the teacher themselves. In these cases, the whole class is likely to be doing the same assignment. This module will require some directed teaching but the expectation will be that students complete most of the work independently.

The ideas in this chapter are based on a coursework module rather than an individual assignment. However, many of the ideas can be applied to both. Student-led tutorials could pick up research methods and schools of historiography that might apply to many different research topics. The teaching ideas are also transferable to other examined modules, especially at A2 when students will be expected to be more independent.

Recipes for reading really well

Is it a particularly British disease to find failure more interesting than success? Only in England could rising examination pass rates be a cause for annual mourning for the good old days when more teenagers failed. My college always requires me to produce reasons why my students underperformed in their exams, but rarely asks me to explain why they succeeded. When wondering why so few students are prepared to read regularly outside lessons, I decided to reverse this trend and concentrate on two success stories.

George was an outstanding student in all respects. He arrived at college with ten A*s at GCSE and soon was making astute classroom contributions and producing stylish analytical essays. It was no surprise that he applied to study history at Cambridge at the start of his second year. But what really impressed about George was his willingness to read and research way beyond the requirements of the specification. He was happy to study the French Revolution for a history society debate and wrote a voluntary extended project on the role of political parties in the reign of Queen Anne. George read widely for his research, picking up volumes in second-hand bookshops and ordering books from his local public library. When asked why he chose this unusual topic from the neglected eighteenth century, he answered: 'Because I knew so little about it'. This is surely the historical equivalent to the mountaineer's 'Because it's there'.

Barry arrived for college enrolment determined to study history. With only Ds in history and English literature at GCSE, and a C in English language, I thought he was unlikely to pass and denied him a place. After two terms of successful study in college, he reapplied and this time I spent a few lunchtimes with him, coaxing him through some practice AS papers. He struggled, but his determination won me round and he started the course the following year. Barry finally emerged with a B grade at A level and went off to study history at university. Barry's story is a credit to his hard work but what really impressed me was his response to the question 'How well do you think your studies at AS/A2 prepared you for studying history at university?' – 'Really well. It got me used to reading a lot outside of college which helps prepare you for the amount of reading required at university.'

These case histories confirm that reading lies at the core of A-level success and that it is a habit not confined to the most able. Both Barry and George read most for their independent project or coursework; enjoying the freedom of finding their own material and following their own leads. They were initially motivated by a confident belief that reading would improve their grades – 'My desire to achieve high grades more than anything else' (George), developing later an appreciation of the wider benefits of reading. When I first started teaching, an older colleague's constant advice to students was to 'read around the subject', which even then caused some bemusement. She meant, of course, that students should go to the library and find a few books to skim and scan to add to their knowledge and understanding. Now that electronic communication is ubiquitous, giving this instruction is like suggesting a teenage boy should get exercise by joining the local ramblers' group. Even at higher education, students admit to never reading a history book from cover to cover (Pearce, 2003: 54–57), so this is a stiff challenge. Students need a kick start into reading but, once there, will enjoy selecting their own journals and books.

Several practitioners have helped me to develop more effective reading inside and outside the classroom. Both Kitson (2003) and Harris (2001) have highlighted the importance of explicitly stating the purpose of reading and using structured tasks to focus and motivate students to read longer and more challenging material. Ways in which a reading culture can be developed are described in a wide-ranging article by Hellier and Richards (2005). They argue persuasively that the perception of difficulty should not be an excuse to neglect reading and that students need to be taught the skills of reading for understanding. Their chart provides a very useful summary of different reading objectives, activities and outcomes, and has been a useful backdrop to this series of lessons. Loy (2008) has developed this with a range of strategies for motivating students to want to read.

Young people in modern Britain are highly privileged in all sorts of ways but none more so than in their access to information. There is a plethora of high-quality textbooks, biographies, fiction and articles provided for them in public, school and college libraries. Online there is much more. Yet reading is not cool and libraries are sadly underused. The activities below are based on the paradox that students can learn to value books by being deprived of them.

The best chefs still need kitchens: getting independent learning right

Most coursework and independent assignment modules have always been based on the principle of independent learning. Teachers are often wary of the concept. In traditional independent-learning projects, the academically gifted seize the opportunity to research on their own, while weaker students may waste time and seriously underachieve. Those in the middle frequently muddle along, leaving too much to the end and not pushing themselves in either their reading or their thinking. These problems happen when there is too stark a contrast between this mode of learning and others; when examination modules are entirely teacher directed and then suddenly a coursework or independent assignment is left to students as isolated individuals. Invariably, it is the student study that is regarded as 'independent' and not the management of the process, which stays firmly in the hands of the teacher. There is also an assumption that 'independent' means 'isolated'; an off-putting concept for less self-motivated learners. Handing over responsibility of both study and management to the students as a group can be a powerful bridge over this difficulty.

Nicol's (2007) work at Strathclyde University has broadened my own understanding of the differing forms and nature of independent learning. He has demonstrated how first-year students made much better progress as a cohort when empowered to manage their own studies and assessment. His framework and ten principles for assessment and feedback in the first year (Figure 4.3) demonstrates assessment and feedback models which influence student performance in their first year at university.

The upper two quadrants of this diagram give examples of activities which empower students, thereby improving both their motivation and their performance. Nicol explains his principle 7 (giving learners choice in assessment processes):

> The provision of choice in the topic, methods, weightings, criteria and timing of assessment tasks is about offering flexibility in what, how and when students study. Greater flexibility gives students control over their own learning and prepares them for their future as lifelong learners. It also supports the moral and legal requirements for fairness, equality and inclusivity of assessment practices.
>
> *Nicol (2007: 3)*

Activities 2 and 3 of this teaching module combine this principle of providing choice with the goal of creating a learning community. Most students are confident communicators online and are used to using message boards to exchange ideas and views. Nicol's REAP project found that 'the mere setting up of a shared discussion board for first year students in a single course stimulated and enhanced the natural development of learning networks' (Nicol, 2007: 3). Finding IT-competent students to design and manage your message board will further enhance their sense of ownership and responsibility for it.

Figure 4.3 *Nicol's ten principles for assessment and feedback*

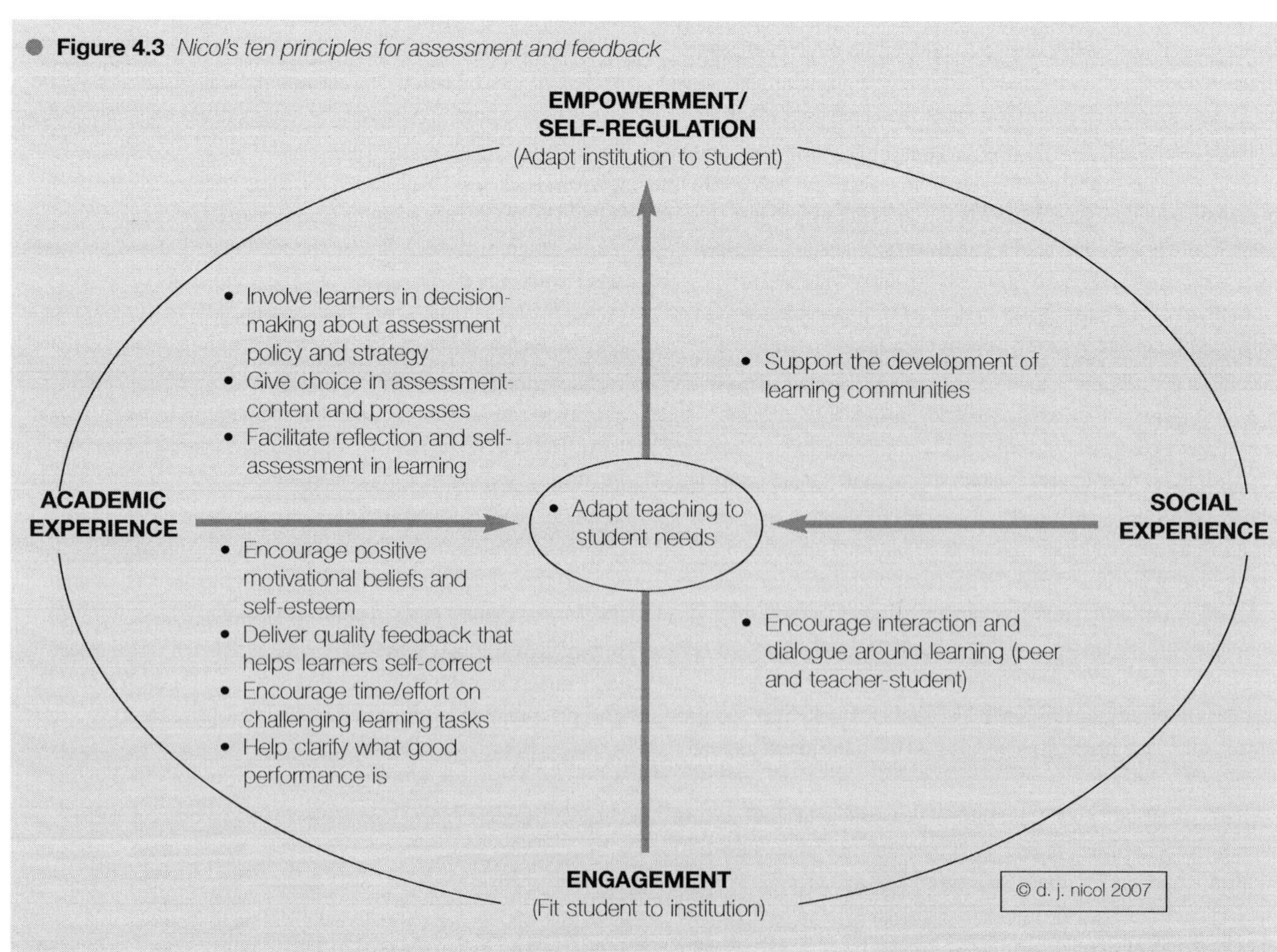

Making the most of the microwave: convenient technology may be just what you need

PowerPoint presentations are as popular with educationalists as the microwave-ready meal is with television chefs. Yet, used well, they can be highly effective. My key rule for PowerPoint presentations is this: the fewer the words, the better the learning. If you provide your students with all the text, why not give them a handout to read? Learning from a PowerPoint presentation requires four processes in sequence: hearing, understanding, recording and reflecting. Build in a fifth requirement – questioning – and effective learning will take place. Active and reflective listening is a very useful skill and one many will need to put into practice at university. Get students started by refusing to put wordy presentations on your intranet and forcing them to concentrate hard in the lesson.

Roast dinner or tikka masala? The problem of polarised views

Students like putting forward their own arguments and can usually support these with relevant evidence. On the whole, they can grasp the main points of a historian's view and understand why he or she has arrived at it. Very often, however, their handling of the interpretation tends to be superficial. Putting forward a coherent argument which integrates the use of historiography with real discernment – that's a real challenge. It is a challenge this series of lessons sets about achieving.

My students have to complete a coursework assignment on the Munich Crisis of 1938. This requires them to find and analyse a range of source material and to handle contrasting interpretations. They have already studied British foreign policy in the 1930s, so do not need more factual background before tackling the key issue. Their first attempts at this assignment were competent but unexciting, with many students getting bogged down in detailed analysis of evidence without showing real engagement in historical argument. They had listened carefully to advice about structure so that this came to be the overarching feature of their work, a problem well explained by Fordham (2007), who argues that we need to cultivate students' sense of agency, so that they are arguing with real purpose. Students were treating the assignment as a jigsaw, fitting the pieces and producing a competent picture, but not having any sense of individual creativity. As Fordham puts it, they were writing 'without any intent' (Fordham, 2007: 32).

The brightest students at this level are expected to produce sophisticated evaluations of historical interpretations. Examination board mark schemes demand that students, at the top marks, judge the historian's view in terms of both content and historical context. This is hard for students aged 16 or 17. Appeasement is an ideal topic with which to address this, however, as views of the policy are so directly linked to both students' and historians' sense of national identity. Finney (2005) has described how historians' opinions on appeasement have reflected developing ideas about Britain's power and role in the world. In a rather simplistic way, student views reflect this too.

On their first attempt at this assignment, there was a degree of student consensus about interpretations, although the group view changed during the course of study. At the start of the exercise, students generally regarded appeasement as an unnecessarily cowardly response to Hitler's aggression. They have grown up in an age when team England rarely wins, the wars we embark on are messy and inconclusive, and our football team does well to reach semi-finals. As a result, they cling fondly to the two apparent successes of the twentieth century: victory in the 1966 World Cup and the Second World War. Churchill was indeed our 'greatest Briton' and his determined resistance to appeasement in 1938 won universal applause. Churchill's view of appeasement was initially compelling.

By the end of their studies, most students seemed to have done a partial or complete volte-face. Sheepishly, they rejected their more naïve initial admiration of Churchill, with his victorious slant on history. Their reading of revisionist historians, study of opinion polls and military statistics convinced nearly all of them that Chamberlain had been maligned and that he followed the best policy in the circumstances. A few students had moved on to counter revisionism and were moderately critical of Chamberlain. Keen to show their credentials as objective, up-to-date historians, they adopted the more pragmatic and apparently 'moderate' views of later historians. They acknowledged the significance of the opening up of the archives in 1967 and recognised the political slant of writers such as Taylor.

Superficially, this looks like progress; students have reviewed their ideas in the light of new evidence and reached developed conclusions. They have moved on from a general grasp of the issue, influenced by a blend of war films and popular references, to a more evidence-based judgement. But underlying this there is timidity, even laziness. Most students have simply played safe, assuming that historians such as Parker (1993) or Charmley (1989) must be more 'reliable' than a passionate contemporary such as Churchill. Following their lead, selecting evidence that supports their stance and ignoring problematic evidence such as *The Gathering Storm*, is an easy way to produce a plausible and competent assignment.

A further problem underlying this is a tendency to categorise evidence in the following way:

- Primary: usually information from the time to be quoted selectively to support an argument
- Secondary: usually a view presented by an academic historian to be accepted or rejected.

Finney's article (Resource 4E) explains how the historiography of appeasement is much more complex. The emergence of counter-revisionism in the 1980s and 1990s happened at a time of growing assertion in British foreign policy under the leadership of Margaret Thatcher and Tony Blair, both of whom have made disparaging references to the 1930s as a time when Britain seemed to lose her way. This has also been accompanied by changing views of the nature of history itself, such as the influence of postmodernism. Finney has shown that, while historians in the last twenty years have appeared to ground their views in new documentary analysis, the evidential basis has not changed significantly. These new interpretations are as much creatures of their times as Churchill's *Gathering Storm*.

Spicing up the shepherd's pie: challenging established views

Reviewing their work, in the second year of teaching, I decided to reverse the intuitive teaching sequence of factual narrative, source analysis and then a final review of interpretations. Instead I started with a source which is very hard to categorise and which would challenge students' preconceived notions of primary and secondary evidence. Mimicking, even overplaying, typical student views at the start and end of the teaching module was used as a way of making them more critical and ambitious. Starting off by provoking the students to reassess their own assumptions would lead to immediate critical engagement. So the interpretation I started with was Churchill's.

And I started out by telling them that it was the only one worth studying.

Activities

The big enquiry question:

Did Chamberlain follow the only realistic policy at Munich in 1938?

Summary of activity stages

1. Is Churchill the only reliable source for studying the Munich Crisis? Teacher PowerPoint presentation followed by student responses on an online message board.
2. What alternative views are there? Finding out alternative views through research and review.
3. How reliable are other views of the Munich Crisis? Supported independent study using rolling tutorials.
4. Is Churchill's view worth using in your coursework assignment?
5. Teacher led plenary which re-examines the arguments put forward in Activity 1.

Activity 1

PowerPoint presentation and student response

Rationale for the activity

The purpose of this teacher PowerPoint presentation is to provoke students into a critical appraisal of the evidence about appeasement, through in-depth examination of one source: Churchill's *Gathering Storm*. It is designed to be really over the top: a worshipful tribute to our 'greatest Briton' as a historian. It builds up the view that his work, *The Gathering Storm*, is a fantastic account of the events of 1938 and ends with the shock conclusion that it is so brilliant that no other view is needed. Physically removing all other books and articles from the library and classroom shelves makes the point more starkly and will guarantee a reaction.

Churchill's *Gathering Storm* is a troublesome work. Is it history? Or is it memoir or even literature? It was written just after the war by a first-hand witness, at the heart of events and with access to lots of information. Added to this, Churchill was a Nobel Prize winner and the hero of the Second World War. It is an apt work to use to tackle that most troublesome of historical concepts: reliability. Through this, the students can be coaxed through the complexity of the historiography of appeasement.

This activity makes strong assertions that a key source is completely reliable to encourage students to consider the concept more carefully. Some assertions are deliberately dubious – such as the view that Churchill is reliable because he was a great writer or because his style of history was correct. It also challenges student views of primary and secondary sources – so often in their minds distinct forms of evidence, but in reality intertwined and indistinct. The case for the reliability for *The Gathering Storm* is based on the following grounds:

1. It is reliable because of proximity to events.
2. It is reliable because of Churchill's political position and power.
3. It is reliable because Churchill was a great man (i.e. character).
4. It is reliable because Churchill was a great writer (i.e. expression, coherence, power of prose).
5. It is reliable because Churchill writes the 'right kind of history' (grand narrative).
6. It is reliable because it was endorsed by others writing at the time.
7. It is reliable because of his method (i.e. employed team of researchers).

Stage 1: The teacher PowerPoint presentation

Each slide of the PowerPoint presentation (Resource 4A) focuses on one of the above reasons. Deliver it all with enough pizzazz to get the class interested but not so much that they become overly suspicious. See Figure 4.4 for suggested teacher expositions. My PowerPoint handouts have sections which highlight the tasks the students have to do: record, reflect and question (see Resource 4B). Make sure you are clear about the rules (Figure 4.5) – students must reflect in silence and write down at least one question for each slide. This waiting time is essential for higher-level thinking (Biggs and Tang, 2007: 121). You can ensure that all students are on board by requesting questions from students at random after they have had sufficient time for reflection.

RESOURCE  4A *PowerPoint slides*

SLIDE 1

Assertion 1:

The Gathering Storm is reliable because of its proximity to events.

Events	Written	Published
1938	1946–47	1948

SLIDE 2

Assertion 2:

It is reliable because of Churchill's position in 1938.

- In 1938 a prominent backbench MP
- Contacts with those in power

SLIDE 3

Assertion 3:

It is reliable because Churchill was a great man.

- A man of great integrity
- A man whose judgement could be trusted
- A man whose memory is still respected

SLIDE 4

Assertion 4:

It is reliable because Churchill was a great writer.

- Won the Nobel Prize for literature in 1953
- Acclaimed journalist and author
- Still recognised as a great writer today

'For his mastery of historical and biographical description as well as for brilliant oratory in defending exalted human values'

SLIDE 5

Assertion 5:

It is reliable because Churchill writes 'proper history'.

Chamberlain returned to England. At Heston, where he landed, he waved the joint declaration which he had got Hitler to sign, and read it to the crowd of notables and others who welcomed him.

The Gathering Storm
Page 286

SLIDE 6

Assertion 6:

It is reliable because his writing was endorsed by others writing at a similar time.

- Bestseller and well reviewed on publication
- Endorsed even by political opponents
- Approved across the world

SLIDE 7

Assertion 7:

It is reliable because he used good research methods.

- Research led by professional historian
- Experts were used
- Access to a range of confidential information
- Process of writing was professional and thorough

Figure 4.4 *Teacher expositions for Resource 4A PowerPoint presentation*

Slide 1
Churchill was a politician at the heart of the events, who kept accurate records including diary entries and letters. The Munich Crisis was fresh in his mind at the time of writing and his accurate memory was prompted by this archive of records from the time. This means that his writing has the benefit of hindsight, in that he was able to explain the significance of the events from a later perspective, but his narrative was not marred by forgetfulness or distortion.

Slide 2
Churchill was a respected and influential Conservative MP in 1938, who was politically active in the House of Commons and elsewhere. Although not on the front bench, he had frequent contacts with government ministers, such as Duff Cooper at the Admiralty.

The fact that he was not actually in government nor in the opposition parties makes him a more objective commentator.

Slide 3
Thousands went to Churchill's funeral in 1965.

One post on the BBC website stated that 'Churchill was a leader who understood that you stand by your principles come hell or high water' (Chris, Canada).

Lord Blake (1988), an eminent biographer, has stated that Churchill was 'by nature a very truthful man'.

Churchill won a poll in 2002 as the greatest Briton.

This consensus means that Churchill is a trustworthy witness to the events of the Munich Crisis.

Slide 4
Churchill was recognised around the world as a great writer. An American reviewer of *The Gathering Storm* in 1949 described him as 'an able writer and sometimes a brilliant one' (Hall, 1949: 357–58).

His power as a writer was recognised with the award of the Nobel Prize for Literature in 1953.

More recently, an Amazon reviewer of *The Gathering Storm* awarded it 5 stars, stating that it was the 'greatest story every told by one of the greatest storytellers ever' (John Ferngrove, Hants, UK, 9 January 2008, Amazon website).

Slide 5
Churchill wrote history which is plain and clear. His style of history was soundly based on a chronological description of the events. His writing is reliable because of this straightforward approach, which removes the danger of confusion or too much theorising.

The Nobel presentation address stated: 'He does not beat about the bush, but is a man of plain speaking' (S. Siwertz, 1953: 2).

Slide 6
The book *Guilty Men* (Cato, 1940), written by three left-wing journalists, argued a similar view to that in Churchill's later book and was a spectacular bestseller, suggesting its views were endorsed by the public at the time. These writers were political adversaries of Churchill's yet agreed with his general thesis.

An American reviewer in 1949 acknowledged the 'essential correctness of Churchill's analysis' (Hall, 1949: 358).

Book reviews and sales of *The Gathering Storm* support the view that his retelling of the Munich Crisis was correct.

Slide 7
It is hard to fault Churchill's methods as a historian. His research team was led by a professional historian and Oxford don, William Deakin. He also had experts in naval and military affairs who had served in high office and had access to a wealth of confidential material. Research was very thorough, for example statistical evidence on German air strength was checked with French and US records; Eden's private secretary provided information from his diary. Churchill read the research essays of his team and then dictated his text. He then reviewed, checked and edited it. This makes his writing accurate and reliable.

RESOURCE 4B *Recording sheet for the PowerPoint presentation*

Assertion ....

The Gathering Storm is reliable because

Record (key examples)

Reflect (e.g. development of those points)

Question (e.g. omissions)

Figure 4.5 *Key rules for delivering the PowerPoint presentation*

- Keep text on slides to the bare minimum.
- Be explicit about the purpose of the presentation.
- Allow reflection time – don't be discomforted by silence.
- Require students to write points in each part of their record sheet and be prepared to wait until everyone has done so.
- Require students to ask questions.

At the end, tell students that they have to 'earn' the return of a textbook by posting a valid and developed criticism of one of the reliability claims on the online message board set up before the next lesson. They are provided with the key pages from *The Gathering Storm* to help them but they need to be reminded that they are not to attack his line of argument, only his reliability as a historian. Of course, it is possible to allocate numbered assertions to different students, taking their abilities into account. On the whole, I prefer a more open kind of differentiation as students appreciate choice and are usually astute at finding their own level.

Resource 4B provides you with a copy of the student recording sheet for the presentation.

Stage 2: Student ripostes using an online message board

In the next lesson, structure your class discussion around student contributions on the message board, picking some examples of strong arguments and prompting the students to develop them further. For each of the reliability points 'knocked out' with a well developed and reasoned attack, the students can be rewarded by having an extra source (book or journal article) provided (see Figure 4.6). If they do an excellent job, they can all be provided with an extended photocopied extract from a useful additional source.

Now turn to any reliability points which are still left standing. With students working in small teams, direct them to challenge these by the end of the lesson with the promise that, if they can do this, the class will win a return of all materials to the library and a copy of a useful summary article for each one of them.

Return to the seven statements about reliability used in the PowerPoint presentation and ask students if any are invalid or if any extra ones should be added. Students are now more aware of the problems of the concept and the inevitable question 'Reliable for what ...?' My students certainly rose to this challenge, as can be seen in the examples shown in Figure 4.7.

Figure 4.6 *Group reward system*

Target
Present a convincing attack on each of the seven assertions about the reliability of *The Gathering Storm*.

Reward
For each winning argument, one source (book or article) is replaced in the library.
If the whole class manage to address all seven points well, the summary article on historiography (Resource 4E) is given to each student and all material returned to the library.

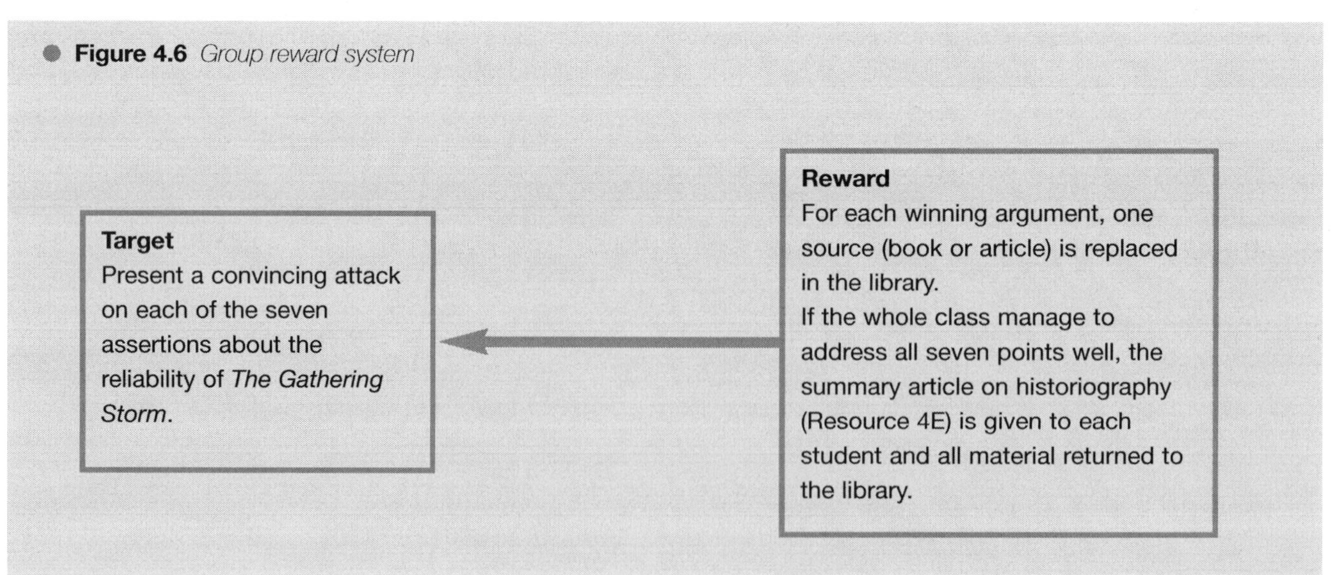

Figure 4.7 *Examples of student responses to the reliability questions*

Gavin's contribution

Assertion 1: Churchill's view is reliable because of his proximity to events

With regards to Churchill's proximity to events, he was actually a back bencher during the Munich Crisis with a poor reputation as being an eccentric at the end of his career. This means he is likely to have been 'kept out of the loop' to a certain extent. Also with higher security at the time he would probably not have seen any top secret documents which front benchers would have had privileged access to.

Furthermore Churchill wasn't at the Munich Crisis so he would have got no information from the people there. He is writing after World War Two, Chamberlain is dead, Hitler is dead so only Daladier and the interpreters really know what happened. Any information he has on the Munich Crisis would not be first hand and is therefore less reliable. I would find evidence by Daladier to be far more reliable in terms of first hand experience.

Martin and Paul's contribution

Assertion 4: The Gathering Storm is reliable because Churchill was a great writer

It is widely acknowledged that Benito Mussolini was a great writer, being a professional journalist before seizing power. This would seem to suggest that Mussolini's work is reliable.

However, he had full control over the press in Italy and managed to sedate any real opposition in the form of journalism. He used this control to great effect to aid his regime, however, we would not say that Mussolini's writings are at all reliable, despite there being no doubt that he was a great writer.

Whether Churchill was a great writer or not, this has no real bearing on whether what he writes is true or reliable.

Ben's contribution

Assertion 6: **The Gathering Storm** ***is reliable because it was endorsed by others writing at the time***

'The Gathering Storm' may well of been endorsed by others writing at a similar time but this does not make a case for it to be the only historical text used to evaluate the time. 'The Gathering Storm' enjoyed great reviews and even some people who openly opposed Churchill praised the book, these were most likely due to the fact the book came out so close to the events and it was written so in-depth, people may well of reacted the same way to any book of this type if released by a well known figure. On top of these reasons is one phrase said by Churchill himself that justifies questioning the sources reliability 'History will be kind to me, because I intend to write it.' This quote shows how he might well slant views a little to make him or others look different compared to what actually happened.

Emma's contribution

Assertion 5: **The Gathering Storm** ***is reliable because Churchill wrote the right kind of history***

Why is Churchill's interpretation of events seen as 'proper history'? Churchill was not an academic historian – he was a politician. He had no training in how to properly gather and use sources. The fact that he had to use a historian in order to find all of the information that he used suggests that he had no idea of how to write a 'proper' historical account.

Why does Churchill's style of writing affect how good his history was? Just because it was clearly written and factual doesn't necessarily mean that it was good history – his writing didn't give different points of view, e.g. the point of view of the Germans or the Czechs. Surely 'proper history' wouldn't be so confined to one point of view. And since Churchill seemed to have such a strong opinion of Munich and appeasement at the time, was he even the best historian to produce such a 'history'?

Activity 2

Student researching and reviewing of alternative views

At this stage the students should read and research more widely, finding alternative views to Churchill. Have a class discussion about how you find out about different writers by studying references and bibliographies in other books you come across. If possible, put a link from the message board to your library records to help students find appropriate material. Encourage them to use their public libraries and also, if possible, university libraries, which are generally open to all. Harris (2001) has suggested the use of a reading sheet to encourage focused and appropriate use of reading material, and these ideas can be used to help your students to devise an appropriate review document (Resource 4C is an example).

This stage falls in the summer holiday for us and this is where the online message board can be such a bonus, as it enables students to swap notes and ideas from home. Insisting that each student writes at least two reviews before returning in September and posts them on the message board motivates the students to read more critically and more extensively. Showing them an example of an argumentative academic book review and the author's response will start them on the right track.

Figure 4.8 *Coursework assessment criteria*

AO1a: Recall, select and deploy historical knowledge and communicate that knowledge in a clear and effective manner

AO1b: Demonstrate understanding of the past through explanation, analysis and making substantial judgements

AO2a: In relation to the set historical enquiry, analyse and evaluate a range of appropriate source material

GCE Examinations 2008/9 Teachers' Guide, WJEC Unit HY3

Figure 4.9 *Key rules for good peer tutorials*

- Prepare your tutorial around one interpretation of appeasement.
- Be well prepared. Have your notes, resources and equipment ready.
- Present your ideas clearly.
- Keep your presentation short: 5–10 key points or PowerPoint slides.
- Always allow time for reflection.
- Expect questions.
- Put your notes on the message board after your tutorial.

Activity 3

Learning through tutorials

In the coursework study, students can be given responsibility for setting deadlines for stages of their assignment, running peer tutorials and interpreting assessment criteria. Set aside 15 minutes of a lesson at the start of the module and use the 'think, pair and share' method to agree reasonable staged deadlines in order for the assignments to be completed for the final hand-in date. On their return from their summer holiday, give the students one-sentence assessment criteria for each level of response and ask them to expand them (see Figure 4.8 for typical examination board criteria). Do a little careful checking and editing and then put their ideas on the message board. Finally, structure your remaining lessons around peer tutorials and teacher mentoring.

Before embarking on the peer tutorials, remind your students of the model set in the earlier teacher presentations based on the idea of recording, reflecting and questioning (as shown in Figure 4.9). Effective tutors need to be well prepared and confident of their material; they should be prepared to provide further explanation and information for other students by posting their preparatory notes on the message board after the tutorial session. This will help prevent it becoming a copying exercise and encourage use of the time for genuine dialogue.

The organisation of your tutorial programme will partly depend on the size of your class. Our average class size is around twenty and the tutorial programme is based on six lessons of 90 minutes. The method I have used is shown in Figure 4.10.

All students have to run at least one tutorial, either on their own or in a pair. All tutorials are peer reviewed, with the students devising their own peer review form (Resource 4D is an example), which is posted on the message board. Students also decide the mode of giving feedback and whether this should be shared with their teacher or not. My class wanted the teacher to know, so their efforts could be recognised.

Peer tutorial sessions can be organised by the students on their message board after a class discussion, with students signing up for ones they want to lead. After consideration of the purpose of the tutorials – primarily to understand and assess one interpretation of the Munich Crisis – the students come up with some golden rules for successful presentations. All tutorials should last for 20–25 minutes. Students have to sign up for tutorials in advance and none should have a class of more than eight. In my class, there was also some teacher-led instruction on referencing, plagiarism and assignment structure, the main points of which were posted on the message board so that all students could refer back to them.

Figure 4.10 *The rolling tutorial system*

This is based on a class of about twenty students in a sequence of six lessons. Each lesson is for 90 minutes and this is divided into three timed 30-minute slots. Every student must do at least two different activities per lesson. Peer tutorials need to be signed up for in advance and can be led by students on their own or in pairs.

Peer tutorial	Teacher supervision session	Private study
Student presentations on PowerPoint or using whiteboard, flipchart or other teaching aids. Tutorials will allow time for reflection and questions. They will be peer assessed and the reading and notes will be posted on the message board afterwards.	The teacher will see individual students to discuss their progress, recommend reading and respond to queries.	Students will study on their own with access to the library and computers.

Built into the programme was a teacher mentoring system, which was also based on reward for responsibility. Students saw the teacher on a one-to-one basis three times over the six-week period but if the work was up to date on the first appointment the second session became optional, with the student gaining an extra half-hour private study if they wished. Most welcomed teacher input but valued it more as a choice. Those who failed to meet the agreed deadlines were not allowed out of the classroom for private study and might have more appointments imposed.

This mode of teaching and learning helped to create a genuine learning community. There was regular peer support without collaboration. Of course, lazy students will let the class down, but fear of peer disapproval is often stronger at 17 than fear of a teacher's telling off. Most students thrive on greater responsibility and develop the skills they need to move on to the world beyond A levels.

Activity 4

Plenary

Mini question:

Is Churchill's view worth using in your coursework assignment?

Towards the end of this unit of study, set aside a lesson for reappraisal of Churchill's thesis. Propose the opposite view: that *The Gathering Storm* is so unreliable that it should not be used at all. Revisit the student objections to the text in an updated PowerPoint presentation and use the same process of listening, reflection and questioning. Churchill is now treated with a scepticism bordering on contempt. This should result in a lively debate which goes beyond the difficulties of Churchill as a historian into discussion of the nature of history and historical evidence. At the end of the session, ask each student to state if they would use the source in their assignment and, if so, how they would use it. This should provide them with the motivation and understanding to write a more ambitious and interesting assignment.

RESOURCE 4C *Student book review form*

Author:

Title:

Date of publication:

Background to the author: (e.g. personal, political, academic)

Background to the publication (e.g. political and international context, type of journal or book and its audience)

Useful for:

Not so useful for:

Your comments:

Star rating:

(From 'Essential reading for all the class' **** to 'Only worth browsing'*)

 © HODDER EDUCATION

RESOURCE 4D *Peer tutorial review sheet*

Interpretation (historian, date and title of key book/article)**:**

Student tutor(s):

Please provide feedback on the following:

The knowledge and understanding of the interpretation:

– the key viewpoints in the interpretation

– explanation of the personal context of the historian

– explanation of the broader context of the interpretation (e.g. political, international)

The tutorial presentation:

– clarity

– timing (e.g. was there enough time for reflection?)

– questions (did the tutor respond well to questions?)

How useful was this tutorial for understanding this interpretation of the Munich Crisis?

RESOURCE  *Extract from Finney's article on the historiography of appeasement*

The underlying point of this essay is to argue that historiography is never innocent; rather it is both shaped by broad ideological forces at work within society and has ideological implications, even if these are not always immediately apparent. This point tends to be obscured by the terms in which we typically conduct our debates. Although the literature on appeasement is replete with references to the role of non-documentary forces and recognition that interpretation changes to 'reflect shifting needs and changing outlooks',[137] these insights are seldom developed. Instead, they are marginalised in prefatory sections or their operation is acknowledged in certain cases but with the implication that there exists some alternative realm of proper historical discourse where they do not pertain. (Typically this occurs when historians analyse the assumptions and prejudices that shaped the views of a previous generation without subjecting their own positioning to similar scrutiny.) So debates are still predominantly conducted solely in terms of empirical factors, as if all that was at stake was 'the weight of the evidence'. Now, it is of course still legitimate to discriminate between texts according to how they negotiate the empirical record, but since there is much more to them than this they can also be engaged fruitfully on numerous other levels.[138] To concentrate exclusively on the empirical dimension obscures the complexity of the constant interactions between past and present within historiography, and the degree to which both interpretations and 'the evidence' alike are subjective ideological constructs, created by historians as they interact with the archival record under the influence of present-centred factors including personal positioning (in terms of race, class, gender, beliefs and their pre-existing interpretations), the current protocols and methodologies of the discipline, and political and social context (including ideas about national identity).

Writing on British appeasement cannot be satisfactorily understood solely by reference to documentary factors or without serious consideration of a range of cultural and ideological forces. Ever since its inception in the perceptions and rhetoric of the 1930s, the appeasement debate has revolved around two contrasting viewpoints grounded in two of the most archetypal forms of narrative emplotment: a negative one emphasising contingency, agency and morality, and a positive one emphasising determinism, structural constraints and realpolitik.[139] The public record of British diplomacy in the 1930s provided sufficient material to support either of these interpretations, and in the light of subsequent archival revelations historians have filled them out in ever greater detail and nuance rather than supplanting them.[140] Over time, there has been a clear correlation between the dominance of one or the other of them on the one hand, and shifts in disciplinary fashion – that is, the methodological and interpretive concerns which historians bring to bear on the documentary record – and in prevailing conceptions of national identity on the other. So it is problematic to conceive of recent interpretations, however impeccable their scholarship, as simply incarnating empirically derived conclusions. Of course, this does not mean that all historians at any given point have cleaved to precisely the same viewpoint, since dominant discourses can be negotiated in different ways, and there are in any case many other variables at work. Nonetheless, it would still appear that fluctuations in the historical verdict are very closely correlated with changes in the social contexts in which inquiry has occurred, rendering one approach or mode of emplotment more plausible than another, and that it makes little sense to conceive of this writing as making any sort of linear progress towards truth.

Source: Finney, P. (2005) 'The romance of decline: the historiography of appeasement and British national identity'

References

137. Skidelsky, R., 'Going to War with Germany: Between Revisionism and Orthodoxy', *Encounter*, 39 (1972), p. 56.

138. For a demonstration of this, see D. Campbell, *National Deconstruction. Violence, Identity and Justice in Bosnia* (Minneapolis, 1998), pp. 33–81.

139. This article has not essayed a detailed narratological analysis of these texts, but it is tempting to see revisionism and orthodoxy/counter-revisionism as examples respectively of romantic and tragic emplotment. These are characterised by Alun Munslow (glossing Hayden White) thus: 'A romance would be identified by the power of the historical agent/hero as ultimately superior to [adverse] circumstances, questing with ultimate success, seeking and achieving redemption or transcendence. In tragedic emplotments the hero strives to beat the odds and fails, eventually being thwarted by fate or their own fatal personality flaws. The end result is usually death (actual or metaphoric).' (Munslow, *The Routledge Companion to Historical Studies*, London, 2000, p. 83).

140. That the appeasement debate has revolved around familiar oppositions almost since its inception is also implied in W. Wark, 'Appeasement Revisited', *The International History Review*, 13 (1995), pp. 545–62. For stimulating reflections on how historians are constrained by the narratives of previous interpreters, see K. Platt, 'History and Despotism, or: Hayden White vs. Ivan the Terrible and Peter the Great', *Rethinking History*, 3 (1999), pp. 247–69.

Sample lesson sequence

Rationale

The teaching of this second-year coursework study falls naturally into two parts. The first section occurs at the end of the summer term and is teacher led. The summer holiday acts as a bridge towards the student-centred learning which occurs in the autumn term. The idea in the planning is that in the first stage the teacher will model the key skills and techniques which the students will need to employ in the second. In the concluding lesson, there is a teacher-led review of the learning and a reappraisal of original views. Study of *The Gathering Storm* is used as a starter and plenary activity to hold the module together.

Prior learning

Students should already have studied British foreign policy in the 1930s and know the key events in the Munich Crisis but will not have discussed differing views of the crisis nor delved into contemporary evidence.

Enquiry question

Did Chamberlain follow the only realistic policy at Munich in 1938?

Outline of learning flow

Two-and-half weeks of lessons (about ten hours of teaching) before the summer break. Reading and research in the summer break with use of the message board to exchange ideas. On return, one lesson a week for seven weeks (a further ten hours or so), with tutorial work and one plenary teacher-led lesson to finish before the final writing up. (See Figure 4.11).

Figure 4.11 *Coursework module*

Did Chamberlain follow the only realistic policy at Munich in 1938?	
Lessons 1–2 *Mini question:* Is Churchill the only reliable source on the Munich Crisis?	Get your students to prepare a simple timeline of events of the Munich Crisis before launching into your PowerPoint presentation to ensure a basic grasp of the events. Take the full first lesson for your PowerPoint (**Activity 1**, stage 1) and remember to insist on reflection with each slide. Ensure all students can access the message board so that technical hitches don't prevent you moving onto the discussion in the next lesson. In the second lesson, begin stage 2, starting with your structured discussion and then setting up your small-group work attacking the remaining reliability assertions.
Lesson 3 and summer holiday reading and research *Mini question:* What alternative views are there on the Munich Crisis?	Before they disappear for the summer, insist that students (a) understand how to find new material by using references, reviews and bibliographies, (b) design a reading review sheet which will be posted for all to use on the message board, (c) have examined an academic online review and responses as a model (**Activity 2**). Also, introduce the idea that students should determine their own deadlines for stages in their assignment.
Lessons 4–11 *Mini question:* How reliable are other views of the Munich crisis?	In these lessons, use your rotating teacher and peer tutorial system (**Activity 3**). Make sure students have taken on the key attributes of successful speaking and listening, and that they devise a suitable peer review form. Keep a watching eye over the message board and adjust student monitoring according to the degree of responsibility they have shown for their own learning. Try hard not to interfere too early or too much – the more you stand back, the more the students will rise to expectations.
Lesson 12 *Mini question:* Is Churchill's view worth using in your coursework assignment?	In your final lesson, return to *The Gathering Storm*, dismissing it as unworthy of consideration (**Activity 4**). Make sure you have planned some questions to develop the students' thinking if this does not flow naturally from the presentation. Set aside some time at the end for any final concerns about the writing up of their assignment and ensure all students know the deadline.

CHAPTER 5 Getting personal with postmodernism

Chapter summary

* This chapter suggests ways of improving student writing, particularly the writing of developed and qualified conclusions. By focusing on the diverse experiences of individuals, students will confront the problems of moving from the particular to the general, thus helping them to add range and depth to their judgements.
* At the beginning and end of the study, students are introduced to two differing approaches to history, postmodernist ideas and microhistory. They are encouraged to use these when considering the validity of their own judgements.
* The sequence of lessons includes an extended role-play activity, based on real and fictional characters. This forces students to think about how values and attitudes might differ over time and according to region, class and gender during their study of the main themes.
* The lessons are based on the broad enquiry question: Is it possible to reach any general conclusions about the impact of Fascism on Italy in the years 1922–39?

Context

Great Uncle Harry: the power of the personal

> You will also have heard of the fighting and magnificent victory – our infantry (the 9th Queenslanders) doing wonderful work, but they suffered sorely, but never mind, victories don't come without losses and sacrifices, do they?
>
> You must not get anxious if you do not hear from me every week for you must remember under what conditions one has to write.

My great uncle Harry wrote this on 1 May 1915. The 'magnificent victory' was the landing at Gallipoli and, shortly after he wrote this, Harry was seriously wounded. He was the black sheep of the Stone clan, who, according to family folklore, was sent off to Africa after getting the rector's daughter into trouble. He did not succeed there and ended up on an Australian sheep farm. At the outbreak of the war he enlisted and was sent to train in Egypt. He wrote regularly to his sister, my maternal grandmother, in Edinburgh. Last year my sister and I rummaged through a family chest in the hall and found Harry's postcards and letters. For me, it was one of those 'hairs on the back of the neck' moments.

Much has been written about the power of the personal in history (Kitson, 2004; Haydn, 2005). *Teaching History* has dedicated a whole edition to this theme. Lomas (2005) reminds us that it is people and the stories of their lives that engage our students and pupils. In my own practice I have always been impressed how the individual experiences of people such as Harry make history meaningful. Students may know that 6 million perished in the Holocaust or that 600,000 British soldiers died in the trenches but it is the individual stories that help them to understand. It is the people that make them care.

Individual experiences are also very useful for highlighting the complexity of history. Family photos, soldiers' diaries and life stories can challenge the official consensus. Harry was confident that the opening days of the Gallipoli campaign were victorious, despite witnessing the cruel slaughter of his comrades. And he was very keen for more action. Yet my students, influenced by Wilfred Owen and their own conviction that suicide would be preferable to living with rats, stress continually the low morale of the troops in the First World War. Look at the writings of fighting men on all fronts, and not just the possibly sanitised letters home, and you will not find this widespread 'low morale', even in 1918. Personal experience poses a constant reminder of the danger of generalisation (Bradshaw, 2009).

Yet where does this leave us? With essay questions demanding broad sweeps and general judgements, is there a place for individual storytelling at post-16 level? Personal experiences are, by definition, unique and, if allowed to dominate, could distort or confuse students' understanding of their history. Students may identify with characters from the past but emotional attachment, as Cunningham (2004) has shown, poses problems as well as benefits. After all, a modern British teenager would react with revulsion at the thought of sharing a bed with several siblings as Cosimo Arrichiello did in 1930s Naples, yet his perception was that his family was relatively well off and he was much more bothered about church festivals and trips to the cinema. A preoccupation with the obvious and with material contrasts of past and present can be a barrier to genuine understanding of attitudes, values and beliefs. While students may empathise in an anachronistic and sometimes superficial way, however, Cunningham argues that a degree of identification with an individual in the past often serves as 'a useful way station to understanding' (Cunningham, 2004: 28). Bellinger (2008) carried out action research into her own practice using Figes' work on personal accounts of Stalin's Russia. She concluded that this developed her post-16 students' historical thinking and knowledge in significant and unexpected ways. Handled carefully and critically, engaging students with personal life stories enriches their historical understanding.

Passion about postmodernism: the power of big ideas

While stories are popular with teenagers, theories on the whole are not. University history departments report (Booth, 2005; Pearce, 2000) that modules about historiography and methods are the least popular for first-year students, especially when they are not linked to particular topics of study. Other than the few who take on Advanced Extension Award or similar courses, the majority of history students in schools do not have to consider the historians' underlying principles or methods, except in the kind of general labelling such as 'Marxist' or possibly 'Whig'. Descriptions of the ideas and methods of the Annales School or the groundbreaking ideas of E. H. Carr in the 1970s have limited appeal to students, and most would fail to grasp how such learning could help them write essays on Elizabeth I's religious settlement or Nazi economic policy. The suggestion that we somehow add historiographical theory into our already crowded schemes of work would raise a legitimate groan from the history teaching community.

This was certainly my position until quite recently when two articles changed my mind. An article in *Teaching History* (Hammond, 2007) has shown how lower secondary pupils can get to grips with historical theories and methods. If Year 9 can do this, then it should certainly be possible in post-16 studies. Hammond shows how Year 9 pupils can become more critical and reflective learners about American slavery by using the methods of cliometrics (the study of history using economic models and statistical analysis) and microhistory.

Then I came across a passionate exchange on the Institute of Historical Research website from 1999. Professor O'Brien's eloquent attack on postmodernism, and the riposte by Dr Alun Munslow, highlight how much historians care about the nature of their subject. Although the two disagreed, both arguments enshrined a deep knowledge and respect for the evolution of history as a discipline. Each models what good historical writing is all about: integrity, clarity and search for truth. It suddenly seemed that my own students were missing out on something precious.

Partialities of the peasantry: the power of role play

> if everyone's got to vote then obviously . . . everyone's got to think . . .

This was Hannah's comment in a plenary discussion on the completion of my action research project (Laffin, 2006; Laffin, 2008) using extended role play with remote voting pads. I had been worried by the quiet disengagement of a small minority in my Tudor history classes and the aim of the project was to improve student participation and confidence. Students in the group chose real or fictional characters from Henry VIII's reign and voted on their satisfaction levels at various stages of his rule. Guidance was provided to ensure there was a variety in class, age, region and gender. The remote voting added value by giving students a visual focus for discussion (the results display as bar charts on the whiteboard) and they liked being able to see immediately if their character fitted in with the class consensus. However, it was the role-play element which moved on their thinking and created a strong sense of involvement. Initially there were mistakes and some fairly basic misunderstandings, but by the end most of the class had a good sense of the viewpoint of their character. The best moment came at the end, and almost accidentally. I had put the students into 'focus groups' of social classes to agree a group review of Henry's policies. One of the more reserved girls in the class, in the role of a shepherd from Northumberland, refused to accept the conservative conclusions of the rest of her group on the matter of religion:

> I know that most peasants liked the mass and all that, but not all of them did. What about the Lollards? They weren't all merchants, were they?

What made this final activity so effective was the transition from the personal to the group view. The tensions in this process brought to the fore the problems of generalising from individual to group; a very useful lesson for all the students involved (Bradshaw, 2009; Anthony, 2009).

There is strong research evidence that role play can be highly effective at improving engagement and understanding in the learning of history. Phillips (2002) lists the benefits of role play as motivation, insight into historical situations, improved recall and 'empathetic appreciation'. In his research using multiple intelligences in the history classroom, Rhys Davies (2006) found that pupils listed role play as one of their favourite history activities as it was regarded as 'fun, enjoyable and engaging'. This is confirmed by course questionnaires at my own college which repeatedly show that role-play and decision-making activities are both popular and memorable. Many practitioners (Dawson and Banham, 2002; Luff, 2001) have demonstrated that this form of learning can add value at examination level by helping young people to understand the range of experiences of people in the past and how this could affect their attitudes and values. In particular, Luff's role-play activity (Luff, 2001: 14) based on McCrae's poem 'In Flanders Fields' explains how pupils can understand the range of viewpoints of people involved in the Great War by providing selected knowledge of that particular context in 1915. This helped his class to develop a much deeper understanding of both the contrasting views of different civilians and how they changed over time. These examples have given me the confidence to incorporate these methods in my own practice.

Fantastic finales: the importance of powerful conclusions

Examiners often stress the importance of a good conclusion in an essay. This is for all sorts of reasons. An obvious point is that these sentences will be the last ones read before a mark is awarded. More than that, though, it is where the writer makes a judgement. It is the quality of that judgement which will weigh heavily with the examiner as it is so often a reflection of the maturity of the analysis throughout the essay. The following extract from an awarding body mark scheme for an essay paper shows what is expected at the highest level.

> Candidates will offer an analytical response which directly addresses the focus of the question and which demonstrates explicit understanding of the key issues contained in it. It will be broadly balanced in its treatment of these key issues. The analysis will be supported by accurate, relevant and appropriately selected factual material which demonstrates some range and depth.
>
> *Edexcel Unit 1: Generic Level Descriptor, level 5, 436 Sample Assessment Materials, September 2007*

High-quality conclusions are the natural result of high-quality thinking. You can teach your students a formula such as 'link, rank and qualify' (see Figure 5.1) but, without a rich vein of knowledge and understanding to draw on, their assertions will lack conviction.

Figure 5.1 *What makes a developed and qualified conclusion?*

Linking: showing that you understand the relationship between aspects or factors by explaining how they are connected and the significance of their interplay

Ranking: making judgements about the relative importance of an aspect or factor and supporting the judgement by referring to evidence included in your essay

Qualifying: recognising the limitations and exceptions which may apply to your general judgement, such as change over time or variations according to region or social class

Figure 5.2 *Sample student conclusions*

Essay question

'Despite the revolutionary myth of the Fascist March on Rome in October 1922, Fascism owed its accession to power largely to conservative forces.' (Martin Blinkhorn, a British history professor writing in the 1980s who has specialised in right-wing politics and violence in Mediterranean Europe)

How valid is this interpretation of the Fascist acquisition of power in 1922?

Conclusion A: The unsupported assertion (David)

Overall, I agree with the statement made, that Fascism did owe its rise to power to conservative failures, weaknesses, decisions and blunders.

David has not developed his ideas at all and makes do with a general undeveloped judgement.

Conclusion B: The timorous fence sitter (Anna)

In summary the validity of Martin Blinkhorn's statement appears to be very valid on the surface however it does not take into account any of the many others' views. The point that conservative forces indeed played a part in the rise of Fascism is valid however to mention this and not anything else is not a true reflection of what caused the rise of Fascism. I think all these views make some contribution and like what is often the case in history many factors are involved. The poor state of affairs in Italy led to resentment amongst the people and the rise of Socialism encouraged the working classes but worried the Conservative elites and bourgeois. This brought about popularity for Fascism. Whether Martin Blinkhorn's view is the most valid and most important is hard to say, even in hindsight.

Anna recognises the multi-causal nature of history but lacks the confidence to make a clear judgement. She summarises a few reasons and suggests how they contributed to the Fascist rise to power but fails to reach a conclusion about relative importance.

Conclusion C: The narrow judgement (Mark)

In conclusion, I feel that although conservative forces did play a role in Mussolini's rise to power it cannot be said they played the major role. This is due to the fact that without the strong leadership of Mussolini Fascism would never have been put on the map in Italy and could have fallen away like it did in Britain during this period. His strong leadership therefore outweighs the role of the conservative forces because if he had not been able to exploit their weaknesses in the way he did Fascism would never have came to power.

Mark confidently puts forward a judgement but this lacks breadth. He recognises only one other major factor and his concentration on this makes him lose focus on the key issue of the role of 'conservative forces'.

Conclusion D: The developed judgement (Ian)

Overall, the march on Rome in 1922 was fairly insignificant in comparison to the other activities and factors involved in helping Fascism take power over Italy. The King was a weak force in attempting to stop Mussolini and the blackshirts, being indecisive and fearful of the Fascist party. The rise of Socialism helped Fascism in that it helped the party gain support from the higher classes in society because they were in fear of the rise of Socialism, allowing Mussolini to exploit them. The agreement with the Church gained the Fascist regime respect and more support, again helping its rise. Therefore, I believe that Blinkhorn's interpretation of Fascism's accession to power is valid, as it was a combination of all these factors which culminated in Mussolini's appointment as Prime Minister, rather than just the march on Rome.

Ian's conclusion shows elements of the developed evaluation required at this level. He makes cautious judgements, explains the role played by various 'conservative forces' and breaks these forces into different individuals or groups.

My own students often fail to get to grips with 'range and depth', getting confused by instructions to make clear judgements but avoid assertive generalisations. In Figure 5.2, I have illustrated some common problems using examples from my own students' writing. Students need to combine the confidence of making a firm judgement with the recognition of the complexity of the issue. Their capacity to write in this way is directly linked to the balance between the overview and depth in their study of the module.

History teachers (e.g. Ward, 2006) have shown how post-16 students' writing can be greatly improved by studying the prose of leading historians and using this as a model for their own writing. In the following activities, I have used a mix of academic historians and standard textbooks to encourage students to engage critically with different forms of historical writing.

Activities

Rationale for the activities

Teaching Fascist Italy is a difficult challenge. At first, students are a little daunted by its strangeness, only Italian football and cuisine being familiar. The language, the earlier history and the ubiquity of Catholicism are all alien territory. Once they learn a little about Mussolini, they feel more comfortable. Here we go again – medals for mothers, a leader who is always right, aggressive invasions – it's the Nazis all over again, isn't it? One of the many problems with teaching this topic is the student perception that, because they learned about Nazi Germany first, Fascist policy is Nazi-inspired rather than the other way round. A deeper difficulty is the differing nature of the two regimes and cultures.

Like many historians of Italy, Bosworth has emphasised the problems of treating Italy and the Italians as one homogeneous people and nation:

> The richly textured histories of these people will be full of loyalties and perceptions that were not merely Fascist. Time and again, Italians proved able to give lip service to totalitarianism while retaining a sense of self. I shall talk of an everyday constituted by Catholicism, the family, gender understandings, the special flavour of different regions, towns and villages and by those who found an identity or identities outside the nation. Comprehending the fluctuating story of 'lite' Fascist totalitarianism, sceptical Fascist fundamentalism, a Fascist liturgy that failed to make itself catholic and universal, Fascist wars that were frequently more toughly fought with words than with weapons, can act as a counter to the pervasive power of Hitler's ghost. Reviewing the uneven experience of a people pent-up for two decades under the sway of a dictatorship of this Fascist sort may help us to the happy realization that, even at the worst of times, human fallibility, human hope and human struggle somehow obscure, delay and derail those determined to apply a simple and single answer, a seamless solution to any question that matters.
>
> *Bosworth (2005: 7–8)*

Italy seems an ideal case to confront students with the problems of making any generalisations in history. It is a young country, with deep and significant regional differences to the extent that many historians, like Bosworth, write of 'italies' rather than the singular 'Italy'. It offers an opportunity to trace a historical path from the contemporary record of individual experience through to general conclusions reached by later historians and to use this to consider the validity of some of the ideas of the postmodernists.

The first activity introduces students to different approaches to history that will be applied to their study of Fascist Italy in the sequence of lessons which follows. Each of the following activities covers a main policy area in four stages:

- A spotlight with a teaching idea for a particular aspect
- A summary of other aspects to be covered
- A voting and discussion session
- A final task using students' learning to develop their essay-writing skills.

The aim is to provide full coverage of Fascist rule and develop the skills of essay writing while, throughout the study, embracing the theme of the relationship between the particular and the general.

Activity 1

Are postmodernist ideas useful for learning history?

Rationale

In this exercise, I was keen for the students to understand the broader debate about the nature of history which surfaced particularly at the end of the 1990s and then to look at one particular aspect of that debate. The issues raised by the postmodernists and their attackers in the two initial articles (Resource 5A) are very broad and complex and I was concerned that students could be put off. To get over this problem, I set the first task as an optional competitive challenge for homework. Thus it neither intruded too much on lesson time nor unnecessarily confused weaker students.

Stage 1

Set up a voluntary challenge to summarise the key points in the concluding paragraphs of Professor O'Brien and Dr Munslow's articles (Resource 5A). Point out the links to the full articles as well, so students can access the broader context. Insist that the summary is no more than one page of A4 and must sum up the gist of the arguments in a clear and accessible way. Divide up the challenge to ensure that you get some good responses for both articles and ask the winning students to explain their summaries to the class. In this way, all students learn the basic areas of debate as a starting point to their studies. Finish off the lesson with a summary plenary in which each student has to write one positive and one negative comment on the postmodernist approach to history, and then select a range to be read out.

RESOURCE  *An online debate about postmodernism*

Read the articles carefully and summarise the main points made on no more than one side of A4. Your summary may be in any form you like: diagram, bullet points or continuous prose.

● Source 1

'An Engagement with Postmodern Foes, Literary Theorists and Friends on the Borders with History'

Patrick Karl O'Brien, February 1999
www.history.ac.uk/discourse/pob.html

Meanwhile, I propose bluntly to list the points that I have already elaborated upon in this encounter, before concluding that I anticipate the established epistemological foundations and practices of modern history will survive best firstly by rejecting the philosophical and historical premises of postmodernism (particularly the linguistic turn) by modifications to rhetoric of the 'truth claims' that some 'elders of the tribe' have rashly made for history; and secondly by adapting two or three major insights derivable from literary theory.

Encounters between intellectuals committed to producing historical knowledge and scepticism about its status (relabelled as postmodernism) go back centuries but in recent decades they have generated an unmanageable bibliography of statements, responses and rejoinders, which have now been neatly summarised and positioned in the form of several well designed textbooks and readers published by Routledge.

Historians will be pleased that their subject has been treated seriously and at length by postmodernists. Many share common political and cultural concerns with their eloquent antagonists and can only protest at being labelled as ideologically conservative or complacent. On three substantive issues, historians are likely, however, to maintain obdurate resistance to intellectual fashions that already look dated. First the entire and mildly patronising suggestion that the practices and claims as currently formulated for history are anachronistic in a postmodern world will be resented by a profession who are perhaps overly attached to exposing anachronisms of all kinds. Very few of us will be at all impressed with the rhetorical deployment of a meta narrative mislabelled as the 'Enlightenment Project' or the 'Episteme of Modernism' that mysteriously came to end in the twentieth century. Secondly, and for decades now, few historians have represented themselves as being in the business of producing 'Truth' about the 'Past' (or even the past). Conjectures, hypotheses, correlations, qualified suggestions, plausible interpretations or at best probalistic [sic] conclusions are the vocabularies they use, except at moments of elation and hyperbole. Thirdly, as working craftsmen and craftswomen, we simply cannot find time to engage seriously with the linguistic turns and spins that have entertained philosophers of language since Plato. That position might indeed be disparaged as 'self referential' because if nothing real or objective exists outside language, history should indeed collapse into fiction and playful semiotics.[41]

Literary theory has and will continue to encourage historians to become more reflexive about the forms and rhetorics deployed to construct histories as texts. The dangers and temptations of using models derived from the social sciences have, if anything, been over-rehearsed by generations of historians now entering retirement, who have long considered narratives to be a more humane, subtle and more objective form for the representation of the past. Reminders that the discursive practices of the discipline, the predicted responses of readers, authorial voices and viewpoints, emplotment and the temptations to build something coherent and rhetorically persuasive and saleable into a book also enter surreptiously into the manufacture of narratives, are nothing but salutary. Nevertheless, at the end of the day, historians will insist that the evidential base supporting and shaping a narrative ensures its acceptance and survival as a provisional story about the past. They recognise (indeed embrace a greater concern with) the 'poetics of history' but believe that any triumphs of form over substance are brief and few and far between. Historical narratives do compete for hegemony. Acclaim for metaphor, rhetoric and fashionable styles of history is transitory because disciplines exist to sort out the wheat from chaff.

Of course, all of the above may be nothing more than the self-referential voice and viewpoint of an elderly, white, male historian, who has been lucky enough to occupy a comfortable niche in the hierarchy of an academic discipline. I hope not!

References

41. If Hilary Putnam, *Reality and Representation* (Bradford Books, Cambridge, 1988) is correct, such an engagement would not resolve the problem one way or the other. We may as well proceed as if language was referential at least for the purposes of the range and quality of conversations that historians wish to pursue with their readers and one another.

 © HODDER EDUCATION

Source 2

Extract from 'The Postmodern in History:
A Response to Professor O'Brien'

Dr Alun Munslow, February 1999 www.history.ac.uk/discourse/alun.html

But even more important than this I do believe history is about ethics and taking up moral positions. Because I have a moral understanding that certain things are right and others wrong, an important feature of my post-empiricist history is that I do not expect my evidence to point me in the direction of objectivised knowledge – the answer. Answers come from moral reasoning as much as empirical realities. This is in part predicated on the ideas of Hayden White and other anti-representationalist philosophers like W.O. Quine, Wilfred Sellars and Richard Rorty, but it primarily derives from my ontological predisposition. History is a story constructed not only by evidence and argumentation but also by ethical positioning. So my history is historicist in that I want to see history as a contemporary and emancipatory cultural practice, and I do not think a narrow concentration on finding out the empirical reality is the only thing required in order to do that – you can use moral argument and non-empiricist positions just as well to know something about the past.

It is in the space created by the diminution of sceptical-empiricism that possibilities open up for writing the-past-as-history, possibilities that explicitly call into question how the history text is organised as a structure of knowledge with truth claims. The point of doing this is not just to raise epistemological questions (crucially important though they are) but also questions about power. History is a political act, and for me it is about challenging various hegemonies such as class, race, or gender. I think it is especially important for those colleagues who write from a critical and materialist perspective intent on deploying history to recover the marginalised and exploited, to understand that conventional historical thinking compresses the possibilities of meaning in the-past-as-history precisely because of the reasoning of sceptical-empiricism. Not only do the 'proper' procedures of history narrow the discipline's boundaries but they disguise those boundaries as universals.

My history is just another cultural practice that studies cultural practice. It is relativist and that in no way worries me. My history collapses knowledge and representation, and representation and being, and enjoys the permeable relationship of past reality and the present. To recognise that we are textualised creatures does not constrain but rather liberates us. I am content that while our interpretations possess referentiality they do not access reality, and so history can never be what it once was.

Stage 2

Provide students with Resource Sheet 5B about microhistory. Read and discuss the questions set. Explore the underlying issues raised by the texts and make links between these and the postmodernist debate. Explain that this module will be taught using three techniques in conjunction:

- macrohistory using the general textbook and articles
- microhistory using the stories of so-called 'outliers'
- using students' own fictional characters in role play.

Explain that by the end of this activity students should be able to comment on:

- the key tenets of postmodernism and its strengths and weaknesses
- the main views of microhistorians and their strengths and weaknesses
- the links between the two different approaches to history.

Before starting on the following activities, introduce the main theme for the module and ask students to record their views on the line shown in Resource 5C. Save the result in order to return to it at the end.

Activity 2

Fascist politics

Mini question:

What was the impact of Fascist politics on the Italian people?

Rationale

The purpose of this activity is to illuminate the range of political responses to Fascism and how they changed over time. Once your students start to study Fascist politics, they will quickly recognise the familiar overlaps with Nazism already alluded to. In fact, Fascist politics is, in many ways, more complex than the Nazi equivalent. For a start, Hitler was never a committed socialist nor would he ever have contemplated sharing power with a king. Students will need to cover a broad range of material on Fascist politics and it is not the purpose of this chapter to suggest how all the material might be taught. Instead, one aspect is chosen to highlight how the individual studies might be integrated into the teaching.

Summary of aspects of Fascist politics

- Key steps which brought the Fascists to power, including the March on Rome
- The consolidation of power between 1922 and 1929, including the Matteotti murder and the Aventine Secession
- ***Spotlight on consolidation of power***
- Fascist control of the legal system and the use of the OVRA (secret police)
- The nature and extent of resistance
- The limitations of Fascist power and the relationship with the monarchy
- The role of the Fascist party in the state.

Stage 1: Spotlight on consolidation of power

(a) *Key features of a dictatorship*
Ask students to define the key features of a dictatorship. Feed these back and create a checklist based on their points for them all to copy down.
Now display the timeline of the creation of the Fascist dictatorship (Resource 5D) and play *The Weakest Link*. Give students the challenge to reduce the timeline to only five events. Organise the class into twos or threes, sharing a mini whiteboard (see Figure 5.3 on why these are so useful). In the first round, ask each pair to vote off one development that they consider less significant in the creation of Mussolini's dictatorship. In the second round, allow them all to vote at the same time and go with the majority verdict. This should lead to lively discussion about the nature and extent of Mussolini's power at different stages in the consolidation process.

Figure 5.3 *Why use mini whiteboards?*

Mini whiteboards are, in my view, an essential tool in every classroom, mostly because of their flexibility and the way they include everyone. Even in these days of exciting starters and plenaries, many lessons begin with a short teacher-led discussion which is all too often dominated by overconfident volunteers or awkward silences, while the targeted student sits silently looking at their feet. Mini whiteboards offer ways round this. The need to record something on the board means that the teacher has to build in thinking time. It is accepted that no one can opt out. The task can be writing a couple of words, or creating a drawing or diagram, covering a range of learning styles. You can ask students to keep it secret and reveal the ideas one by one or you can go for a whole-class response. Another option on the general theme is to start by allowing one board each and then, as you develop the learning and discussion, remove more and more so that students have to reach agreements in pairs, small groups and then larger groups.

Most educational suppliers offer sets relatively cheaply or you can make your own by laminating white card. They are worth every penny.

RESOURCE 5B *Microhistory and its place in the postmodernist debate*

Source 1

'What Is Microhistory?', Sigurður Gylfi Magnússon, August 2006

Microhistory came about, according to the German-US historian Georg G. Iggers in his excellent summary of the development of modern historical practice, *Historiography in the Twentieth Century*, not because the microhistorians considered that the traditional methodology of the social sciences "is not possible or desirable but that social scientists have made generalizations that do not hold up when tested against the concrete reality of the small-scale life they claim to explain."[1] In the light of this perception, monographs and journals began to appear focusing specifically on microhistorical research, and these became a forum for criticism of the kind of social history produced under the influence of the social sciences. Perhaps foremost of the contributors to the debate was the Italian historian Carlo Ginzburg, who delivered incisive criticisms of the prevailing methods in numerous articles in the Italian journal, *Quaderni Storici*, the German journal, *Historische Anthropologie*, in English in *Critical Inquiry*, and elsewhere.[2]

Ginzburg and many of his colleagues attacked large-scale quantitative studies on the grounds that they distorted reality on the individual level. The microhistorians placed their emphasis on small units and how people conducted their lives within them. By reducing the scale of observation, microhistorians argued that they are more likely to reveal the complicated function of individual relationships within each and every social setting and they stressed its difference from larger norms. Microhistorians tend to focus on *outliers* rather than looking for the *average* individual as found by the application of quantitative research methods. Instead, they scrutinize those individuals who did not follow the paths of their average fellow countryman, thus making them their focal point. In microhistory the term "normal exception" is used to penetrate the importance of this perspective, meaning that each and every one of us do not show our full hand of cards. Seeing what is usually kept hidden from the outside world, we realize that our focus has only been on the "normal exception"; those who in one segment of society are considered obscure, strange, and even dangerous. They might be, in other circles, at the center of attention and fully accepted in their daily affairs.

Nearly all cases which microhistorians deal with have one thing in common; they all caught the attention of the authorities, thus establishing their archival existence. They illustrate the function of the formal institutions in power and how they handle people's affairs. In other words, each has much wider application, going well beyond the specific case under examination by the microhistorian. The Italian microhistorian Giovanni Levi put it this way in an article on the methods of microhistory. "[M]icrohistorians have concentrated on the contradictions of normative systems and therefore on the fragmentation, contradictions and plurality of viewpoints which make all systems fluid and open."[3] To be able to illustrate this point, microhistorians have turned to the narrative as an analytical tool or a research method where they get the opportunity to present their findings, show the process by which the conclusions are reached, and demonstrate the holes in our understanding and the subjective nature of the discourse.[4]

Source: George Mason University's History News Network. http://hnn.us/articles/23720.html

References

1. Georg G. Iggers, *Historiography in the Twentieth Century: from Scientific Objectivity to the Postmodern Challenge* (Hanover, NH, 1997), p. 108. See also: Sigurdur Gylfi Magnusson, "The Singularization of History: Social History and Microhistory within the Postmodern State of Knowledge." *Journal of Social History*, 36 (Spring 2003), pp. 701-735.
2. Ginzburg's ideas are put forward in a large number of books and articles, notably "Just One Witness," *Probing the Limits of Representation: Nazism and the "Final Solution"* (Cambridge, Mass., 1992); *The Cheese and the Worms: the Cosmos of a Sixteenth-Century Miller*, trans. John and Anne Tedeschi (Baltimore, 1980); "Proofs and Possibilities: in the Margins of Natalie Zemon Davis's 'The Return of Martin Guerre'," *Yearbook of Comparative and General Literature*, 37 (1988), pp. 114–127; "Microhistory: Two or Three Things that I Know about it," *Critical Inquiry*, 20 (Autumn 1993), pp. 10–35; "Checking the Evidence: the Judge and the Historian," *Critical Inquiry*, 18 (Autumn 1991), pp. 79–92; Carlo Ginzburg and Carlo Poni, "The Name and the Game: Unequal Exchange and the Historical Marketplace," in Edward Muir and Guido Ruggiero, eds., *Microhistory and the Lost People of Europe*, trans. Eren Branch (Baltimore, 1991), pp. 1–10; Carlo Ginzburg, "The Philosopher and the Witches: an Experiment in Cultural History," *Acta-Ethnographica-Academiae-Scientarum-Hungaricae*, 37 (1991–92), pp. 283–292; *Clues, Myths, and the Historical Method*, trans. John and Anne C. Tedeschi (Baltimore, 1989). This last contains several important essays, of which perhaps the best known is "Clues: Roots of a Evidential Paradigm," pp. 96–125.
3. Giovanni Levi, "On Microhistory," in Peter Burke, ed., *New Perspectives on Historical Writing* (University Park, Pa., 1991), p. 107.
4. For good discussions of the importance of storytelling in connection with the methods of microhistory see Guido Ruggiero, *Binding Passions: Tales of Magic, Marriage, and Power at the End of the Renaissance* (New York, 1993), pp. 18-20.

Source 2

Extract from 'An Engagement with Postmodern Foes, Literary Theorists and Friends on the Borders with History', Patrick Karl O'Brien, February 1999 www.history.ac.uk/discourse/pob.html

Indeed the recovery of previously silenced viewpoints and the related proliferation of sub branches of history (now already splintering into 'sects') has raised legitimate anxieties about synthesis, synoptic overviews and the very possibilities for reaching multi-vocal and inclusive generalisations about major questions and themes that have been the staples of history for generations past.

One way out of our current embarrassment of histories has been to ignore, even to denigrate, the 'staples' of traditional history, eschew the subject's ambition, to explain big things and (with proper humility towards the complexity of the past and the inexplicable 'other') to embrace micro history. Micro histories are now fashionable and effectively support and circumvent several postmodern objections to traditional, larger scale historical analysis and explanation. They are often biographies based upon a cache of sources, marshalled to reveal their 'own' story and thereby minimise 'intrusions' by historians. Close to literature, micro histories attract readerships beyond the reaches of a hierarchically organised discipline; deliberately refuse to 'patronise' subjects by aggregating people's lives along with others for inclusion into a model or even to contextualise or position the 'dead other' as 'mere examples' within a narrative.

Source 3

Extract from Sigurður Gylfi Magnússon, 'Social History – Cultural History – Alltagsgeschichte – Microhistory: In-Between Methodologies and Conceptual Frameworks', *Journal of Microhistory*, June 2006 www.microhistory.org/pivot/entry.php?id=20

Of this kind of research [microhistory], Giovanni Levi writes: "Phenomena previously considered to be sufficiently described and understood assume completely new meanings by altering the scale of observation. It is then possible to use these results to draw far wider generalizations although the initial observations were made within relatively narrow dimensions and as experiments rather than examples."[78] Here Levi is touching on the question of how small units connect with and fit into larger wholes, and as previously noted many microhistorians have turned the identification of such connections into one of the chief identifying features of their method: microhistorical research would be of little value if it was not used to shed light on the greater wholes of society.[79]

References

78. Giovanni Levi, "On Microhistory," p. 98.
79. In this connection it is worth mentioning an article by Guðmundur Hálfdanarson in the history journal *Saga* in 1993 which seems to exhibit undeniable indirect links with microhistory. In this article he takes a single, specific court case from the most easterly part of Rangárvallasýsla in the southern plains of Iceland, one incident in a dispute between the sheriff and local farmers, and shows how it sheds light on highly complex and multifaceted changes in the international mental world of the 19th century: see Guðmundur Hálfdanarson, '"Is it any business of the sheriff...?" On the development of state authority in Iceland in the 19th century', *Saga* 31 (1993), pp. 7–31.

Read the three extracts carefully. Using the extracts and your own ideas, jot down some points for a seminar discussion on these key issues:

- ways in which microhistory can be said to have undermined 'traditional' history
- ways in which microhistory supports the ideas of the postmodernists
- ways in which microhistory undermines the ideas of the postmodernists
- ways in which this approach to history might be helpful for studying Fascist Italy

 © HODDER EDUCATION

RESOURCE 5C Record of student views

Is it possible to reach any general conclusions about the impact of Fascism on Italy in the years 1922–39?

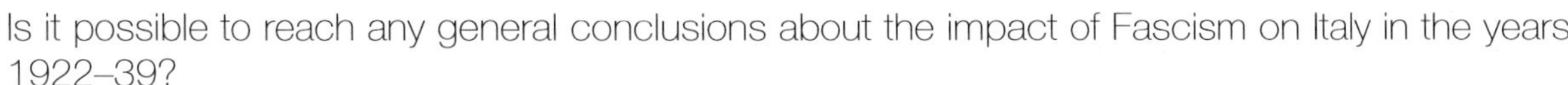

Yes, you can — No, impossible

RESOURCE 5D Basic timeline 1922–29

Steps of political control from the March on Rome to 1929

1922	**A**	Mussolini granted emergency powers for one year
	B	Fascist Grand Council set up
1923	**C**	Merger with Nationalist Party
	D	Acerbo Election Law
1924	**E**	Elections take place with accusations of vote rigging and intimidation
	F	Press censorship introduced
	G	Murder of Matteotti
	H	Opposition party meetings no longer allowed
1925	**I**	Mussolini's speech to parliament takes responsibility for Fascist violence
	J	Powers to control the press are increased
	K	Elected mayors replaced by appointed podestas
	L	Squads merged into national militia
	M	The Civil Service is purged
1926–27	**N**	Mussolini given the power to rule by decree
	O	Parliament loses the right to debate laws or criticise the government
	P	The special police, the OVRA, is set up
	Q	New Special Tribunal for political crimes
	R	All non-fascist parties suppressed
	S	Trade unions, strikes and lockouts made illegal
1928	**T**	The Fascist Grand Council can exclusively decide who becomes a Deputy or Senator

(b) *Introduction of Salvemini*
Provide students with Salvemini's real life story (Resource 5E) and his view of Mussolini's dictatorship:

> From that moment [the March on Rome in 1922] Italy no longer had free and representative institutions, but a dictatorship. From that moment Italy no longer had a King – but only a 'prisoner of war' with the title of King.
>
> *Salvemini (1928: 158)*

Use this as the basis of a class discussion evaluating which features of a dictatorship were in place by 1922 and what elements of democracy remained. Now return to the timeline and ask students to write their initials on the point where they think the dictatorship was established.

Stage 2: Voting and discussion

When you have covered the political topics above, ask the students to invent characters in Fascist Italy. You will need to give guidelines to different groups within the class to ensure you get a range in terms of age, gender, region, class and ethnicity. However, they will enjoy the freedom of inventing names and backgrounds and, with prompting, will find an interesting diversity of locations. Set this as homework and ask them to come to the lesson with some idea of the lifestyle and the political and religious views of their individual, using intelligent guesswork and some imagination. If you are using the remote voting system, you can set them up as a class and allocate their characters to numbered voting pads so that their views are automatically recorded (see Figure 5.4). However, this is not essential and getting students to plot their own graphs can be more effective.

Organise the students into social classes, issue the graphs and ask them to plot the information on their character record sheets (Resource 5F). Then take them through the PowerPoint (Resource 5G), asking them to vote at each stage while interweaving the story of Salvemini and his changing political views.

Take the opportunity to explore key turning points in Fascist power. For Salvemini it was the Matteotti murder but for other Italians it may not have been. If using the remote voting system, you can review the bar chart of support for the Fascists on the whiteboard. Alternatively, this can be done by providing coloured voting slips to be held up and noting the totals on a conventional board. During the voting, challenge individuals to explain why they held consistent views or changed their minds. This should bring out some of the underlying hopes and fears of many Italians at this time: dread of civil war, concerns about property and business or worries about civil rights and religious faith.

Figure 5.4 *Using remote voting systems in the classroom*

There are numerous electronic voting systems for educational use on the market. In the package there will usually be a set of keypads and a base station linked to a computer. Using a data projector or interactive whiteboard, you can display your question and, after students have voted by pressing a button on their keypad, a graph can be generated displaying the class response. Most students are familiar with this from their use in *Who wants to be a millionaire?* when the 'Ask the Audience' option is used.

For extended role play, it is possible to set up your class in advance so that a numbered keypad is registered to a particular individual in your class and their voting pattern is recorded. You can then print out a record of their votes at the end of the study.

The manufacturers of these products market them mainly as tools to test knowledge in multiple-choice quizzes. In fact, this is the least imaginative way of using them. A project led by Walsh and sponsored by the Historical Association has been looking at ways to base voting around 'What do you think?' rather than 'What do you know?'. His report is published on the Historical Association website at www.history.org.uk

At the end, give students the group discussion task (Resource 5H). Ask them to write down their agreed responses and take them in.

Stage 3: Written task

This is a good point to set the first essay for formative assessment (see Figure 5.5). Your students will be ready for an essay on the impact of Fascist politics on the people of Italy. Challenge them to adapt their knowledge and understanding by changing the focus to one of the extent of control. Set the question: 'How far had Mussolini's government won control of the Italian people by 1929?'

- Provide students with a summary of feedback from all the groups and ensure they all have the information about Salvemini's life.
- Make the main feature of the feedback the student's balance between general judgements and specific examples.
- Before your one-to-one feedback with each student, ask them to highlight examples of general assertions and specific examples in their own work.
- Use this as the basis for your one-to-one discussion alongside your comments.

RESOURCE 5E *Real lives in Fascist Italy*

Gaetano Salvemini

Salvemini was born in 1873 in the extreme south of Italy into a poor peasant family. He was the eldest of nine sons and his parents both died when he was a child. He was looked after and educated by his uncle, who was a Roman Catholic priest. This uncle was a supporter of the former monarchy of Naples and felt some resentment at the enforced unification of Italy under the leadership of Piedmont. Aged 17, Salvemini won a small scholarship which enabled him to study at the University of Florence and after graduating he became a history teacher. Salvemini had joined the Socialist Party in 1895 and his writings revealed his commitment to the poor and to democratic ideals.

In 1902 Salvemini became Professor of History at the University of Messina in Sicily. When an earthquake struck the town in 1908, his wife and five children all died. He worked for two days trying to remove the rubble with his own hands to find them and commented: 'I made a mistake in not killing myself on the first day.' Many believed that Salvemini himself had died and Mussolini (then a Socialist leader) even sent a telegram stating his regret at the loss of one of the 'finest figures of Italian socialism'.

After this, Salvemini became Professor of History at Florence, where he completed research on the French Revolution, on the Italian nationalist, Mazzini, and on medieval Florence. However, he was also politically active, being highly critical of the corruption of the Liberal leader, Giolitti, and leaving the Socialist Party in 1911 because of its failure to support his campaign. After 1921 he withdrew from the political scene and concentrated on his academic work.

The murder of Matteotti in the summer of 1924 ended his silence. He wrote: 'I too feel responsible for this murder, for I have not withstood the Fascist dictatorship as I should have done.' He continued to speak out against Mussolini and the Fascist press campaigned for him to be removed from his post. He was arrested in Rome in 1925 and spent more than a month in prison. Although he was released, his lawyer and friends were beaten up by *squadristi*. Shortly after this, he left Italy and spent some years in Britain and France before taking up the position of Professor of History at Harvard University in the USA in 1930. He became an American citizen in 1940 but returned to Italy after the war.

During his years in exile, Salvemini wrote several books about the Fascist dictatorship, including *The Fascist Dictatorship in Italy* (1928) and *Under the Axe of Fascism* (1936).

What did Salvemini say?

From *The Origins of Fascism in Italy* (published 1973), based on a series of lectures given at Harvard in 1942. Here Salvemini is writing about the political situation in 1925, after Matteotti's murder:

> Mussolini's victory set the seal on his supreme and absolute control not only over his opponents, but over his own party. Whatever other minor Fascist leaders had said and done to save fascism in the hour of danger, it was Mussolini who, by assuming the whole responsibility for Fascist deeds and by openly challenging the opposition to a final duel, had brought the crisis to an end. From that moment on, there was nothing that he could not dare to do. His victory intensified in the rank and file of his party the faith in the myth of the 'invincible *duce*' and the conviction that blind obedience to him was essential to the existence of fascism. The party became more and more a military organisation in which the first duty was the old military slogan, 'obey first and do not try to understand'.

Salvemini, G. (1973) The Origins of Fascism in Italy, *p. 408*

Character record sheet

The impact of the Fascist government on your life

General character details

Name: ....

Age in 1922: ....

Gender: ....

Region of Italy: ....

Employment: ....

Other details ....

Put a dot where your character lives

The impact of Fascist politics

Your character: •••••••••••••••••••••• Gaetano Salvemini: — — — — — — — — — —

Committed Fascist											
Sympathetic to Fascism											
Indifferent to Fascism											
Strong opponent of Fascism											
	1919	**1922**	**1924**	**1926**	**1929**	**1931**	**1935**	**1936**	**1938**	**1939**	**1940**
	Post-war recession	March on Rome	Matteotti murder	Dictatorship	Lateran Pact	Height of depression	Abyssinian War	Spanish Civil War	Anti-Semitism	Pact of Steel	Joins war

Commitment Graph

 © HODDER EDUCATION

RESOURCE 5G *The impact of Fascist politics on the Italian people*

PowerPoint slides

<table>
<tr><th>Fictional character</th><th>Gaetano Salvemini</th></tr>
<tr><td>SLIDE 1

How has the Fascist state affected your life?

Focus on: Politics</td><td>SLIDE 2

Gaetano Salvemini

• Background in South
• Education
• Family
• Intellectual Socialism</td></tr>
<tr><td>SLIDE 3

It is 1919. The war is over but has left Italy with serious problems such as inflation and unemployment. Elections are on the horizon and it looks like the Socialists will do well. The Fascist Party has just been founded in Milan with a radical (mostly socialist) agenda.

What is your view?

A. I will support the Fascists.
B. I like some of the Fascist ideas but am not sure if I will vote for them.
C. All the political parties are corrupt and I'm just not interested.
D. I dislike the Fascists and what they stand for. I will support one of the opposing parties.</td><td>SLIDE 4

What did Salvemini think?

In 1919 Salvemini supported the Socialists, although with some misgivings. He was worried about the violence of some radical socialists – for instance, the aggressive land seizures in the countryside. The Fascist Party was small and insignificant at this time and would not have attracted him.

Plot him between 'indifferent' and 'sympathetic' on the commitment graph (Resource 5F).</td></tr>
<tr><td>SLIDE 5

It is 1922. Mussolini has been appointed prime minister. The country seems to be more settled but there have been serious restrictions in political and civil rights.

What is your view?

A. I will support the Fascists.
B. I like some of the Fascists' ideas but am not sure about some of their policies.
C. All the political parties are corrupt and I'm just not interested.
D. I dislike the Fascists and what they stand for. I will campaign against them.</td><td>SLIDE 6

What did Salvemini think?

Salvemini was very concerned about the violence and ineptitude of the Biennio Rosso. He was also critical of the weak and corrupt liberal governments. Therefore he thought that it was worth giving Mussolini and the Fascists a chance, even if just for a short time, to settle the country down.

Plot him between 'indifferent' and 'sympathetic' on the commitment graph (Resource 5F).</td></tr>
</table>

<table>
<tr><th>Fictional character</th><th>Gaetano Salvemini</th></tr>
<tr><td>SLIDE 7

It is 1924. The Socialist leader, Matteotti, has been murdered. The Socialists and some Liberals have walked out of the Chamber of Deputies. The King has done nothing.

What is your view?

A. I support the Fascists.
B. I like some of the things the Fascists have done but also have some doubts.
C. All the political parties are corrupt and I'm just not interested.
D. I dislike the Fascists and what they stand for. I will campaign against them.</td><td>SLIDE 8

What did Salvemini think?

In 1924 Salvemini was shocked by the murder of Matteotti and the failure to punish the perpetrators. He already had serious worries about the lawless and undemocratic nature of Fascist rule. At this point he wrote and spoke directly against Fascism and Mussolini personally.

Plot him on the commitment graph (see Resource 5F).</td></tr>
<tr><td>SLIDE 9

It is 1929. Mussolini now has the full powers of dictator. He has control over the press, has disallowed all opposition parties and dismantled local and national democratic systems.

What is your view?

A. I support the Fascists.
B. I like some of the things the Fascists have done but also have some doubts.
C. All the political parties are corrupt and I'm just not interested.
D. I dislike the Fascists and what they stand for. I will campaign against them.</td><td>SLIDE 10

What did Salvemini think?

Salvemini had been imprisoned and his friends and lawyer beaten up as a result of his opposition to Fascism. He was removed from his post at Florence University and left the country. He became a persistent opponent of Fascism from abroad, writing papers and giving lectures in the USA and Europe.

Plot him on the commitment graph (see Resource 5F).</td></tr>
</table>

RESOURCE 5H *Group discussion task*

Impact of Fascism on politics, according to social class

Record a response for your social group underneath each question.

1. On the whole, how much did this social class support the Fascists in 1922?

2. How much did they support them in 1929?

3. What were the main reasons for this?

4. Are there any individuals who disagree with the general view of the group? Why do they disagree?

Figure 5.5 *Use of formative and summative assessment*

- **Summative assessment** is the use of marks or grades to provide feedback to the student. Its main purpose is to judge the student's performance.
- **Formative assessment** is the use of comments to provide feedback with the main purpose of helping the student to improve their work.

There has been a tremendous amount of discussion at my college, as in most schools around the country, about the use of formative and summative assessment. Black and Wiliam's 'Working inside the Black Box' (2001) argued persuasively that the use of assessment for learning can have a significant impact on improving achievement. As a result there has been a trend away from continual awarding of marks and grades and greater use of comments-only feedback alongside self and peer assessment. At post-16 level this has met with a mixed response. On the negative side, students dislike not knowing how they are doing and some find peer assessment more intimidating than teacher assessment. Teachers feel less confident at parents' evenings and at review times without the support of a set of marks in the mark book. On the other hand, involving students in assessment as an interactive process ensures they take more responsibility for their own progress and gain a sharper understanding of assessment criteria. For most students this form of assessment is better for motivation.

My own view is that the first assessment in any module should be formative, with detailed feedback, actively involving the student and, if possible, involving a one-to-one discussion. The final assessment should be summative, as preparation for the looming external assessment. In between I use a mix of methods, as suggested in this module.

Activity 3

Fascist social policies

Mini question:

What was the impact of Fascist social policies on the Italian people?

As before, one aspect is provided as an in-depth example in a broader survey of social change.

Summary of key social policies

- Education and youth policies
- The relationship between the Fascist state and the Church, including the Lateran Pacts, Catholic Action and conflicts over anti-Semitism
- The role of women in the Fascist state, including Fascist policies on female employment, health, births and marriage and education
- ***Spotlight on minority groups***

Stage 1: Spotlight on minority groups

This activity starts with the contrasting life stories of Wanda Newby and Ettore Ovazza (Resources 5I and 5J). Both are outsiders in Fascist Italy but their level of integration into society changes over time. Newby is a Slovene schoolgirl, whose family was forced to resettle in central Italy and whose father disliked all that Fascism stood for. Despite this she finds herself taking part in Fascist celebrations and even cheering the Duce. Ovazza is a committed Italian patriot, the son of a proud First World War veteran and an eager volunteer for the Abyssinian War. In 1938 he is horrified at the turn towards anti-Semitism and, as a Jewish businessman, his family suffers severely in the ensuing persecution.

(a) *The life story of Wanda Newby*

This is a listening activity. Tell the class a little of her family background, her simple life in a Slovene village and the deaths of numerous brothers and sisters. This area had been made part of Italy in the Treaty of St Germain, having formerly been part of the Austro-Hungarian Empire. Explain the brutal change imposed by the Fascists when the family had to relocate to a village near Parma. Describe the family's anti-Fascist stance, with a brother emigrating and her schoolmaster father quietly critical of the regime. Remind students that Newby herself is exposed to Fascist propaganda at school and at her compulsory youth group. Then read from Newby's book (see Figure 5.6).

After listening, ask your students to write down individually and in silence a few ideas in answer to these questions:

1. What made Newby feel an outsider in Fascist Italy?
2. What made Newby feel a part of Fascist society?

Then pair them up to exchange ideas so that they have contributions to make to the class discussion. Most students will have experiences of being an outsider in an established group and these memories can be used, with care, to help them to understand Newby's position. (Hold back Resource 5I.)

(b) *Research into Fascist treatment of minorities*

The most important minority to study here is the Jewish population and students can be given a note-taking task from a range of sources covering the motives, key developments and effects of anti-Semitic measures. You can provide a summary of the Fascists' treatment of other minorities, such as those in the north-east region (Slovenes, Slavs and Germans) and homosexuals.

RESOURCE 51 *Real lives in Fascist Italy*

Wanda Newby

Wanda Newby was born in 1922 in a small village not far from Trieste in Slovenia. She was her parents' eleventh child and only one other, an older brother, survived to adulthood. Her father was the local schoolmaster, a well respected member of the close-knit community. At the end of the First World War, under the Treaty of St Germain, Slovenia had been made part of Italy. Although there were strong cultural traditions and most families spoke a Slovenian dialect, it was a mixed community and Wanda's parents spoke Italian and German as well as their native tongue. However, once Mussolini came to power, these minority groups were persecuted. There were raids on the school house, searching for subversive materials. In 1930 Wanda's anti-Fascist brother decided to emigrate to Argentina to avoid conflict with the authorities.

In the early 1930s the Fascist government began to relocate non-Italian nationals employed in public service who lived in territories which had been annexed after the war. Schools were to have only Italian teachers, who used the Italian language in the classroom. Wanda's father was moved to a new teaching job in a village near Parma and the whole family were forced to leave Slovenia and resettle. For the first time Wanda (now aged 10) was exposed to a Fascist education:

> During that first year in Fontanellato I was obliged to join the most junior of the Fascist organisations and become a *Piccola Italiana*, a little Italian. This meant that on special occasions I had to wear a black pleated skirt, white blouse and black beret, with white socks and black shoes and, when the weather was cold, a black coat. At twelve I would become a *Giovane Italiana,* and at eighteen a *Giovane Fascista.* If you didn't join one of these organisations you couldn't go to school.
>
> Fascism was not thought of as a separate subject on the school curriculum, but the history of how Mussolini came to power was dealt with at length at the end of the modern history textbooks. We learned Fascist songs, and at the end of each term we would hold a gymnastic display for the Fascist authorities and our parents. On days of national holiday we had a parade, marching up and down and singing patriotic songs. I found it all very boring, especially when I got older, but kept my thoughts to myself.
>
> *Newby, W. (1991)* Peace and War: Growing up in Fascist Italy, *p. 72*

Wanda learnt Italian quickly and won a scholarship, which paid half her fees to attend secondary school in Parma. Her father disliked Mussolini, particularly objecting to his rewriting of school history books and his aggressive foreign policy. Wanda was a reluctant member of the Fascist Youth group and was warned that she could lose her place at school unless she attended more regularly. However, she and her schoolmates took a day off school to join in street demonstrations celebrating victories in the Abyssinian War in 1935. In her village of Fontanellato, along with her father, the local doctor and priest expressed anti-Fascist views, for which they were to suffer. The priest, a kindly man who organised activities for the young people, was beaten up and finally moved to an isolated parish. However, most of the members of this small community showed little interest in Mussolini's policies at home or abroad. Wanda herself was more interested in her studies, her family and her friendships.

Wanda was still at school when Italy joined in the Second World War in June 1940. She qualified as an accountant and went to work in a bank. During the war her family helped Jews and escaped prisoners of war, including Eric Newby, an English officer, whom she later married.

Figure 5.6

In 1938 Wanda was in Trieste at the time of a visit by Mussolini and she could not resist going to see him:

Before I left Fontanellato my father had told me that although he was not against my trying to see Mussolini he would be very upset if I indulged in any kind of cheering or applause. I promised I wouldn't and in fact had no intention of doing so, as I secretly regarded the Duce as a bit of a buffoon. He was known for wanting to be photographed from every conceivable angle and vigorously applauded when making his inflammatory speeches, and I was looking forward to seeing in the flesh this extraordinary man of whom my parents had brought me up to disapprove.

When the day came I got up very early and managed to get myself into what was almost the front row of the crowd, immediately underneath the platform in Piazza Unita where he was to appear. When he finally did so the impression he made was unforgettable. Wearing a rather absurd black tasselled fez, an army officer's uniform jacket, riding breeches and a black shirt, he delivered his speech slowly, articulating the words very clearly. He stood in a familiar, flamboyant posture with his hands on his hips and his chin stuck out, constantly turning his head from left to right and back again, to take in his entire audience. He looked taller than I had imagined him: it was said that the platforms on which he stood always had an elevated section in the middle to raise him up. The effect he had on me was unexpected. I found his personality irresistibly magnetic and at the end of his speech I joined the rest of the huge crowd in tumultuous cheering. It was an experience I will never forget, and one of which, when I returned home, I felt deeply ashamed. I never told my parents.

Newby, W. (1991) Peace and War: Growing up in Fascist Italy, *pp. 105–06*

(c) *The life story of Ettore Ovazza*

This time give students the summary sheet (Resource 5J) of Ovazza's life up until 1939 and ask them in groups to make a storyboard of the key events of his story, focusing on how much he felt an insider or outsider in Italian society at different stages in Fascist rule. To ensure they do this, insist on a speech bubble in each portion of the storyboard describing how Ovazza feels. Give them some choice about whether to do this in booklet or poster form. When completed, put the stories on display and ask students to speculate about what happens to Ovazza and his family after 1939. Finally, show the class a clip from *Italian Fascism: Revealed* (Channel 5) which tells the tragic story of what happened to the family.

Return to the questions asked before about Newby:

1. What made Ovazza feel an outsider in Fascist Italy?
2. What made Ovazza feel a part of Fascist society?

Use this as the basis for discussion and comparison with Newby and record, as a class, the main 'push' and 'pull' factors influencing these two individuals. (At this stage, you can let students have copies of Resource 5I.)

Stage 2: Voting and discussion

Group students according to the age groups of their fictional characters at the start of Fascist rule in 1922 (under 21, twenties and thirties, forties and fifties, and over 60) and get them to consider the three multiple-choice questions (Resource 5K), making decisions as a group, and noting down their decisions and any who disagreed. This can be set up on the remote voting system or using mini whiteboards or can be a simple group activity on paper. Use the results as the focus for discussion, encouraging dissenters to explain why they disliked the majority verdicts.

Stage 3: Written task

Focus on the essay question: 'How far did Fascist social policies unite the people of Italy?' Emphasise the importance of breadth and balance.

- Require students to make a plan of this essay on no more than one side of A4.
- Remind them to use all their notes, including the life stories of Newby and Ovazza, and their record of the group voting.
- For each of the policy areas they cover, they should write a general judgement, have two examples of supporting evidence and a qualification of that judgement, i.e. some exception such as time, region or class.
- Then ask your students to come up with their own checklist of key features of good essay plans (essential topics to include, precision of evidence, clear structure) and comment on each other's work.

Activity 4

Fascist policies on culture, leisure and propaganda

Mini question:

How much impact did Fascist policies on culture, leisure and propaganda have on Italian lives?

This time the focus for the in-depth study is sport.

Summary of key areas

- Fascist propaganda and the cult of the Duce
- The OND (leisure organisation) and its impact
- Fascist policies on culture and the arts

RESOURCE 5J *Real lives in Fascist Italy*

Ettore Ovazza

The Ovazza family was a successful Jewish banking family based in Turin. The state of Piedmont, in northern Italy, had a long history of toleration and the Ovazzas had been strong supporters of Italian unification in the nineteenth century. Ettore Ovazza's father had been proud of his Italian and Jewish background and had the words 'Fatherland, Faith and Family' carved on his tombstone. He had, along with his three sons, voluntarily enlisted to fight in the First World War. The family was well integrated into Italian society and, while they followed Jewish traditions such as celebrating Passover, they spoke Italian rather than Hebrew at home.

Ettore Ovazza had studied law at university and then travelled to Germany with a view to a diplomatic career. At the outbreak of war he had volunteered and trained as an officer, only to suffer humiliating defeat at Caporetto. His patriotic letters from the front were published in 1928 and received general praise. After the war, the city of Turin was badly affected by the turmoil of the *Biennio Rosso* with repeated strikes, lockouts and violent demonstrations. The Ovazza family was alarmed by these developments.

Aged 30 when Mussolini came to power, Ettore Ovazza was a committed Fascist from the start. He was not unusual in this respect. Two Jews held office in the Fascist government and 10,000 were members of the Fascist Party, about one in three of the adult Jewish population. Ovazza took part in the March on Rome in October 1922 and in 1929 he was invited to meet Mussolini as part of a delegation of Jewish war veterans. He described the encounter later:

> On hearing my affirmation of the unshakeable loyalty of Italian Jews to the Fatherland, His Excellency Mussolini looks me straight in the eye and says with a voice that penetrates straight to my heart: 'I have never doubted it'. When Il Duce bids us farewell with a Roman salute, I feel an urge to embrace him, as a fascist, as an Italian, but I can't; and approaching him at his desk I say: 'Excellency, I would like to shake your hand'. It is not a fascist gesture, but it is a cry from the heart… Such is The Man that Providence has given to Italy.
>
> *Stille, A. (1992)* Benevolence and Betrayal: Five Italian Jewish Families Under Fascism, *p. 47*

In the 1930s Fascist attitudes to the Jewish population began to change. Hitler came to power in Germany and, although Mussolini rejected his racist views, they influenced some leading Fascists in Italy. In 1934 several Jews were arrested in Turin for smuggling in anti-Fascist literature. Ettore Ovazza reacted by redoubling his efforts to support the Fascist regime. He founded a newspaper called *Our Flag*, reminding Italians of the Jewish sacrifice for Italy in the Great War and attacking the idea that all Jews were Zionists. Taking a leading role in the Jewish community in Turin, Ovazza ensured that all the key positions were held by Fascist supporters. When Mussolini invaded Abyssinia, he immediately volunteered for service, an offer that was turned down probably due to his age (43). Despite the beginnings of anti-Semitism, Ovazza was still being rewarded for his patriotism. In 1935 he was honoured for his contribution to the colony of Libya and in the following year was invited to be part of the honour guard at the tomb of the royal family in Turin.

In 1938 a series of anti-Semitic laws were passed; the Ovazza family was hit hard. They were no longer allowed to marry 'Aryan' Italians, to send their children to state schools, to employ Italian servants or be in the army. Much more damaging were the rules that stated they could not employ more than 100 people, or own valuable land or buildings. This put an end to the Ovazza business and banking operations. Ettore Ovazza was expelled from the party and his brother from the military. In 1939 Jews were banned from all skilled jobs, and cafes in Turin displayed signs saying that Jews were no longer welcome. Jewish organisations were disbanded and many Jews converted to Catholicism or emigrated abroad. However, Ettore Ovazza accepted the racial laws without renouncing his faith. He was reluctant to leave the country, hoping that the Duce would alter his views. He wrote an anguished letter to Mussolini, expressing his pain:

> Was it all a dream we nurtured? I can't believe it. I cannot consider changing religion, because this would be a betrayal – and we are fascists. And so? I turn to You – DUCE – so that in this period – so important for our revolution, and you do not exclude that healthy Italian part from the destiny of our Nation.

The family began to live on savings and sales of possessions. Permission had to be asked to own a radio or take the family to the seaside. Yet, despite the growing danger, and the emigration of his brother, Ettore Ovazza kept his family in Italy.

RESOURCE  *Multiple-choice questions for group voting on social policies*

Reviewing the situation from the year 1939, circle your group answer and fill in your answer to the question underneath.

1 What has been the impact of Fascist policies on education and youth?

A Very beneficial **B** Generally positive **C** Made little difference **D** Generally negative

Did anyone in your group disagree? If so, why?

2 What has been the impact of Fascist policies on the Church?

A Very beneficial **B** Generally positive **C** Made little difference **D** Generally negative

Did anyone in your group disagree? If so, why?

3 What has been the impact of Fascist policies on women?

A Very beneficial **B** Generally positive **C** Made little difference **D** Generally negative

Did anyone in your group disagree? If so, why?

 © HODDER EDUCATION

- ***Spotlight on sport***
- Attempts to introduce new customs.

Stage 1: Spotlight on sport

There is a pervasive lack of coherence and consistency in Fascist policies on culture and leisure. This comes from muddled ideology, combined with a reluctance to risk unpopular restrictions and a willingness to accommodate institutions such as the Catholic Church and vocal groups such as artists and designers. Female sport is an ideal topic to highlight this.

(a) *The case of Ondina Valla*
Valla was the only Italian athlete to win gold at the Berlin Olympics. She had been forbidden to go to the Olympics in 1932, along with all the female athletic team, not because of the Fascist state but because of an edict of the Pope. There is a photo showing her leaping over a hurdle, an image which highlights the conflicting views of the Fascists towards women. The Fascists wanted their ladies at home with numerous children and wearing modest long skirts or dresses. But they also wanted their women to be physically strong and patriotic Fascists. Provide students with the life story of Valla (Resource 5L) and then ask them to make a judgement about the influences on Valla's career by writing their name on the triangular diagram on the board (Resource 5M).

(b) *Female sport*
Now provide students with the extract (Resource 5N) from De Grazia's book, *How Fascism Ruled Women*. Ask them to highlight statements which echo Valla's experience in one colour and statements which contradict her experience in another. Make this the basis for a class discussion of how far Valla's life story can be used to make general conclusions. This will lead naturally to the next task.

(c) *Fascist policy on sport*
Broaden this out to a more complete survey of Fascist policy on sports, including boxing and football, with a focus on (i) aims, (ii) consistency, (iii) success. Set this as a homework research task, encouraging careful use of the Internet, which has lots of information about Italy's victories in the football World Cup and their impact at home.

Stage 2: Voting and discussion

Finally, return to the problem of making general judgements. Organise your classroom into four main groups, each focusing on one of the policy areas listed at the start of this activity. Ask students to sit at a policy table that they consider would have affected their character particularly strongly, and even out the groups if they end up unbalanced. Students fill in the summary chart (Resource 5O) on their policy area and, as a group, put their policy on the success/failure line (Resource 5P), justifying their decision to the rest of the class. Display the diagram on the board and discuss the results.

Stage 3: Written task

This time focus attention on writing coherent paragraphs. Set the essay title: 'How far did the Fascists achieve their aims in their control of culture and leisure?'

- Using the PEGEX formula of writing paragraphs (see Figure 5.7 and Harris, 2001: 16), ask students to write a model paragraph within the essay which considers whether Fascist policies on sport were successful.
- With students working in threes, ask one to write the P, the next to write the EG and the third to write the EX.
- Ask them then to merge the three together and improve each other's contributions as they do so. Make explicit that this 'paragraph sandwich' is building on the theme of general and specific writing already addressed in this module.

Figure 5.7 *PEGEX paragraphs*

Students can be helped to write well structured paragraphs using the following formula:

1. Start the paragraph with a Point which relates directly to the question asked.
2. Follow up with Examples (EG) illustrating the point.
3. Finish off with an EXplanation which develops and qualifies the point.

Summary of ideas in Harris (2001: 15–16)

Activity 5

Fascist economic policy

Mini question:

How much impact did Fascist economic policy have on the Italian people?

Many students regard economic policy as the driest aspect of their studies. Putting their character at the centre of their work on this topic will help to engage them more. Organise your students into teams, broadly around the kinds of employment on their character cards (agriculture, public service, manufacturing, and so on). Divide the economy into the main themes outlined, starting with autarky.

Summary of key economic policy areas

- ***Spotlight on autarky***
- The Corporate State: its aims, main features and effects on the economy
- The nature and extent of state intervention in the economy: de Stefani's laissez-faire approach, the management of the depression and the drive to rearmament
- The impact of economic policy on living standards: welfare, taxation, consumption, prices and wages.

RESOURCE  *Real lives in Fascist Italy*

Ondina Valla

Trebisonda Valla was born in 1916 in a village near Bologna, where her father was the local blacksmith. She was the youngest of five children, having four older brothers. She was naturally athletic and liked to copy her older brothers, who were keen high jumpers. Spotted by the local Fascist Party secretary, she was given special training and took part in her first athletics competition aged 11. In 1929 she won fifth place in both high jump and long jump at an international athletics meeting and in the following year she was the Italian record holder for both hurdles and high jump. However, in 1932 the Italian women's team were forbidden by the Pope to take part in the Olympic Games in Los Angeles, a big disappointment for Valla. The Church was disapproving of female sport because it was thought to encourage sensuality. Some experts had suggested it affected female fertility and others stated that it encouraged lesbianism. Light and graceful physical exercise was recommended for young women instead. Valla's family, however, continued to support her training and she was able to compete despite religious disapproval and lack of official encouragement.

While the Fascist state had been generally encouraging of female health and fitness, their main priority in competitive sport was the male teams. However, in the 1936 Olympics the only athletics gold medal was won by Valla (now nicknamed 'Ondina', which means little wave), in the 80 metres hurdles. The women's team consisted of only seven women but they also won fourth place in the 80 metres hurdles and in the 4 x 100 metres relay. Their victory was celebrated in the national press and they were greeted as heroines on their return home. On her return from Berlin, Valla dedicated her victory to the fatherland and to the achievements of female Italian sport. The success in the Berlin Olympics altered the views of Fascist commentators, who now came round to the idea that competitive sport was healthy and did not contradict Fascist ideals of womanhood. Even the Pope congratulated Valla on her success.

Valla continued to compete until the early 1940s, when she developed back problems. There had been rumours about her sexual orientation, so when she married and had a baby, there were numerous photos in the press of her with her baby to disprove these claims.

 © HODDER EDUCATION

RESOURCE 5M *Which were the biggest influences on Valla's career?*

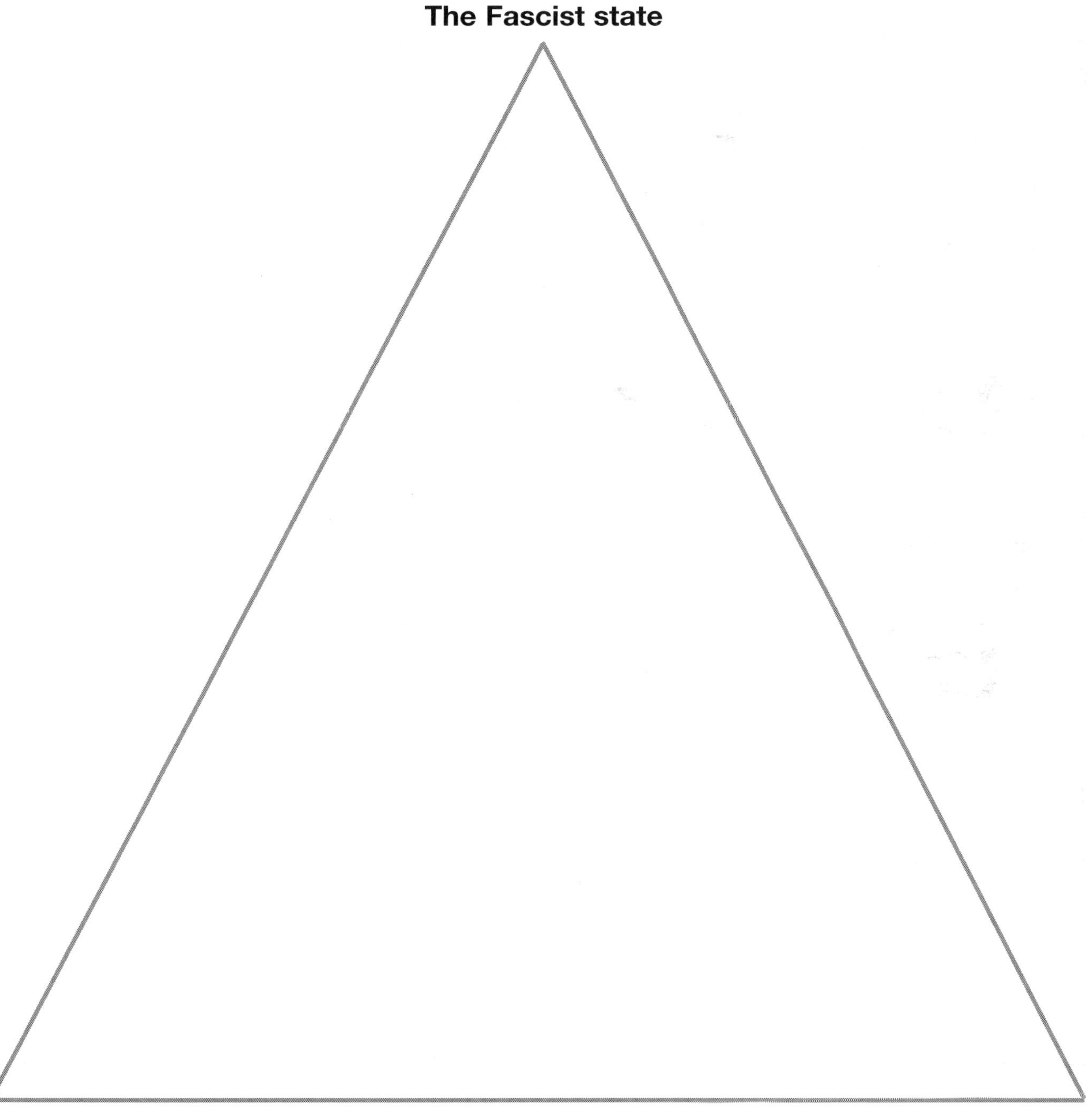

RESOURCE  *De Grazia's assessment of Fascist policy on female sport*

Initially, fascist sports promoters were enthusiastic about female participation; modernity meant sports for women as well as for men. Sports policy thus contemplated women's involvement in the fascist recreational clubs and youth groups. By 1930, however, faced on the one hand with Church protests and on the other hand with the threat that women would treat sports as a step towards emancipation, the regime backed off. In the 1930s, it promoted instead a highly regulated, medicalized model of physical culture for women. ...

By the mid 1920s, Catholic modernizers, Father Gemelli in the lead, endorsed promoting 'a Catholic gymnastics' and in 1923, under the leadership of Professor Teresa Costa, the Gioventu femminile began forming 'Strength and Grace' sections. But this 'feminine' version, as Gemelli specified, meant 'no shorts, no athleticism, and above all no competition with men's sports'. Its ultimate purpose was to form 'good, Christian mothers who were physically and morally healthy, hence capable of creating a generation of equally good and healthy Italians'. This development was cut short, however, when on April 9, 1928, the fascist government banned all non-fascist sports groups. Shortly thereafter Pius X1, alarmed at the rapid growth of the fascist sports movement after 1926 and outraged at public parades of girl athletes in the Holy City, condemned fascism's moral sensibility as 'weaker' than that of pagan Rome and, possibly, of 'the even more corrupt' towns of ancient Greece.

Pius's fulminations worked, but perhaps only because fascist officials themselves suspected that women's sports lowered birth rates and fostered promiscuous behaviour. On October 16, 1930, the fascist Grand Council undertook a much-bruited [well publicised] reassessment of sports politics. The stated purpose was not to rule against female gymnastics and physical education, which it claimed to accept, but to scrutinize female 'athleticism' meaning competitive sports. Out of a desire to avoid public polemics, the Grand Council in effect medicalized the problem by ordering the head of the Italian National Olympic Committee (CONI), in consultation with the National Federation of Sports Doctors, to determine activities appropriate for women. The main principle to guide them was that 'nothing distract women from her fundamental mission: MATERNITY'...

The rules governing women's sports were thus part positivist physiology, part Catholic prudery, the whole well dosed with fascist opportunism. Females, current medical opinion insisted, were starkly different from males of the species. From their brains to their bones, they were products and prisoners of their reproductive systems, which were the basis of their social roles and the source of their most common ailments. Physical recreation, if properly administered, ensured the gracefulness that made women attractive, perhaps increased their longevity, and helped, or at least did not hinder, their reproductive performance. Ultimately childbirth was the best exercise, of course, and all physical culture was to facilitate that purpose.

By the mid 1930s, a host of rules, injunctions, and customs distinguished women's sports from men's 'in all circumstances and at every event'. As the ONB head Renato Ricci specified, this meant 'separate itineraries, events, hours, days and personnel, which should only be female'. Budgets too were separate, he might have added. Women travelled to meets second class, while male athletes and their trainers went first class. So-called male games, in particular soccer, were discouraged; with trepidation Arpinati acquiesced to the formation of a single 'woman's soccer group' at Milan, on the condition that it never play in public. Lest girl athletes caused public scandal, the Italian Field and Track Association ordered that female members 'never for any reason go outside the sports field without putting on long pants and keeping them on until their event began. ... Not the least of the sports trainers' duties was to stand guard lest the female friendships encouraged in the name of team camaraderie degenerate into lesbian relationships.

The effects of this fascist-promoted female sports culture were far-reaching. Far more young women practiced [sic] sports of some kind than ever before. On fascist Saturdays in the 1930s, school groups massed for callisthenics and parade routines. For the first time, there were regional and national competitive meets in track and field, basketball and swimming. ... Women's journals followed international and local sporting events, treating the feats of Amelia Earhart and other women as accomplishments on behalf of their sex.

De Grazia, V. (1992) How Fascism Ruled Women: Italy, 1922–1945, *pp. 219–20*

 © HODDER EDUCATION

RESOURCE 5O *Summary review of leisure, culture and propaganda*

● **Policy area ....**

1. What were the key aims?

2. In what ways did they fail?

3. In what ways did they succeed?

4. Which character in our group would have been most affected by this policy and in what way?

RESOURCE 5P *How successful were Fascist policies on leisure, culture and propaganda?*

Total triumph

Neutral

Complete failure

Position these items on the continuum: OND | Propaganda | Arts | Sport | New customs

Stage 1: Spotlight on autarky

In their employment teams, students complete the forms recording general points on the aims and impact of autarky alongside its impact on their own lives (Resource 5Q). As a group at the end they need to assess the influence of autarky on their aspect of the economy. They can then feed this back to the class as the basis for a structured class discussion on the effectiveness of the policy.

Stage 2: Voting and discussion

As homework, prepare your students by asking them to consider how Fascist economic policy would have affected their character and how their fortunes in 1939 would have differed from their position in 1922 when the Fascists first came to power.

At the start of the lesson, take them through the life of Antonio Origo (Resource 5R). Then get them out their seats and ask them to line up from the one who has benefited the most from Fascist government to the one who has gained the least. Take on the role of Antonio Origo yourself and ask them to place him in their line. This should cause some lively discussion and require them to make comparisons about the standard of living between the real and fictional characters. When you have reached consensus, number the students/characters from the one who has benefited the most to the one who has suffered the most under Fascism and ask them to note it on their record sheet (Resource 5S).

Stage 3: Written task

Make conclusions the focus for this written task. Set the question: 'How far did the Fascist government fulfil its aims in economic policy?'

- Ask students in pairs to think of the key ingredients of a strong conclusion to this essay. Remind them once more of the theme of this module and to think about how their judgements might demonstrate linking, ranking and qualification of their views.
- Give them the two concluding paragraphs from the textbooks (Resource 5T) and ask them to consider their strengths and weaknesses, highlighting the features on their checklists (Resource 5Q).
- Having studied the two conclusions, now ask them to write their own.

Activity 6

Fascist foreign policy

Mini question:

What was the impact of Fascist foreign policy on the Italian people?

Summary of key areas

- Fascist foreign policy in the 1920s, including Fiume, Corfu, Albania and the Locarno Pacts
- Diplomacy in the early 1930s, including Four Power Pact, Stresa Front, attempted Anschluss
- ***Spotlight on the Abyssinian War***
- Involvement in the Spanish Civil War, 1936–39
- Partnership with Germany1936–39, including the Axis, Anti-Comintern Pact, the Anschluss, the Czech Crisis and the Pact of Steel.

Stage 1: Spotlight on the Abyssinian War, 1935

(a) Start with a brisk review of the historical background, the reasons for the war and the key events during the war. Then divide the class in two and give half the extract from Arrichiello (Resource 5U) and half the passage from Levi (Resource 5V). As the extracts are long, you could set this as homework.

Both these characters were based in the south of Italy, but in very different contexts. Arrichiello was one of a large working-class family in Naples, while Levi was a socialist, sent into exile in a tiny mountain village. Their contrasting responses to the war once again highlight the problems of generalisation while also demonstrating some common points.

After they have read their extract carefully, ask students to fill in their part of the chart (Resource 5W).

(b) Once back in the classroom, pair students up and ask them to exchange their points and suggest reasons why the two commentators might differ.

(c) Broaden their knowledge by using a combination of video (relevant clip from the BBC's *Road to War: Italy*) and textbooks to gain an overview of the causes, key developments and effects of the war.

(d) Ask students to go back to their character roles in the year 1935 on the outbreak of war and to line up in front of one of four options displayed on A4 posters:

1. Volunteer to fight
2. Enlist willingly when asked to do so
3. Avoid conscription as far as possible
4. Oppose the war.

If they are the wrong age or gender to join in the war themselves, ask them to go with what they would advise a male relative of fighting age to do.

Sitting in groups, students can now fill in the analysis of their group (Resource 5X), ready to feed back into the class discussion. Set up a chart on the board to record their numbers and then use this as the basis for analysis of class and regional differences in reactions to the war.

Stage 2: Written task

Pose the question: 'How successful was Mussolini's foreign policy?'

- This time focus on writing a good introduction to an essay. Think up a range of possible foreign policy questions such as those shown in Figure 5.8 and number them. Give your students five minutes to write an introduction on a piece of paper with the number of the question but not the question itself.

RESOURCE 5Q *Spotlight on autarky*

Complete this form by explaining how the policy of autarky affected your character and others working in the same area.

Aims	Policies	Impact on your character
• To reduce dependence on foreign imports	• Protectionism: tariffs on imports • Production of substitutes, e.g. rayon for cotton • Search for new sources, e.g. AGIP set up to find oil	
• To boost domestic production of basic raw materials	• Government sponsored Battle for Grain and land reclamation	
• To find new or alternative sources of materials	• Production of substitutes, e.g. rayon for cotton • Search for new sources, e.g. AGIP set up to find oil	
How has this policy affected your character's team?		

RESOURCE  *Real lives in Fascist Italy*

Antonio Origo

Origo was born in 1892, the illegitimate son of a cavalry officer, Marchese Clemente Origo, who had run off with the Russian-born wife of an Italian duke. His parents married in 1899 but he was only formally recognised as his father's son in 1921. As a result, he spent a large part of his childhood in a Swiss boarding school and he was only allowed home for one holiday a year. He worked for a bank and a champagne firm before the outbreak of war, when he served in the Italian cavalry. In 1922 Antonio met his future wife, Iris Cutting, and was able, with funds from her family, to buy a small landed estate in Tuscany in the following year. The house and estate were in poor condition, having been left derelict for many years and there was no electricity, telephone or bathroom.

The traditional system in Italy at that time was for the landlord to keep the land and houses in a good state and to provide half of everything needed to farm the land. In return, the peasant farmers contributed half of their produce to their landlord. Antonio Origo's estate involved 200 people, many very poor because of the infertile and arid nature of the land.

In 1921 Mussolini had reassured landowners that their property would be respected and had promised to support farming. Despite knowing little about farming or estate management, the Origos set about improving their property and supporting their tenants.

In the first five years after buying the estate, Origo made major improvements. New roads were built, over 30 new farmhouses were constructed, as well as many bridges and dykes. New methods were used to improve irrigation, such as diverting water from the River Orcia and sinking artesian wells. Trees were planted and new machinery such as tractors and bulldozers were bought. The Origos took advantage of government grants for many of these schemes, although they had to pay for much of it themselves, including the introduction of telephones and electricity. The estate became prosperous and, with the help of a family inheritance, Origo was able to buy an adjoining estate of over 2000 acres in the mid 1930s.

The director of the Agricultural Institute in Florence, who was also the Under Secretary of State for Agriculture, Professor Serpieri, took a great interest in the improvements made by Antonio Origo and was a frequent visitor to the estate. He was in charge of the implementation of the Bonifica Integrale (Battle for the Marshes) and encouraged local landowners to form a consortium to promote good land use in the area. Antonio Origo was named president of the consortium and retained the position for 40 years. In 1932 he was mentioned by name in the Council of Delegates in Rome.

Antonio Origo was never interested in politics and liked to spend nearly all his time and effort on his family estate. In a speech to the Academy in Florence he said:

> I am not a technician, and I am not an academic. I am simply a passionate and amateur farmer, who at a certain moment in my life, perhaps the most romantic as it coincided with my marriage, experienced the eternal fascination that comes from the earth, and who wished to make of this, and of those people eking out their lives from the earth, the object of my life's work.

However, there is no doubt that he had benefited greatly from Fascist agricultural policies, especially government grants for machinery, land drainage and grain production. Photographs show that when Fascist officials visited, Origo wore a Fascist black shirt. When Origo met Mussolini personally at a diplomatic party, he discussed his farming plans with the Duce with enthusiasm.

In 1925 the couple had a little boy, Gianni, and in the 1940s two daughters were born. Sadly, Gianni caught meningitis while on a family holiday to Switzerland and died, aged only 7. When war broke out, Antonio Origo was called up and served in the army. After the war he returned to farm the estate once more. He died in 1976.

Information taken from Moorehead, C. (2000) Iris Origo, Marchesa of Val d'Orcia

 © HODDER EDUCATION

RESOURCE 5S *The differing impact of Fascist economic policies on the people of Italy*

How far had Fascist economic policy made Italians better off by 1939?

Circle your character's position on the line in red.

Circle the position of Antonio Origo in green.

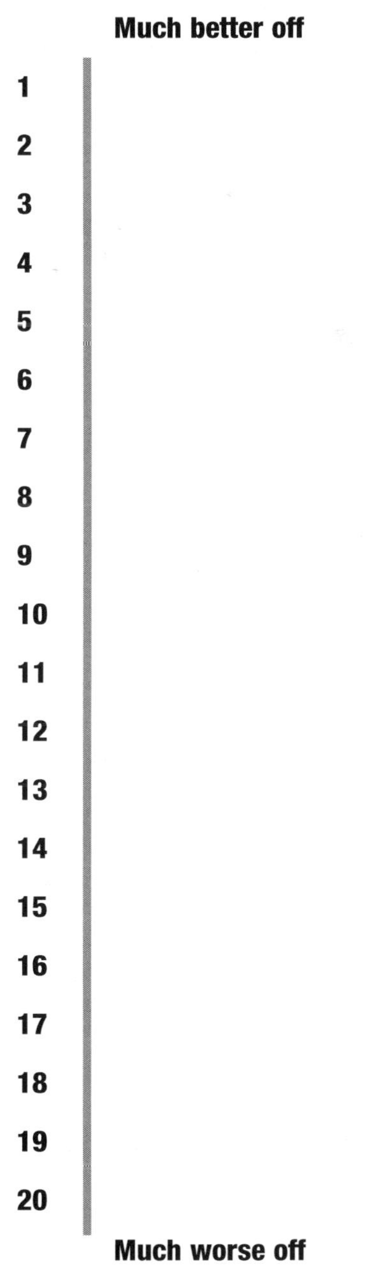

RESOURCE 5T *Textbook assessments of the success of Fascist economic policy*

Read these paragraphs carefully and highlight strengths in one colour and weaknesses in another, using the checklist you have made.

Source 1

Overall, there was precious little transformation of the Italian economy and this was apparent at the time. As de Grand points out, 'large numbers of Italians understood (by the 1930s) that Fascism lacked any real commitment to economic change'. Nevertheless, it is important to point out that despite Fascism's failures the development of Italian industry and agriculture up to 1940 was not disastrous. Output did increase in both agriculture and industry, and big companies did well. In the field of communications, Fascism made real progress, building *autostrade* [motorways], electrifying 5000 kilometres of railway line, and improving the efficiency of the railway system. On the other hand, it should be remembered that such improvements were made principally for propaganda purposes and Italy remained relatively backward compared to Germany, France and Britain.

Robson, R. (2006) Italy: The Rise of Fascism, *p. 92*

Source 2

To what extent did Fascism fulfil these [economic] aims? The clear answer is that it failed to do so monumentally. The Corporate State became nothing more than a propaganda exercise which masked the exploitation of workers. Whilst Mussolini never gave up his belief in state intervention as a modernising force, the intervention which took place had only very limited impact on the direction of Italian economic development. It failed to address Italy's structural problems, lacked clarity, did not integrate workers into the economic (or political) system and, whilst setting boundaries to industrial growth, allowed capitalist enterprises a relatively free hand within those boundaries to pursue their own profit. Mussolini's obsessions with an economic policy that would sustain foreign policy adventures finally dominated all other objectives, and ultimately failed to achieve its goals.

This is not to say there were no achievements. Rather it is to assess them as achievements on a small scale, compared to the betrayal of the apparent radical objectives of the Corporate State and the ultimate failure of the Italian economy to sustain the unrealistic demands that Mussolini's foreign policy placed upon it.

Whittock, M. (1998) Mussolini in Power, *p. 30*

 © HODDER EDUCATION

RESOURCE  *Real lives in Fascist Italy*

Cosimo Arrichiello

Cosimo Arrichiello was born in June 1920 and was only two years old when Mussolini came to power. He was one of a large working-class family growing up on the outskirts of Naples. As job opportunities were so poor in the area, Cosimo's father worked abroad for long periods, sending the family money to live on. Despite this the family were very overcrowded with four children sharing a one-bedroom flat with their parents. It was only in 1928, when the family now had ten children, that they were able to move to a two-bedroom flat. While Cosimo was indoctrinated in Fascist values at school, Catholic teachings and practices were also a big influence on his childhood and the family took part in all the traditional parades, saint's days and services organised by their local church. He was also able to afford occasional trips to the cinema, where he saw Hollywood films which portrayed America as a rich land of opportunity.

Although three of the children and Cosimo's father suffered serious illnesses, requiring expensive medical care, all but one of the family survived the war. Cosimo served in the army and at the end of hostilities emigrated to Indonesia.

Arrichiello on the Abyssinian War

From about the end of 1934, the Fascists began reminding us of Italy's abortive attempt to conquer Abyssinia at the end of the nineteenth century. At that time a force of twenty thousand men under the command of General Barettieri was sent there. They had been greatly outnumbered by Abyssinian warriors and had suffered heavy losses – in fact eight thousand of our soldiers were massacred at Adowa. As a result of this disaster, Italy had to give up all hope of conquering that country.

Feeling strong and bold now, the Fascists revived the Abyssinian question. They said they wanted to avenge the deaths of those Italian 'heroes'. The Fascist campaign gradually spread throughout the whole of Italy and aroused nationalistic feelings which took people's minds away from their domestic tribulations.

The campaign continued persistently and tried to persuade us that, by conquering Abyssinia, thousands of kilometres away, we were going to enjoy a better standard of living some time in the future. Besides this, our military achievement, they said, would enhance our prestige in the eyes of other countries.

During 1935 the British and the French, especially, were determined to thwart Mussolini's ambition to conquer Abyssinia. However, he defiantly went ahead and made preparations to invade. He called to arms thousands of men in their late twenties and early thirties who had already served as conscripts.

Vast numbers of unemployed men volunteered to join the army. They received twenty lira per day. At that time it was equivalent to the daily pay of a skilled worker. These men wore impressive uniforms and, while waiting to embark for Africa, swaggered round our towns, squandering their money in restaurants, bars, cinemas and brothels. They certainly put on a good show. They seemed jolly, handsome, prosperous and full of vitality.

The poor wretched men who had to toil long and hard for a crust of bread envied these young, flamboyant soldiers bound for Africa. Unfortunately only those who were very fit were eligible to join them.

In the afternoon of 2nd October, 1935, sirens wailed all over Italy, as if we were expecting a huge air attack. Guns of warships anchored in the harbour of Naples boomed and military aircraft flew overhead. People in the streets, alarmed and surprised, scattered in all directions. These were signals of which we had been warned days and weeks previously. When this happened, Blackshirts and the rest of the Italian population were to assemble in the main squares of our towns and listen by radio to what Mussolini had to tell them.

The dictator was eloquent and full of bluster as he delivered his historic speech from the famous Venice Palace in Rome. He announced to the crowd gathered there that the Abyssinian conflict had begun, and that the economic sanctions applied against Italy would not deter him from carrying on with his great military campaign.

People had no choice but to put up with the dictator's decisions; nobody would dare to oppose him. So he decided and went ahead, fully convinced that whatever he did was right and undisputed.

About a quarter of a million soldiers were sent abroad to fight the costly Abyssinian war. Wives and mothers were seriously concerned for the safety of their husbands and sons, and prayed fervently that the war would not end in tragedy as the Italian campaign of 1896 had done.

I was visiting some friends in Naples that day when the sirens wailed and the warships guns' boomed. I saw hundreds of people who, having stopped work, were hurrying through streets and lanes or jumping on public transport, trying to get home as quickly as possible.

I had never witnessed such an event before – it was a kind of stampede – I was awe-struck. I was fifteen when this occurred and was a member of the Fascist organisation called the *Avanguardista* (avant – gardist). Soon after the wailing of the sirens, I was supposed to be wearing my *Avanguardista* uniform and playing a drum on one of the street corners of our town. The drum had been lent to me by the Fascists a couple of weeks before this day of national upheaval. I was very angry indeed because, when the alarm came, I was in Naples, and unable to play my part in that historic and dramatic hour.

I caught the tram to go home, but most of the trams were very old, only fit for the scrap heap. It was impossible to make them go fast, especially when passengers were packed in like sardines. The tram coughed, spat, got all worked up and hardly made any progress. I almost foamed with rage and frustration. How could I get home quickly, wear my black shirt and join my comrades? The tram moved along like a snail, especially when it was toiling uphill; then it had to stop several times, because its motor protested with sporadic bangs and then refused to budge.

'The bloody tram has had it,' shouted a number of exasperated passengers. 'Let's push it, otherwise we won't be able to get home.'

Besides the appalling performance of our tram, the main road was heavily congested with traffic. I could hardly control my anger. I yearned to be in uniform and play my drum, which would have made me feel important. *Il Duce* certainly needed my support, and he was telling us that the war with Abyssinia had begun.

It took the tram over an hour to get to the vicinity of my home. It reached a town called Miano and could not proceed any further. I got off and ran the kilometre or so to my home. I was gasping for breath, my chest ached, my lungs were on the verge of bursting. The main street, Corso Umberto Primo, which ran alongside our two balconies, was crammed with Blackshirts gathered behind their flags and pennants. They were still listening to *Il Duce*'s speech on the radio when I arrived at my house. Mother let me in, but she was very concerned when she noticed that I was puffing and gasping for breath like an asthmatic.

'What's the matter with you? Are you sick?' she asked.

'No, I'm not,' I replied, but I was still breathing with difficulty. 'I've been running.'

'Sit down, have a rest,' she ordered me. I obeyed.

Having rested for a minute or two, I rushed to the wardrobe, but my uniform and drum were missing!

'The Fascists were looking for you,' Mother said, 'but you weren't here, so your brother Tony put on your uniform and took the drum with him.'

I was furious for being late and resentful towards Tony. Previously I had never allowed him to wear my uniform – he could not even touch it; but now he was swaggering in it, while I badly wanted to wear it. Still seething with rage, I rushed downstairs, went out in the street and searched for Tony in the dense crowd. After a few minutes I found him, seized him by his arm and dragged him home.

'Hurry up,' I shouted menacingly. He meekly obeyed, for he knew that when I was in a fit of temper, I wouldn't hesitate to treat him roughly. I dressed up rapidly and soon felt as if I were a general or *Il Duce*'s second-in-command.

In no time I was among my comrades who were still gathered in the main street, and in unison with them I shouted, '*Viva Il Duce!*' (Hail the Duce!)'. We sang Fascist songs. Later our superiors, dressed in flamboyant uniforms, packed us into trams which took us to the city of Naples. Once there we marched a couple of kilometres and showed our patriotic feelings by praising *Il Duce* and singing. We endeavoured to make an impression on a poor and densely populated section of Naples.

I returned home late, exhausted, hungry and with a raucous voice. I wolfed down the frugal supper which Mother had kept warm for me in the oven and then I went to bed. I dreamed of our majestic Duce – in his dictatorial pose – on the balcony of the Venice Palace and hailed by the crowd on the square below. They boisterously acclaimed our attack on Abyssinia. Was it perhaps the first step forward towards that greatness the Fascists and *Il Duce* so badly wanted?

During the following days, weeks and months the attention of the Italians was devoted to the progress of the war. Most people seldom bought a newspaper but when there was exciting news from the front, the sales of our daily shot up dramatically. We ourselves did not buy the newspaper; we learned about the news from what we overheard by chance, or from what we could gather from newspapers on display outside newsagents' shops. Everybody, literate or illiterate, was interested in the news.

Newspaper vendors shouted at the top of their voices about our military successes such as the capture of an Abyssinian town, the surrender of a large Abyssinian army unit and so on. Victory after victory boosted our morale. People were jubilant that our armies, under the command of Generals Badoglio and Graziani, were making great progress. Everybody, Fascist or not, became patriotic overnight. They praised the army, our generals and *Il Duce* who was the promoter of the campaign.

Wherever I went, people were enthusiastic about our victories. Students saluted every major military feat by walking out of their classrooms or university lecture halls, assembling and staging patriotic demonstrations through the main streets of our cities.

The Italians could not be indifferent – all those

 © HODDER EDUCATION

victories seemed too good to be true. Under this influence, patriotism mounted very high. Who could perceive or envisage that about seven years after the glorious and costly Abyssinian campaign, our patriotism and all our military achievements would end in ruins?

While our army was doing well in Abyssinia, Mussolini was overjoyed and had something to boast about. No doubt he thought that we were invincible, and adequately equipped to avenge the loss of the Roman Empire about fifteen hundred years before.

When the Italian Army attacked Abyssinia, the League of Nations applied economic sanctions against Italy, and we had to pay in gold to get military supplies through the Suez Canal. Bearing this in mind, the Fascists organised a ritual ceremony called 'Gold to the Fatherland'. They assembled with their brass bands, flags and banners in front of the Town Halls, where married women paraded ceremoniously. As they did so, one by one, they took their gold wedding rings off their fingers and proudly donated them to the fatherland. We all applauded their patriotic gesture and were deeply touched by it. They had given to their country what was precious to them – a symbol of love, fidelity and devotion to their husbands and families. In exchange, they obtained rings made of base metal.

On the 5th May, 1936, after a campaign of seven months and three days, Marshal Badoglio, who had been promoted from general presumably as a reward for his victorious campaign, entered Addis Ababa triumphantly. This brought about the conclusion of the Abyssinian war. There was a great national celebration all over our country. *Il Duce* spoke again to the dense crowd amassed on the square below Venice Palace. He stated categorically: 'The Italian people have conquered an empire with their blood. They will be prepared to defend it against anybody.'

After the Abyssinian war, the Fascists became more arrogant and boisterous: it looked as if they were ready to challenge the whole world. The misery of poor people increased, the cost of living went up, while wages and salaries were static. Sicknesses raged, afflicting downtrodden workers who could hardly provide themselves with basic necessities. They were supposed to look after their large families, but how could they do so without nourishing food and free medical assistance? Since they could not afford to buy good food and medical care, mortality, especially among young people and elderly people, was alarming. We had few modern hospitals; hardly any new ones were built. The conditions of our people were ignored, yet Mussolini was wasting our meagre resources on Abyssinia. We conquered a white elephant which made us feel great, but left us with empty hands; our treasury was in dire financial straits. At the end of the war it was costing us a fortune to keep an army there. Most of our colonies seemed to be nothing but liabilities, yet the Fascist propaganda made us wallow in a false glory which could only aggravate our misery.

Arrichiello, C. (2000) Italian Heartbreak: Life Under Mussolini, *pp. 114–19*

RESOURCE 5V Real lives in Fascist Italy

Carlo Levi

Levi was from a wealthy Jewish family in Turin. He went to university in his home town, graduating with a degree in medicine in 1924. Instead of working as a doctor, he took up painting and became involved in Socialist politics. In 1929 he was one of the founding members of Justice and Liberty, an anti-Fascist organisation. In the mid-1930s he was arrested and sentenced to *confino* – exile to a remote village in southern Italy. There he recorded his experiences while painting and acting as an unofficial doctor. After the war he published his memoir of his life in exile: *Christ Stopped at Eboli*, which was an immediate bestseller.

Levi on the Abyssinian War

Levi describes the peasants' reaction to the outbreak of war in 1935:

> So the 'fellows in Rome' wanted war and left it up to the peasants to do the fighting? All well and good. It couldn't be much worse to die in an Abyssinian desert than to perish from malaria in a pasture by the Sauro river. It seemed that schoolchildren and their teachers, Fascist scouts, Red Cross ladies, the widows and mothers of Milanese veterans, women of fashion in Florence, grocers, shopkeepers, pensioners, journalists, policemen and government employees in Rome, in short, all those generally grouped together under the name of the 'Italian people', were swept off their feet by a wave of glory and enthusiasm. Here in Gagliano I could see nothing. The peasants were quieter, sadder, and more dour than usual. They had no faith in a promised land which had first to be taken away from those to whom it belonged; instinct told them that this was wrong and could only bring ill luck. The 'fellows in Rome' didn't usually put themselves out on their behalf and this latest undertaking, in spite of all the fuss made over it, must have a remote purpose in which they had no part.
>
> 'If they had money enough for a war, why don't they repair the bridge across the Agri which has been down for four years without anyone moving a finger to fix it? They might make a dam to provide us with more fountains, or plant young trees instead of cutting down the few that are left. We've plenty of land right here, but nothing to go with it.'
>
> War they considered just another inevitable misfortune, like the tax on goats. They were not afraid to go; 'To live like dogs here or to die like dogs there is just the same,' they said. But no one except Donna Caterina's husband enlisted. It soon became clear that not only the purpose of the war, but the way it was being conducted as well, was the business of that other Italy beyond the mountains, and had little to do with the peasants. Only a few men were called up, two or three in the whole village, besides those who had reached the age for military service, and one other boy, Don Nicola, a priest's son, brought up by the monks of Melfi and a regular non-commissioned officer, who was one of the first to go. A few of the very poorest peasants, who had neither land of their own nor food to eat, were attracted by [the Fascist school master] Don Luigi's speeches and the promise of large salaries. They applied for manual labour as civilians but never received an answer. 'They don't know what to do with us,' those wretched fellows said to me. 'They don't even want us to work. The war is for the benefit of those in the north. We're to stay at home until we starve. And now there's no chance of going to America.'
>
> The third of October, which marked the official opening of the war, was a miserable sort of day. Twenty or twenty five peasants, roped in by the Carabinieri and the Fascist scouts, stood woodenly in the square to listen to the historical pronouncements that came over the radio. Don Luigi had ordered flags to be displayed over the town hall, the school, the houses of the well to do; their bright colours waving in the breeze made a strange contrast to the black death pennants on the doors of the peasants' huts.

Levi, C. (1947) Christ stopped at Eboli, *pp.131–32*

 © HODDER EDUCATION

RESOURCE 5W *Did Italians agree about the Abyssinian War?*

Aspect	Arrichiello	Levi	Agree/ Disagee	Ideas about why this might be the case
Causes of the war				
The community's reaction				

RESOURCE  *Group response to the Abyssinian War*

Circle your decision.

Our group decided to:

- volunteer
- enlist when required
- avoid conscription
- oppose the war

The number in our group is: ..../20

In our group: ... live in rural areas

... live in urban areas

In our group: ... live in the north

... live in central Italy

... live in southern Italy

In our group : ... are in agriculture

... are involved in industry

... other, such as:

....

....

 © HODDER EDUCATION

Figure 5.8 *Possible questions on foreign policy*

1. 'Successful in the 1920s, a failure in the 1930s'. Is this a fair assessment of Fascist foreign policy?
2. How far would you agree that involvement in the Spanish Civil War was Mussolini's biggest error?
3. To what extent do you agree that Mussolini's alliance with Germany was mutually beneficial?
4. How far did Mussolini achieve his aims in foreign policy?
5. How far would you agree that Fascist foreign policy helped the Fascist regime while damaging the Italian state?
6. To what extent was Mussolini's decision to invade Abyssinia in 1935 a key turning point in Fascist foreign policy?
7. How far would you agree that Mussolini's partnership with Germany was his only serious mistake in foreign policy?
8. 'Economically damaging but politically useful'. Is this a fair summary of Mussolini's conquest of Abyssinia?
9. 'The most serious effect of Mussolini's wars in the 1930s was to end all hopes of an alliance with France and Britain.' How far do you agree with this assessment of Mussolini's participation in the wars in Abyssinia and Spain?
10. How far do you agree that the success of Mussolini's diplomacy in the 1920s has been greatly underrated?

- Set them the task of matching the written introductions to the correct questions. This should help them clarify what makes a good introduction (see Figure 5.9).
- Now ask them to write a perfect introduction to the question above in a maximum of five minutes and share the best examples.

Figure 5.9 *What makes a good introduction?*

- Clearly focusing on the key words and issues in the question, showing that they have been understood
- Being concise
- Indicating the main areas which will be covered in the answer

Activity 7

Are the methods of microhistorians useful for learning history?

As preparation, divide the class into seven and give two or three students one of the real-life characters studied in this module to read over and reflect on for homework. Ask them to return to the general question about how much Fascist policies influenced the character's life and be prepared to talk in that role to the rest of the class.

Numbering the students 1 or 2, prepare a hot seat and roll a dice to determine which student has to speak. Ask them to go in the hot seat for 'Just a Minute' as if they were in 1939, reflecting on how Fascist rule changed their lives over the last 17 years. Focusing on three or four of the life stories, rather than all seven, will stop the class getting restless.

At this stage review the problems of moving from individual to group and then the national experience and discuss how these relate to Fascist Italy.

Now set the summative essay: 'How far do you agree that Fascist rule had a positive impact on the lives of most Italians?'

Finally return to the big theme:

Is it possible to reach any general conclusions about the impact of Fascism on Italy in the years 1922–39?

Does the integration of the study of outliers during the module support or undermine the case of the postmodernists? Require your students to come up with a structured argument on this point by insisting on ten minutes' quiet reflection and recording of ideas. Finally return to the saved version of their original view (Resource 5C) and ask them to consider if they have changed their minds.

Sample lesson sequence

Rationale

The first and last activities focus on the broader issue raised by this module. The idea is to give students an intellectual challenge which will frame their factual studies. The five intervening activities enable the students to study key policy areas and the nature and extent of their impact on the Italian population. Of course, your study of the topic may require a broader range in time period or in topics but this model can easily be adapted to these needs. It is helpful in the lessons with voting if you can organise the students into their voting groups at the start by setting out the room appropriately and directing them to the right seats. This helps them to work as a group during the lesson and avoids time wasting.

Prior learning

Students will have had some introductory background lessons, giving them a basic grasp of Italian geography and economy as well as an understanding of the impact of the First World War. Most students will have studied Nazi Germany at some time and this can be used as a contrast.

Enquiry question

Is it possible to reach any general conclusions about the impact of Fascism on Italy in the years 1922–39?

Outline of learning flow

In my course this study unit is half a module or about six to seven weeks of teaching (around 30 hours). See Figure 5.10.

Figure 5.9 *Half a module*

Is it possible to reach any general conclusions about the impact of Fascism on Italy in the years 1922–39?	
Lesson 1 *Mini question:* Are postmodernist ideas useful for learning history?	Start with **Activity 1**, organising the introductory competition in advance, and introduce your first lesson with the winning students presenting their summaries. Follow up with the summary sheets on microhistory and a structured discussion of the links between them. Explain the rationale for the teaching of the module with the combination of personal and general approaches. Ask students to write their names on the line diagram setting the general question for this module.
Lessons 2–4 *Mini question:* What was the impact of Fascist politics on the Italian people? *Key character:* Gaetano Salvemini	Take the class through the background Fascist ideology and then the key events in the establishment of the Fascist state: the March on Rome and the Matteotti murder. At this stage, move on to **Activity 2** and agree the timeline of key events. Follow this up with the introduction of Salvemini and a debate about the year when the dictatorship was established. This is a useful way of drawing out the key features of a dictatorship and a critical assessment of whether Mussolini ever achieved this. Continue with the remaining political topics: Fascist control of the legal system and the use of the OVRA (secret police); the nature and extent of resistance; the limitations of Fascist power and the relationship with the monarchy; and the role of the Fascist party in the state. Set them the task of creating character cards as homework. Students will need to produce their characters in preparation for the voting session (stage 2) with the conjunction of Salvemini's views and the views of the fictional character. Follow this up with the group discussion, remembering to collect and copy the students' responses. Use this for your final formative essay task: 'How far had Mussolini's government won control of the Italian people by 1929?' and provide one-to-one feedback when marked.
Lessons 5–8 *Mini question:* What was the impact of Fascist social policies on the Italian people? *Key characters:* Wanda Newby and Ettore Ovazza	**Activity 3** fits in best at the end of your survey of social policies covering women, youth and the Church. Start off with the story of Wanda Newby, using this as the basis for drawing out ideas of insiders and outsiders in society. Follow this with independent research and note taking on anti-Semitism and finish off with the storyboard activity using the life of Ettore Ovazza. The video clip will help to bring his experience to life. In the plenary voting, group students/characters by age and make them vote together, to force a majority verdict. Finally, give them the essay plan to write, with the focus on ensuring breadth and balance in their coverage of the topic.
Lessons 9–11 *Mini question:* How much impact did Fascist policies on culture, leisure and propaganda have on Italian lives? *Key character:* Ondina Valla	Cover the major topics of this question first: Fascist propaganda and the cult of the Duce; the OND (leisure organisation) and its impact; and Fascist policies on culture and the arts. Introduce **Activity 4** with the case study of Ondina Valla, filling in the triangle diagram and discussing its significance. Next comes the comparison with the comments on female sport by De Grazia. Broaden the study to sport generally and complete the judgement exercise to remind students of the problems of moving from one experience to general judgements. Complete the study with an examination of the new customs introduced in the later 1930s. In the plenary voting, allow students to choose an aspect which affects their character and ask them to note down answers to the questions as a group. Put the chart (Resource 5P) on the board and ask students to record their group's view to provide an overview of the relative success and failure of each aspect of social policy. Finish off with the exercise on writing PEGEX paragraphs.

Lessons 12–14 *Mini question:* How much impact did Fascist economic policy have on the Italian people? *Key character:* Antonio Origo	Set up teams according to the students' fictional employment from the start and keep them in these groups throughout this topic. Introduce the main aims and problems of the Italian economy, the corporate state and the main phases of Fascist management of the economy through the 1920s and 1930s. Then introduce **Activity 5**, completing the study of autarky in the same groups. Follow this with a survey of how Fascist economic policy affected living standards. Introduce the character of Antonio Origo, explaining clearly which policies affected him and in what ways. Now finish off with the continuum line from the standpoint of 1939, making the class decide how their fictional characters' living standards might be affected and placing Origo in the line. The final written task is the comparison of textbook conclusions and the writing of their own.
Lessons 15–17 *Mini question:* What was the impact of Fascist foreign policy on the Italian people? *Key characters:* Carlo Levi and Cosimo Arrichiello	Cover the earlier period and the diplomacy which started in the 1930s. Provide a brief summary of the background to the Abyssinian War and then set the reading in **Activity 6** as a homework. Mix up pairs of students who have studied the contrasting scripts and complete Resource 4W. Use the video and textbooks to provide a factual overview. Now move students into character, requiring them to choose one of the four responses to the war. Get them to analyse their own group composition and record this on the board. Use this as the basis of discussion, drawing in the views of Levi and Arrichiello and contrasting their attitudes with other probable responses to the war. Complete the foreign policy module with a study of the Spanish Civil War and the German alliance. Finish off with the practice in writing introductions.
Lesson 18 Is it possible to reach any general conclusions about the impact of Fascism on Italy in the years 1922–39?	Introduce **Activity 7** by returning to the original theme at the start of the unit and remind students of issues raised by postmodernism and microhistory. Give them a real-life character to review and prepare their 'Just a Minute' talk. Hot seat several members of the group to remind them of the variety of personal experiences. Set the summative essay, reminding students to use all the materials from the module, including their real-life characters and notes from group discussions. Return to the main module question, asking students to reconsider their position on the line. Reintroduce the postmodernist position and allow enough time for a developed discussion using the module learning as a base.

Bibliography

Adams, T. (1 July 2007) 'For your information' in *The Observer*, an interview with Jimmy Wales, the co-founder of Wikipedia.

Anderson, D. (2002) *The Falklands War 1982*, Oxford: Osprey Publishing.

Anthony, K. (200) 'Were individual towns "death-traps"? Year 9 learn to question generalisations and to challenge their preconceptions about the "boring" 19th century', *Teaching History*, 135, *To 'they' or not to 'they' Edition*.

Arrichiello, C. (2000) *Italian Heartbreak: Life Under Mussolini*, London: Minerva Press.

Arthur, M. (2002) *Last Post: The Final World from our First World War Soldiers*, Weidenfeld & Nicolson. Audio CDs: (2007) Orion Publishing.

Badsey, S., Havers, R. and Grove, M. (eds) (2005) *The Falklands Conflict Twenty Years On: Lessons for the Future*, London: Routledge.

Banham, D. (2000) 'The return of King John: Using depth to strengthen overview in the teaching of political change', *Teaching History*, 99, *Curriculum Planning Edition*.

BBC News 'Churchill voted greatest Briton'. http://news.bbc.co.uk/1/hi/entertainment/tv_and_radio/2509465.stm

BBC News Online (Education). http://news.bbc.co.uk/1/hi/education/7311917.stm

Beilin, E. V. (ed.) (1996) *The Examinations of Anne Askew*, Oxford: Oxford University Press.

Bellinger, L. (2008) 'Cultivating curiosity about complexity: what happens when Year 12 start to read Orlando Figes' *The Whisperers*?', *Teaching History*, 132, *Historians in the Classroom Edition*.

Belshaw, D. and Dennis, N. (unpublished) 'Using podcasts, blogs, wikis and new media to solve learning problems', a workshop session at Schools History Project Conference, 2007 http://teaching.mrbelshaw.co.uk/index.php/2006/10/03/20-ideas-setting-up-a-teaching-and-learning-wiki/

Bereiter, C. and Scardamalia, M. (1987) *The Psychology of Written Composition*, Hillsdale, NJ: Lawrence Erlbaum Associates.

Bernard, G. (unpublished) 'When did England become a Protestant country?', talk to the Reading branch of the Historical Association given in 2005.

Biggs, J. and Tang, C. (2007) *Teaching for Quality Learning at University*, 3rd edn, Glasgow: Open University Press, p. 121.

Black, P. and Wiliam, D. (2001) 'Working inside the Black Box: assessment for learning in the classroom', London: King's College School of Education. Published online at: http://weaeducation.typepad.co.uk/files/blackbox-1.pdf

Blake, R. 'Winston Churchill the Historian', address to the International Churchill Societies, May 1988.

Booth, A. (2005) 'Worlds in collision: university tutor and student perspectives on the transition to degree level history', *Teaching History*, 121, *Transition Edition*.

Bosworth, R. J. B. (1998) *The Italian Dictatorship; Problems and Perspectives in the Interpretation of Mussolini and Fascism*, London: Arnold.

Bosworth, R. J. B. (2005) *Mussolini's Italy*, London: Allen Lane.

Bradshaw, M. (2009) 'Drilling down: how one history department is working towards progression in pupils' thinking about diversity across Years 7, 8 and 9', *Teaching History*, 135, *To 'they' or not to 'they' Edition*.

Bramley, V. (2006) *Forward into Hell*, London: John Blake Publishing.

Browning, C. R. (2001) *Ordinary Men: Reserve Police Battalion 101 and the Final Solution in Poland*, London: Penguin.

Browning, P. (2002) *The Changing Nature of Warfare: The Development of Land Warfare from 1792 to 1945*, Cambridge: Cambridge University Press.

Burleigh, M. (2001) *The Third Reich: A New History*, London: Pan Books.

Byrom, J. (1998) 'Working with sources: scepticism or cynicism? Putting the story back together again', *Teaching History*, 91, *Evidence and Interpretation Edition*, p. 32.

Cato, (1940) *Guilty Men*, London: Victor Gollanz.

Chapman, A. (2006) 'Asses, archers and assumptions: strategies for improving thinking skills in history in Years 9 to 13', *Teaching History*, 123, *Constructing History Edition*.

Charmley, J. (1989) *Chamberlain and the Lost Peace*, Chicago: Ivan R. Dee.

Churchill, W. (2005) *The Gathering Storm*, London: Penguin Classics. (First published 1948.)

Cohen, E. (1994) *Designing Groupwork: Strategies for the Heterogeneous Classroom*, New York: Teachers College Press.

Coman, P. (1999) 'Mentioning the War: does studying World War 11 make any difference to pupils' sense of British achievement and identity?', *Teaching History*, 96, *Citizenship and Identity Edition*.

Conway, R. (2006) 'What they think they know: the impact of pupils' preconceptions on their understanding of historical significance', *Teaching History*, 125, *Significance Edition*.

Cooksey, J. (2004) *3 Para Mount Longdon: The Bloodiest Battle*, Barnsley: Pen and Sword Books Ltd.

Corrigan, G. (2003) *Mud, Blood and Poppycock*, London: Cassell.

Counsell, C. (2000) Editorial, *Teaching History*, 100, *Thinking and Feeling Edition*.

Counsell, C. (2004) 'Looking through a Josephine Butler-shaped window: focusing pupils' thinking on historical significance', *Teaching History*, 114, *Making History Personal Edition*.

Counsell, C. (2004) *History and Literacy in Year 7: Building the Lesson Around the Text*, London: John Murray.

Cunningham, D. L. (2004) 'Empathy without illusions', *Teaching History*, 114, *Making History Personal Edition*.

Davies, R. (2006) 'Multiple Intelligences in the Classroom: An evaluation of the effectiveness of the "MI approach" through the teaching and learning of History', national teacher research panel, DFES.

Dawson, I. and Banham, D. (2002) 'Thinking from the inside: je suis le roi', *Teaching History*, 108, *Performing History Edition*.

Dawson, I. Thinking History website. www.thinkinghistory.co.uk/ActivityKS/ActivityALevel.html

De Grazia, V. (1992) *How Fascism Ruled Women: Italy, 1922–1945*, California: University of California Press.

Delarue, J. (1962) *History of the Gestapo*, New York: Paragon House Publishers, p. 86.

Dickens, A.G. (1964) *The English Reformation,* London: Batsford.

Dixon, N. (1994) *On the Psychology of Military Incompetence*, London: Pimlico. (First published 1976, Jonathan Cape.)

Duffy, E. (1992) *The Stripping of the Altars,* Yale University Press.

Edexcel GCE History Specification September 2007.

Feinberg, K. (2002) 'Big Paper: Building a Silent Conversation', Facing History and Ourselves www.facinghistory.org/resources/strategies/big-paper-building-a-silent-c

Fines, J. (1994) 'Evidence: the basis of the discipline?' in Bourdillon, H (ed.) *Teaching History,* London: Routledge, p. 125.

Finney, P. (2005) 'The romance of decline: the historiography of appeasement and British national identity', the *Electronic Journal of International History*, published by the Institute of Historical Research. Available online at: www.history.ac.uk/resources/e-journal-international-history/finney-paper

Fordham, M. (2007) 'Slaying dragons and sorcerers in Year 12: in search of historical argument', *Teaching History*, 109, *Disciplined Minds Edition*.

Foxe, J. (1563) *Book of Martyrs,* London: Ambassador (2002 edition).

Freedman, L. (2005) *The Official History of the Falklands Campaign*, Vol. II *War and Diplomacy*, London: Routledge.

Freeman, T.S. and Wall, S.E. (2001) 'Racking the body, shaping the text: The account of Anne Askew in Foxe's "Book of Martyrs"', *Renaissance Quarterly*, Vol. 54.

Gardner, H. (1993) 'Educating for understanding', *The American School Board Journal*, July 20–24, quoted in Biggs, J. and Tang, C. (2007) *Teaching for Quality Learning at University*, p. 40.

Gellately, R. (2001) *Backing Hitler: Consent and Coercion in Nazi Germany*, Oxford: Oxford University Press.

Gray, P. W. (2005) 'Air Power: Strategic Lessons for an Idiosyncratic Operation', in Badsey, S., Havers, R. and Grove, M. (eds) (2005) *The Falklands Conflict Twenty Years On: Lessons for the Future*, London: Routledge.

Grunberger, R. (1971) *A Social History of the Third Reich*, London: Penguin.

Haffner, S. (2002) *Defying Hitler: A Memoir*, London: Weidenfeld and Nicolson.

Hall, W. P. (1949) 'The Second World War: The Gathering Storm by Winston S Churchill' (book review), *The Journal of Modern History*, Vol. 21, No. 4 (Dec).

Hammond, K. (2001) 'From horror to history; teaching pupils to reflect on significance', *Teaching History*, 104, *Teaching the Holocaust Edition*.

Hammond, K. (2002) 'Getting Year 10 to understand the value of precise factual knowledge', *Teaching History*, 109, *Examining History Edition*.

Hammond, K. (2007) 'Teaching Year 9 about historical theories and methods', *Teaching History*, 128, *Beyond the Exam Edition*.

Harris, R. (2001) 'Why essay writing remains central to learning at AS Level', *Teaching History*, 103, *Puzzling History Edition*.

Harris, R. and Kitson, A. (2002) 'Basket weaving in Advanced level History: how to plan and teach the 100 year study', *Teaching History*, 109, *Examining History Edition*.

Hart-Dyke, D. (2007) *Four Weeks in May: A Captain's Story of War at Sea*, London: Atlantic Books.

Hastings, M. and Jenkins, S. (1983) *The Battle for the Falklands*, London: Pan Books.

Haydn, T. (2005) 'Pupil perceptions of history at key stage 3', Final Report For QCA. www.qcda.gov.uk/6391.aspx

Hellier, D. and Richards, H. (2005) '"Do we have to read all of this?" Encouraging students to read for understanding', *Teaching History*, 118, *Rethinking Differentiation Edition*.

Hibbert, B. (2006) 'The articulation of the study of history at General Certificate of Education Advanced Level with the study of history for an honours degree', Leeds University, PhD thesis, p. 267. Available online at www.barbarahibbert.org/

Hibbert, C. (1985) *The Destruction of Lord Raglan: A Tragedy of the Crimean War 1854–55*, London: Penguin. (First published 1961, Longman.)

Historical Association (2005) 'Historical Association Curriculum Project: History 14–19', London: Historical Association, p. 52 – highlights problems of lack of reading.

Historical Association (2005) The Historical Association Curriculum Development Project, London: Historical Association, p. 50.

Hite, J. and Hinton, C. (1998) *Fascist Italy*, London: John Murray.

Howells, G. (2000) 'Gladstone spiritual or Gladstone material? A rationale for using documents at AS and A2', *Teaching History*, 100, *Thinking and Feeling Edition*.

Howells, G. (2007) 'Life by sources A to F: really using sources to teach AS History', *Teaching History*, 128, *Beyond the Exam Edition*.

Husbands, C. (1996) *What is History Teaching?*, Buckingham: Open University Press, pp. 90–91.

Husbands, C., Kitson, A. and Pendry, A. (2003) *Understanding History Teaching,* Open University Press, p. 132.

Italian Fascism: Revealed (2007), Channel 5, UK broadcast in July 2007. Richmond College provides a service for all subscribers of recordings of any TV programme from the last ten years. Information at: www.richmond-utcoll.ac.uk/facilities/video.asp

Johnson, R. (2002) *The Changing Nature of Warfare 1792–1918*, Somerset: Studymates.

Keegan, J. (2004) *The Mask of Command: A Study of Generalship*, London: Pimlico.

Kitson, A. (2003) 'Reading and enquiring in Years 12 and 13: a case study on women in the Third Reich', *Teaching History*, 111, *Reading History Edition*.

Kitson, A. (2004) Editorial in *Teaching History*, 114, *Making History Personal Edition*.

Kitson, L. (1982) *The Falklands War: A Visual Diary*, London: Mitchell Beasley.

Klemperer, V. (1999) *I Will Bear Witness 1933–1941: A Diary of the Nazi Years*, London: Weidenfeld and Nicolson. Translated by Martin Chalmers.

Koonz, C. (1987) *Mothers in the Fatherland: Women, the Family and Nazi Politics*, New York: St Martin's Press.

Laffin, D. (2006) 'Using extended role play to develop confidence in learning Tudor history', published on the Action Research project section of the Farnborough Sixth Form College website. http://actionresearch.farnboroughsfc2.ac.uk/Pages/a65626ae-295a-4208-9a11-0ec7990bd820

Laffin, D. (2008) 'If everyone's got to vote then, obviously … everyone's got to think': Using remote voting to involve everyone in classroom thinking at AS and A2', *Teaching History*, 133, *Simulating History Edition*.

Laffin, D. and Wilson, M. (2005) 'Mussolini's marriage and a game in the playground: using analogy to help pupils understand the past', *Teaching History*, 120, *Diversity and Divisions Edition*.

Lang, S. (2003) 'Narrative: the under-rated skill', *Teaching History*, 110, *Communicating History Edition*.

LeCocq, H. (1999) 'Notemaking, knowledge-building and critical thinking are the same thing', *Teaching History*, 95, *Learning to Think Edition*.

Lee, P. and Shemilt, D. (2003) 'A scaffold not a cage: progression and progression models in history', *Teaching History*, 113, *Creating Progress Edition*.

Levi, C. (1947) *Christ stopped at Eboli*, London: Penguin.

Levi, G. 'On Microhistory', in Burke, P (ed.) (1991) *New Perspectives on Historical Writing*, London: Polity Press.

Lomas, T. (2005) 'New ideas in developing pupils' learning in key stage 3 and 4 History', plenary session at Schools History Project Conference.

Loy, M. (2008) 'Learning to read, reading to learn; strategies for moving students from "keen to learn" to "keen to read"', *Teaching History*, 132, *Historians in the Classroom Edition*.

Luff, I. (2001) 'Beyond I speak, you listen, boy! Exploring diversity of attitudes and experiences through speaking and listening', *Teaching History*, 105, *Talking History Edition*.

Luff, I. (2003) 'Stretching the straitjacket of assessment: use of role play and practical demonstration to enrich pupils' experience at GCSE and beyond', *Teaching History*, 113, *Creating Progress Edition*.

Lyon, G. (2007) 'Is it time to forget Remembrance?', *Teaching History*, 128, *Beyond the Exam Edition*.

Magnusson, S. G. (2006) 'Social History – Cultural History – Alltagsgeschichte – Microhistory: In-Between Methodologies and Conceptual Frameworks', *Journal of Microhistory*, June. www.microhistory.org/pivot/entry.php?id=20.

Magnusson, S. G. (2006) 'What is Microhistory?', published on George Mason University's History News Network. http://hnn.us/articles/23720.html

Mallman, K. M. and Paul, G. (1994) 'Omniscient, Omnipotent, Omnipresent? Gestapo, society and resistance' in Crew, D. (ed.) *Nazism and German Society 1933–1945*, London: Routledge.

Mason, T. (1976) 'Women in Germany, 1925–40: Family, Welfare and Work', *History Workshop Journal*, Issue 1.

Massie, A. (2004) *The National Army Museum Book of the Crimean War: The Untold Stories*, London: Pan Books.

McAleavy, T. (1998) 'The use of sources in school history 1910–1998: a critical perspective', *Teaching History*, 91, *Evidence and Interpretation Edition*, p. 12.

McCully, A. and Pilgrim, N. (2004) '"They took Ireland away from us and we've got to fight to get it back". Using fictional characters to explore the relationship between historical interpretation and contemporary attitudes', *Teaching History*, 114, *Making History Personal Edition*.

McManners, H. (2007) *Forgotten Voices of the Falklands: The Real Story of the Falklands War*, Ebury Press. (Also available on CD.)

Megill, A. (2007) *Historical Knowledge, Historical Error*, Chicago: University of Chicago Press.

Middlebrook, M. (1985, revised edition 2001) *The Falklands War 1982*, London: Penguin.

Moorehead, C. (2000) *Iris Origo, Marchesa of Val d'Orcia*, London: John Murray.

Munslow, A. (1999) 'The Postmodern in History: A Response to Professor O'Brien', published on the website of the Institute of Historical Research. www.history.ac.uk/discourse/alun.html

Newby, W. (1991) *Peace and War: Growing up in Fascist Italy*, London: Collins and Sons.

Nicol, D. (2007) 'Principles of good assessment and feedback: Theory and practice', from the REAP International Online Conference on Assessment Design for Learner Responsibility, 29–31 May, 2007. Available at www.reap.ac.uk/public/Papers/Principles_of_good_assessment_and_feedback.pdf

Noakes, J. and Pridham, G. (1984), *Nazism 1919–1945*, Vol. 2: State, Economy and Society 1933–39, Exeter: University of Exeter.

O'Brien, P. (1999) 'An Engagement with Postmodern Foes, Literary Theorists and Friends on the Borders with History', published on the website of the Institute of Historical Research. www.history.ac.uk/discourse/pob.html

Overy, R. (2001) *Interrogations: The Nazi Elite in Allied Hands, 1945*, London: Penguin.

Owings, A. (1995) *Frauen: German Women Recall the Third Reich*, London: Penguin.

Parker, R. (1993) *Chamberlain and Appeasement: British Policy and the Coming of the Second World War*, Basingstoke: Palgrave Macmillan.

Pearce, R. (2000) 'History at University 2000', *History Today*, Vol. 50, Issue 8.

Pearce, R. (2003) 'University History 2003' *History Today*, Vol. 53, Issue 8, pp. 54–57

Pemberton, W. R. (1962) *Battles of the Crimean War*, London: Batsford.

Peukert, D. J. K. (1989) *Inside Nazi Germany: Conformity, Opposition and Racism in Everyday Life*, London: Penguin. Translated by Richard Deveson. (First published 1987, Yale University Press.)

Philip, D. (2002) 'Falklands Conflict 1982 – The Air War: A New Appraisal', in Badsey, S., Havers, R. and Grove, M. *The Falklands Conflict Twenty Years On: Lessons for the Future* (Sandhurst Conference Series), London: Routledge.

Phillips, R. (2002) *Reflective Teaching of History 11-18*, London: Continuum.

Prince, S. (2002) 'British command and control in the Falklands Campaign', *Defense and Security Analysis*, 18: 4.

QCA (2006) GCE AS and A level subject criteria for history, QCA/06/2854.

Raudzens, G. (1990) 'War-Winning Weapons: The Measurement of Technological Determinism in Military History', *Journal of Military History*, Vol. 54, 403–34.

Riley, M. (2000) 'Into the Key Stage 3 history garden: choosing and planting your enquiry questions', *Teaching History*, 99, *Curriculum Planning Edition*.

Robson, R. (2006) *Italy: The Rise of Fascism*, London: Hodder Murray.

Rosenzweig, R. (2006) 'Can History be Open Source? Wikipedia and the Future of the Past', *Journal of American History*, Vol. 93, No. 1.

Rudham, R. (2001) 'The new history AS: principles for planning a scheme of work', *Teaching History*, 103, *Puzzling History Edition*.

Salvemini, G. (1928) *The Fascist Dictatorship*, London: Jonathan Cape.

Salvemini, G. (1973) *The Origins of Fascism in Italy*, New York: Harper and Row.

Schoenbaum, D. (1966) *Hitler's Social Revolution: Class and Status in Nazi Germany, 1933–1939*, Garden City, NY: Doubleday.

Sellar, W.C. and Yeatman, R. J. (1982 edition) *1066 and All That*, London: Methuen. (First published 1930.)

Sheils, W. J. (1989) *The English Reformation 1530–1570*, Longman.

Shemilt, D. (1980) *History 13–16 Evaluation Study*, London: HarperCollins.

Shirer, W. (1991 edition) *The Rise and Fall of the Third Reich*, London: Mandarin Paperbacks. (First published 1960.)

Siwertz, S. (1953) Nobel Prize Organisation, presentation speech. http://nobelprize.org/nobel_prizes/literature/laureates/1953/press.html

Small, H. (2007) *The Crimean War: Queen Victoria's War with the Russian Tsars*, Stroud: Tempus Publishing.

Spilsbury, J. (2005) *The Thin Red Line: An Eyewitness History of the Crimean War*, London: Cassell.

Stewart, N. (2001) *The Changing Nature of Warfare*, London: Hodder Murray.

Stille, A. (1992) *Benevolence and Betrayal: Five Italian Jewish Families Under Fascism*, NewYork: Summit Books.

Sweetman, J. (1984) *War and Administration: The Significance of the Crimean War for the British Army*, Edinburgh: Scottish Academic Press.

Sweetman, J. (1990) *Balaclava 1854: The Charge of the Light Brigade*, Oxford: Osprey Publishing.

Thomson, D. (1957, reprinted 1972) *Europe since Napoleon*, London: Longman.

Tinker, H. (1982) *A Message from the Falklands: The Life and Gallant Death of David Tinker Lieut. R.N. From his Letters and Poems*, London: Junction Books.

Troubetzkoy, A. (2006) *A Brief History of the Crimean War: The Causes and Consequences of a Medieval Conflict Fought in a Modern Age*, London: Constable and Robinson.

Walsh, B. (2009) 'Beyond Multiple Choice: Questions and Answers, Pedagogy and Technology in the History classroom', Historical Association. www.history.org.uk.

Ward, R. (2006) 'Duffy's Devices: teaching Year 13 to read and write', *Teaching History*, 124, *Teaching the Most Able Edition*.

Whittock, M. (1998) *Mussolini in Power*, London: Collins Educational.

Willson, P. (2002) *Peasant Women and Politics in Fascist Italy: The Massaie Rurali*, London: Routledge.

Wineburg, S. (2001) *Historical Thinking and Other Unnatural Acts*, Philadelphia: Temple University Press.

Wineburg, S. (2007) 'Unnatural and essential: the nature of historical thinking', *Teaching History*, 129, *Disciplined Minds Edition*.

Wood, D. (1992) 'Teaching Talk: how modes of teacher talk affect pupil participation' in Husbands, C. (1996) *What is History Teaching?*, Buckingham: Open University Press, pp. 92–93.

Woodham-Smith, C. (1953) *The Reason Why*, London: Penguin.

Woodward, S. (with Robinson, P.) (2003) *One Hundred Days: The Memoirs of the Falklands Battle Group Commander*, London: Harper Collins. (First published 1992.)

Woolley, M. (2003) '"Really weird and freaky": using a Thomas Hardy short story as a source of evidence in the Year 8 classroom', *Teaching History*, 111, *Reading History Edition*.